THE NOVEL AND THE NATION

CONTEMPORARY IRISH STUDIES

Series Editor Peter Shirlow (Queen's University Belfast)

Also available

Peter Shirlow and Mark McGovern (eds)
Who are 'the People'?: Unionism, Protestantism and Loyalism in Northern Ireland

THE NOVEL & THE NATION

STUDIES IN THE NEW IRISH FICTION

Gerry Smyth

Pluto Press
LONDON • CHICAGO, ILLINOIS

First published 1997 by Pluto Press
345 Archway Road, London N6 5AA
and 1436 West Randolph, Chicago, Illinois 60607, USA

British Library Cataloguing in Publication Data
A catalogue record for this book is available from
the British Library

ISBN 0–7453–1220–9

Library of Congress Cataloging in Publication Data
Smyth, Gerry, 1961–
    The novel and the nation : studies in the new Irish fiction /
Gerry Smyth.
        p.   cm.
    Includes bibliographical references (p.   ).
    ISBN 0–7453–1220–9 (hardcover : alk. paper)
    1. English fiction—Irish authors—History and criticism.
2. English fiction—20th century–History and criticism.
3. Ireland—In literature. I. Title.
PR8803.S69   1997
823'.914099415—dc21   97–2948
                                                              CIP

Designed, typeset and produced for Pluto Press by
Chase Production Services, Chadlington, OX7 3LN
Printed in Great Britain

CONTENTS

ACKNOWLEDGEMENTS

I would like to thank the following people for their help in the writing of this book and also for their encouragement and inspiration: Peter Childs, Elspeth Graham, Richard Haslam, Glenda Norquay, Michael Parker, Shaun Richards, Peter Shirlow, George Smyth, Roger van Zwanenberg and Roger Webster. I would also like to thank all my colleagues in the department of Literature, Life and Thought at Liverpool John Moores University for covering my teaching and administration duties during the sabbatical leave when the bulk of this book was written. For their patience, love and support, this book is dedicated to Christine and Lizzie.

INTRODUCTION

This book is concerned with the changes that have occurred in the writing, publishing and reading of Irish novels since the 1980s. It explores the new directions and new influences which have overtaken the practice, and attempts to place these within the context of established social and cultural traditions. My intention is to provide people new to the field with an accessible account of the foundations of Irish novelistic discourse, as well as an analysis of a selection of significant modern texts. Part 1 introduces some of the theoretical, formal and conceptual issues surrounding the emergence of the Irish novel since the eighteenth century. Part 2 looks at a number of recent Irish novels in the light of these issues, and especially the ways in which the latest generation of writers challenge established notions regarding the limits and possibilities of Irish identity.

The book's ethos is pedagogical rather than monographic. While my own beliefs and preferences are implicit in the structure and in the texts I have chosen to include, it should be clear that no claims are being made as to the propriety of the critical-theoretical approaches described in Part 1, or indeed as to the 'literary' quality of the novels invoked in Part 2. This text does not represent an exercise in canon-formation, as the absense of some of Ireland's most successful and celebrated contemporary novelists (such as Maeve Binchy and John Banville), as well as some of the more exciting and innovative of the 'new' writers (such as Anne Enright and Colm Tóibín) hopefully demonstrates. The motivation informing the study, rather, is to bring a number of critical, theoretical and historical discourses into active, illuminating cross-fertilisation, and then to discuss a selection of significant documents which I believe reveal something of the complex and changing society from which they have emerged. Part 1 represents for the most part a synthesis of research carried out elsewhere by other scholars, while the textual analyses provided in Part 2 are intended to be suggestive, conceived as broad interpretative overviews rather than nuanced close readings. However, in as much as all criticism is itself a form of fiction, there is a narrative of sorts running throughout the text concerning the significance of 'change' in modern Irish society and the ways in which change is mediated by novelistic discourse. I will return to this issue shortly.

The reader is expected to use this book as a resource, and the ideas and theories described in it as a set of tools which may be flexibly deployed in any critical undertaking. *The Novel and the Nation* is not designed to provide answers as such, but rather the means to enable the reader to ask pertinent questions. The analyses in Part 2 are not slavish readings in terms of the issues raised in Part 1, but rather a set of suggestions which depend for their usefulness upon knowledge of the novel in question and an ability to link creatively the imaginative texts with the analytical material described earlier. The obvious connections between Parts 1 and 2 will not be laboured. It should be reasonably straightforward, for example, to read sections in Chapter 1 ('Theories') on the novel as a site of competing social and political discourses, in Chapter 2 ('Forms') on the impact of the oral tradition on Irish writing, and in Chapter 3 ('Themes') on the recurrence of madness as a figure in the Irish novelistic tradition, and bring these together in an analysis of a contemporary text – say, Patrick McCabe's *The Butcher Boy* – without too much prompting.

THE BACKGROUND

If there is such a thing as the 'new Irish novel', it is reasonable to inquire how it qualifies for this description – that is, in what ways is a particular text new, Irish and/or a novel? Answering these questions requires a brief detour through recent Irish political and cultural history.

A fundamental premise for what follows throughout this book is that Ireland was England's first colony.[1] It is true that the French-speaking Norman knights who landed in Ireland on 1 May 1169 came on the invitation of a local warlord in an effort to boost his own political ambitions. It also seems incontrovertible that the rise to power of these first 'English' in Ireland was facilitated by the lack of a common political and/or cultural identity amongst the natives who were, in any case, not aboriginals but a melting pot of various previous Celtic and Viking invasions. But however much they assimilated, the new invaders continued to owe allegiance to another home across the Irish sea. Therefore, the principle of colonisation has structured relations between the two islands since the twelfth century, and not only for the Irish and the English. The 'Anglo-Irish' were a typical colonialist community in their domination of Irish political and cultural life, and in as much they became increasingly strung out across the constituent parts of their identity. Through the Wars of the Roses, religious upheavals, civil wars, Anglo-Irish Ascendancy and periodic attempts at 'plantation' (the appropriation of Irish land for loyal British settlers) the history of relations between the earlier and the later invaders of Ireland is one of political and cultural strife, interspersed with moments of compromise and accommodation.

Ireland was also one of the first geographical locations in the world to begin the process of *decolonisation* – that is, to move (through a flexible strategy of armed struggle and diplomacy) from being part of a larger political formation (the British Empire) to a situation of increasing political and cultural independence. Although precipitated by an intermittent political revolution lasting from 1916 to 1922, this move occurred slowly and unevenly over an extended period of time. Under a treaty agreed between the British government and the majority of the revolutionary forces, part of the island was offered a measure of political autonomy. After a brief but bitter civil war between those wishing to accept the terms and those holding out for a complete formal break with the Empire, the treaty was accepted and became law in 1922. Initially known as the 'Irish Free State', the name of the state was changed to 'Éire' (the Gaelic word for Ireland) in 1937 before becoming the 'Republic of Ireland' in 1948, at which time the state formally seceded from the British Commonwealth and became to all intents and purposes a different country. During the same period, the six north-eastern counties of the island remained politically affiliated to Great Britain, initially forming a separate state called 'Northern Ireland' but ruled directly from London after the breakdown of civil order in 1972.

For reasons that will emerge throughout this book, this protracted process of decolonisation has had a profound impact on life throughout the island. In the years since the treaty it seemed that the different communities sharing Ireland could not, or did not wish to, shake off the legacy of the past. So traumatic was the rearrangement of relations with Great Britain, and so powerful the emotions and beliefs needed to negotiate those changes, that the revolutionary period maintained a hold on the Irish imagination long after 1922. As a consequence, the peculiar political formation of post-colonial Ireland – a small geographical area having to accommodate all shades of opinion, and complicated still further by the close proximity of the former colonial power – is characterised by insecurity and a constant need for self-identification, conditions which are themselves left over from colonial times: Who am I in relation to the groups and the beliefs and the political affiliations I perceive around me? Who am I in relation to the past from which I believe myself to have emerged and the future towards which I believe myself to be moving?

Subsequent study has revealed that all post-colonial formations are affected by this 'identitarian' imperative.[2] As part of the programme to develop a consistent and coherent resistance to colonialism, identity was structured in terms of similarity (Irishness) and difference (Englishness) during the period leading up to the revolution. This oppositional structure, however, was not modified after the withdrawal of the colonial power, but remained the principal device whereby post-revolutionary Irishness was defined and characterised.

Another basic premise of this book is that Ireland is still decolonising. What this means in effect is that modern Ireland, North and South, remains dominated by questions of political and cultural identity – dominated, that is, by fidelity to a past structured in terms of clearly defined stories about *us* and *them*, even if these stories were quite clearly mutually incompatible. Self-surveillance on such a scale, moreover, requires huge amounts of personal and political energy, and life on the island has suffered seriously as a result. All told, any description of the island as 'post-colonial' might be said to be premature as both 'Irelands' have remained fixated with the colonial link – one deliberately and doggedly, the other unconsciously and capriciously.

During the 1980s, however, there were signs that a desire to take different perspectives on Irish history and its current condition was beginning to take hold of the popular and political imagination. Under the influence of new technologies in the areas of travel, communications and information, Ireland (like the rest of Europe) was changing rapidly at this time. It seems clear in retrospect that new political, social and cultural languages were needed to give voice to these changes. These needs were confirmed by the election of a feminist and civil rights lawyer as President of the Republic in November 1990. Defeating two male candidates – one (Brian Lenihan) from Fianna Fáil, the traditional Republican party, and one (Austin Currie) having links with the 'Troubles' in Northern Ireland – Mary Robinson's election focused the attempt to bring fresh

perspectives to bear on traditional concerns. The President's popu-
larity, moreover, has not diminished over her term of office, a sign
that her election was the result of a deeply felt desire for change
rather than a cosmetic rearrangement of the existing discourses.
Her inaugural speech acknowledged this sense of changing times:

> The Ireland I will be representing is a new Ireland, open, tolerant,
> inclusive. Many of you who voted for me did so without sharing all my
> views. This, I believe, is a significant signal of change, a sign, however
> modest, that we have already passed the threshold to a new, pluralist
> Ireland ... The best way we can contribute to a new integrated Europe of
> the 1990s is by having a confident sense of our Irishness.[3]

Robinson's election, as Carol Coulter explains, 'was widely welcomed as a triumph for those who supported a modernising,
liberal agenda for Ireland, and as a defeat for those associated
with nationalism and Catholic traditionalism'.[4] The mood of the
time is captured in an open letter written to the President by
philosopher and cultural critic Richard Kearney:

> Your election to the highest office of this land was a good day ... I
> believe it marks a significant, indeed irreversible, sea-change in the life
> of this small Republic of ours. The tide has turned ... the story we are
> telling ourselves and others in electing you as President is that we are
> not just natives of an ancient land but citizens of a new society. We have
> come of age. We have performed a rite of passage from past to future ...
> Your election has endorsed this transition from outworn piety to a
> more enabling sense of possibility. The young – and women in
> particular – have decided they want a modern enlightened Republic
> where each citizen enjoys equal rights and responsibilities. And they
> have shown they want it now.[5]

Robinson's election may be seen as the consolidation of a broad
but unfocused movement that had been developing for a number
of years in which the old political pieties of post-1922 Ireland
were seen as increasingly problematic for a small island coming
to terms with life in the late twentieth century. The Ireland of
her vision entailed not only a pragmatic acknowledgement of the
changing circumstances confronting modern Ireland, but also a
re-emphasis upon the most radical elements of the revolutionary
discourse from the earlier part of the century – elements which
under the malign influence of identitarian politics had calcified
into conservative institutions and effete catchphrases. Robinson

offered the possibility of an escape from the discursive *impasse* which always sought to process information in terms of national and racial discourses invented during the nineteenth century. A 'confident' modern Ireland would not need to identify itself constantly in relation to others, whether British, European or indeed other forms of Irishness.

Kearney's use of the story as a metaphor for new perceptions of Irishness picked up on something to which Robinson herself had alluded in the inaugural speech: 'I want Áras an Uachtaráin [the President's Official Residence] to be a place where people can tell diverse stories – in the knowledge that there is someone there to listen. I want this Presidency to promote the telling of stories – stories of celebration through the arts and stories of conscience and of social justice' (p. 255). These comments were both prophetic and instrumental, for not only have a range of diverse, formerly silenced stories emerged in Irish life in recent years, but there has also been a renaissance in that cultural form specifically calibrated to circulate stories throughout modern society – the form known as the novel.

The novel is important in modern Irish culture because as a genre it evolved to formulate narratives in which social, political and historical change could be accommodated. To anticipate later arguments, the Russian theorist of the novel Mikhail Bakhtin wrote: 'The novel is the only developing genre and therefore it reflects more deeply, more essentially, more sensitively and rapidly, reality itself in the process of its unfolding. Only that which is itself developing can comprehend development as a process.'[6] We should not be surprised, then, with the emergence of a 'new Irish fiction' during the period of change which has overtaken the island since the 1980s. Nor should we be surprised that the novel is becoming perhaps *the* pre-eminent Irish cultural form. This is not only to do with the great number of novels currently circulating. Understood (in Bakhtin's work) less as a discrete literary genre than a particular way of engaging with the world, Irish culture is in fact in the process of becoming a novel-driven discourse. So although in 1987 the critic Kevin Barry could claim with some justification that 'Poetry, the most intimate, the most literary, the most free, the most unreliable form in terms of its effects and meaning, is the one we revere', less than a decade later it is doubtful if this is still the case.[7] Of course, a great amount of Irish poetry and plays (and increasingly films) is still produced and consumed, but it is arguable that these genres now answer a specifically novelistic impulse, which in the wider context described by Bakhtin has been underway since the early eighteenth century but which in the Irish context has emerged only in recent years in response to the fact of rapid, exponential social change.

As we shall go on to see, the novel has been a part of Irish social and cultural life since at least the late eighteenth century, if not always happily so. One of the claims of this book, however, is that something fundamentally different has overtaken novelistic discourse in Ireland since the mid-1980s, and especially since the election of Mary Robinson. It is in this sense that the Irish fiction which has emerged in the decade and a half leading up to the millennium can be described as 'Robinsonian'. It is possible, in fact, to consider all the novels studied in Part 2 of this book – even the ones published before 1990 – as 'Robinsonian' in their impetus and/or their outlook. At its most basic, such a description means that the new Irish novelists combine a willingness to confront the formal and conceptual legacies of a received literary (and wider social) tradition alongside a self-awareness of the role played by cultural narratives in mediating modern (or perhaps it would be better now to say *postmodern*) Ireland's changing circumstances.

In Joseph O'Connor's *Cowboys and Indians* (1991), for example, we encounter a character disparaging the received tradition of Irish fiction:

> Oh yeah, the Great Irish Novel, Jesus man, a computer could write that. A bit of motherlove, a touch of suppressed lust, a soupçon of masochistic Catholic guilt, a bit of token Britbashing, whole shitloads of limpid eyes and flared nostrils and sweaty Celtic thighs, all wrapped up in a sauce of snotgreen Joycean wank.[8]

This description is interesting for its comic reduction of what is in fact a wide-ranging and complex tradition. But it is also interesting for the fact that it is a passage from a modern novel which is itself in active dialogue with the very themes and forms that are being attacked. Much in the same way that modern Ireland itself has been obliged to renegotiate a relationship with its own past under pressure from changing circumstances in the present, so we find *Cowboys and Indians* engaging with many of the concerns of traditional Irish fiction while also attempting self-consciously to distance itself from that tradition. The tension generated as a result of this contradictory structure, in which the subject is forced to operate constantly on the interface between discourses of change and discourses of continuity, is the defining characteristic of both modern Irish experience and the new Irish fiction which seeks to represent that experience.

PART 1

1 THEORIES

THE BIRTH OF THE NATION

The idea of the nation-state began to emerge in Europe during the eighteenth century. The nation was invented by scholars and intellectuals as a response to three important elements of human experience which, in their traditional forms, were entering into crisis at that time. These elements were: (a) a form of social organisation; (b) a form of political order; (c) a narrative of historical identity. The nation appeared to answer what were seen as these basic human needs in as much as it presented a model of a geographical community (a) exercising power (b) by dint of its organic links with the land (c). As older models based on dynasty and religion came under pressure from developments such as the growth of explorations and communications, the rise of a print-based culture and the growing awareness of the diversity of human language, the nation was offered by scholars and historians as a new, energetic and highly attractive version of the relations between (a), (b) and (c).

Between 1784 and 1791 the German writer Johann Gottfried Herder published his *Outlines of a Philosophy of the History of Man*, in which he claimed that there exists an organic link between specific geographical locations and the communities which inhabit them. 'Every nation' he wrote, 'is one people, having its own national form, as well as its own language.'[1] This 'national form' – a natural link between geographical unit and state sovereignty – was just what was missing in eighteenth-century Ireland; this form had instead been corrupted by the 'unnatural' enlargement of the English nation. Herder's defence of the nation was taken up by those writers and artists who felt that European achievements in 'civilisation', rather than representing the race's development towards perfection, in fact constituted the decay of the natural order. Together these arguments developed into a fully fledged Romantic theory of nationalism – that is, adherence to the nation as the most natural form of human organisation. In a remarkably short time, national-ism became a highly successful concept in the social, political and cultural thought of Europe.

Over the years since its emergence, however, the nation has become a highly contentious category in political and cultural debate. For some, nationalism represents a historically retrograde and intellectually impoverished organisation of human affairs. Herder's model, it could be claimed, just does not stand up to Irish history, which shows instead a series of invasions and hybrid graftings of different peoples and different cultures. Even the Gaelic/Celtic identity which was to form the basis of Irish nationalist discourse in the eighteenth and nineteenth centuries was an imposition by an invading people upon an aboriginal race which, presumably, already possessed its own culture.

However, the major conceptual flaw, say its opponents, is that despite the historical contingency of its own emergence, national-ism believes as authentic the stories it tells about its own origins, and finds it increasingly difficult to acknowledge alternatives to its own peculiar way of seeing. The nation imposes human form upon the world but then treats that imposition as if it were a (re)discovery. Moreover, the temporal location of the nation is uncertain, say its critics, in as much as it appears to exist in the past, as a point of mystical origin from which all cultural and political legitimacy derives; but also in the future, as the utopian destination of all nationalist activity. Thus, the nation is always present (allowing nationalist activity) and always absent (that which nationalist discourse is working to realise). For many, this represents the central philosophical paradox of nationalism – its inability to constitute itself as a coherent narrative of human activity. Indeed, to some commentators, the nation remains both *the* major puzzle and *the* major problem of modern world history – a puzzle, because despite the paucity of its philosophical and political basis it was an incredibly successful idea in all parts of the world throughout the nineteenth century; and a problem, because long after its death notices were read by anti-nationalist intellectuals and politicians, nationalism resurfaced in more aggressive forms throughout the world and continues to exercise an inordinate influence on politics and culture.

On the other hand, there are those who claim that national-ism is a valid stage in human history, and that it served an important purpose in allowing certain historically marginalised communities to begin the process of decolonisation. The argu-ment is that while it may be legitimate to criticise and combat the *effects* of nationalism – especially those forms which from the nineteenth century became implicated in aggressive, pseudo-scientific discourses of race – it is nevertheless necessary to understand nationalism as a historical process amongst other processes, one which can be wielded for specific ends but which, like any other human activity, possesses no inherent moral identity in and of itself. All versions of the relations between (a), (b) and (c), it could be claimed, are constructions, the result of acts of intellectual will rather than a discovery of real or natural things that exist somehow in the world and remain constant over time. One must remain aware of the different applications and effects of the nation, and of the various ways it functions in various places and various times.

These issues have been hotly debated in Irish cultural criticism in recent times, and two basic positions have emerged. On the one hand, the 'revisionist' stance, drawing upon a wide range of political and critical discourses, questions the legitimacy of nationalism in Irish history. Revisionists see nationalism, with its spurious emphasis on origins and destiny, as responsible for continuing division in Ireland, a third-rate political doctrine with no mandate in Irish (or Gaelic) history. Its historical blindness, they say, is matched only by its philosophical bad faith. Revisionists are equally suspicious of any 'neo-nationalist' affiliations with fashionable modern theories such as post-structuralism, postmodernism and post-colonialism. For the revisionists, such affiliations demonstrate an intellectual opportunism in which critics invent models of Irish literary and political tradition as doubtful as any colonial ones they might hope to replace. Some nationalist critics, however, see revisionist antipathy to postmodernism as ironic, because much of revisionist discourse relies upon a general postmodernist scepticism with regard to traditional 'grand narratives' such as nationalism.[2]

Against revisionism, there exists what might be referred to as a general 'post-national' consensus. Critics from this camp argue that nationalism performed a necessary role in Irish decolonisation, but was never conceived by its adherents as the final word on Irish history or identity. Nationalism, it is claimed, was not the crypto-fascist bogey imagined by revisionists, but an enabling ideal which in its fullest articulations managed to mobilise the various strands of anti-imperial opinion in the service of a liberal, non-coercive notion of Irishness. As an idea and as a movement, nationalism instead can be accommodated within a developmental model which stresses the necessity for any distinctive cultural community to achieve political independence, but the equally pressing need to dissolve the oppositional discourses foisted onto the colonial society by imperialist discourse. Nationalism, then, is a means to an end, a stage in the development of a modern pluralistic society rather that a goal in itself. It is true that post-revolutionary formations are susceptible to the most retrograde elements in society, and it is also true that the version of nationalism which predominated in Ireland from 1922 until quite recently was based upon an arrested notion of Irish identity which gave rise to an exclusivist, conservative society. It is this latter version of nationalism which most often serves as the target of revisionist attack. But criticising these developments is not the same as denying the validity of the decolonising project. Rather, the important thing, as Richard Kearney writes:

> is that one must discriminate between different kinds of political nationalism – those which emancipate and those which incarcerate, those that affirm a people's cultural identity in dialogue with other peoples and those that degenerate into ideological closure – into xenophobia, racism and bigotry.[3]

These positions are fluid. Some critics, having struggled to deconstruct essentialist notions of Irishness, find that they wish to hang on to some notion of identity and are offended at the blasé manner in which the Irish past has become the focus of attack for anyone. These critics wish to reaffirm an identity which, under pressure from revisionism and postmodernism, has been strained to breaking point. Indeed, the monotony of affirmation and refutation becomes another of the binaries that haunt post-colonial criticism.

CULTURAL NATIONALISM

In its earliest eighteenth-century forms, the Irish nation functioned primarily as a *cultural* phenomenon. Culture provided an ideal model of the relations between (a), (b) and (c) in any given situation, and its key task became the facilitation of the passage from colony to nation to nation-state. Culture in this sense, we might say, is *future*-oriented. At the same time, the nation must already exist so that properly 'national' cultural forms can emerge and be identified. Culture is thus also *past*-oriented, as all cultural forms can be measured in terms of their fidelity to the natural national blueprint. Culture, in fact, was forced to assume the dual task of anticipating the virtual nation, while remaining answerable to the historically postponed nation.[4]

It is out of this paradox that one of the most significant and enduring concepts of modern intellectual discourse emerges, that of *cultural nationalism*. At its most basic, this theory holds that there is a natural link between culture and nation – that is, that the kinds of artefacts and narratives produced by individuals and communities are related to the peculiar national system of social organisation, political order and historical identity from which they have emerged. It thus becomes possible to consider German culture, Italian culture or, at a finer level, concepts such as French drama, Spanish music, English poetry. The latter discourse, for example, would be expected to display formal and conceptual characteristics which would allow one to identify it in terms of the social, political and historical formations in which it developed. As the nineteenth century progressed and as the vogue for knowledge of European history grew, this *past*-oriented form of cultural nationalism was shared by most of the modern European nations, regardless of their political status. When political nationalism became *future*-oriented, however, as it did for decolonising formations such as Ireland, cultural nationalism came to signify something different.

In fact, there were few places in Europe where cultural nationalism was as successful as in Ireland. In the last three decades of the eighteenth century there occurred what scholars refer to as the First Celtic Revival, in which a fashion for all things Celtic swept through Europe. In Ireland, this was mostly a *past*-oriented cultural nationalism led by gentrified scholars from the Anglo-Irish settler community. These men and women were attempting to prove the existence of an ancient Irish nation sustaining a fully developed culture as part of their programme to secure improved status for Ireland in its contemporary relations with England. The 1790s, however, also saw the birth of Irish republicanism, influenced by the American and French Revolutions, and dedicated to breaking completely the formal political links with England. Thus was born a specific form of *future*-oriented cultural nationalism, in which the primary purpose of Irish cultural activity was to give form to the virtual political nation which was yet to be. For all subsequent Irish cultural activity, it then became a question of emphasis: culture *of* the nation or *for* the nation?

What occurred in Ireland during the nineteenth century was that the former discourse (*past*-oriented culture *of* the nation) was subsumed by the latter (*future*-oriented culture *for* the nation). Culminating with the Second Celtic Revival of the 1890s, the idea of an authentic culture supported by an established nation exercised a very powerful influence in contemporary Irish affairs, especially when it was appropriated by a *future*-oriented form of cultural nationalism dedicated to reconstituting, if not entirely severing, political links with England. Culture moved from being *representational* to being *interventionist*; the novel, in particular, began to read less like a work of anthropology and more like a polemical pamphlet.

The relations between culture and nation continued to be discussed by writers and critics throughout the nineteenth century, culminating in the intense critical debates of the 1890s and 1900s. Even if one typical gesture is to deny the validity of such debates, the acceptance of a significant link between culture and nation by both revisionists and post-nationalists means that critical encounters have tended to be concerned with the *nature* of that link, rather than its existence. The acceptance of such a link, moreover, means that these critical debates as to the function of literature and its relations with the nation have played a significant role in the imagination of different kinds of Ireland, as well as in the Ireland that actually did emerge.

There are on the other hand many critics and artists who dispute this, claiming that rather than aiding the emergence of a confident independent nation, cultural nationalism has in fact been detrimental to Ireland's political and cultural development. We should be careful to differentiate between those who dispute the existence of a link between culture and nation, and those who argue that even if such a link did exist and exert an influence, it is a spent force in the late twentieth century. The novelist Francis Stuart gave an example of the former line when he argued that 'National literature is to my mind a meaningless term. Literature can't be national. Literature is individual. Nationality has nothing to do with it.' Or again, John Banville, one of the most important Irish novelists of the late twentieth century, has said:

> I must say I've never felt part of any movement or tradition, any culture even ... I feel a part of my culture. But it's purely a personal culture gleaned from bits and pieces of European culture of four thousand years. It's purely something I have manufactured. I don't think any writer ever felt part of a culture.[5]

Stuart and Banville refuse the 'sincerity' of any inherited tradition, emphasising instead the 'authenticity' of their own artistic visions.[6] It is possible to see denials of this kind as a form of Oedipal thrust against the authority of tradition, a gesture which perhaps does more to confirm the existence of cultural nationalism in some form or other. This gesture, however, in which the writer-subject says 'I am myself' rather than 'I am the son of my father' (or nation or tradition) is a characteristic response of much Irish writing, and we shall be returning to it in Chapter 3. In the meantime, we should note that not least of the interesting tensions animating contemporary Irish fiction is the way in which it has inherited and used this anti-traditional tradition. We should also avoid neat critical oppositions such as the one between 'authenticity' and 'sincerity', or between affirmation and denial. The position adopted here by Stuart and Banville, although clearly *against* cultural nationalism, is at odds with the one claiming that cultural nationalism once performed important tasks in the decolonisation of the nation but has now been superseded. One claims that literature can never be national; the other that literature can be national, but that it is a sign of a nation's maturity when its culture becomes less self-conscious and starts to focus on specifically literary issues, such as language, imagination and creativity.

Whether with reference to its existence or its influence, however, it does seem clear that many Irish novelists have felt the burden of cultural nationalism as a curb upon their creative powers. Especially given the enormous changes that have occurred in Irish life in recent years, much of the new Irish fiction with which we are concerned here seems determined to resist the idea of a national literature limited to traditional concerns, and few of the younger writers would look to locate their work in any kind of inherited national literary tradition. Novelists such as Dermot Bolger and Joseph O'Connor resent what they see as the attempts by academics to read their work solely in terms of artificial critical apparatuses – such as postmodernism or post-colonialism – which, they argue, have more to do with Anglo-American cultural angst than modern Irish realities. Reacting to the opinion (of a British critic) that Irish art which does not address the country's post-colonial status is invalid, O'Connor writes:

'The war' is not Ireland's central drama. Ireland's central drama is – and always has been – the conflict between private life and public fantasy ... maybe this new concentration on the dignity of individual lives is what is so powerful – and so profoundly political – in the work of the new Irish writers which my correspondent so roundly chastises.[7]

Again, there is room for confusion here, as these novelists appear to wish to disavow any reductive analysis of their work in terms of 'Irishness', yet continue to saturate that same work with themes and contexts which are recognisably of the nation. It is possible to find examples of this precarious line between denial and dedication throughout post-revolutionary discourse; but this effect has become acute in recent years, during a period in which established models of Irish identity have come under pressure from the cultural and political developments of the late twentieth century, and when, as Fintan O'Toole says, sex and drugs and rock 'n' roll have come to replace 'the old Irish totems of Land, Nationality and Catholicism'.[8]

NOVEL AND NATION

How does the novel figure in the rise of cultural nationalism? Traditional accounts say that the genre evolved in Europe from older forms of narrative – romances, memoirs, letter-collections, historiography – and is linked with diverse social, political and cultural factors such as the emergence of national bourgeois classes, the rise of literacy, technological advances in printing and the formation of modern discourses of gender and individual subjectivity.[9] Howsoever, the novel soon proved itself a highly adaptable and successful form, and from the eighteenth century both the reading and writing of novels became a fashionable occupation for leisured classes across Europe. A variety of positions has emerged on the possible relations between the novel and the nation, of which I wish briefly to describe four which are pertinent to our concerns here.

Novel and nation as imagined communities

Some critics perceive the novel and the nation to be closely linked. As cultural concepts, after all, both emerged around about the same time (the eighteenth century) and place (Europe), and it is likely therefore that both were effects of the same matrix of intellectual and material developments. It could

be claimed, of course, that the novel is an object – a thing in
the world – whereas the nation has no such material reality,
existing only in the collective imagination and rituals of a
given geographical community. But this criticism, argues Benedict Anderson, far from undermining the case for a link
between the novel and the nation, actually strengthens it.[10]

Anderson understands the nation as 'an imagined political
community' which requires an act of faith between large
amounts of people who otherwise would have no sense of, or
reason for, solidarity. These people come to consider themselves part of a social, political and historical community that,
given the population and geographical patterns of the modern
age, can be perceived only in the imagination. Anderson then
goes on to discuss the novel as a particular kind of cultural
practice that came to prominence at more or less the same
time as the nation, and which realises in its form the same act
of faith required by the nation. The novel, he claims, is linked
to the nation in that they imagine similar communities, that in
fact the novel 'provided the technical means for "re-present-
ing" the *kind* of imagined community that is the nation'
(p. 25). The typical novel of the eighteenth and nineteenth
centuries sees the progression of a single hero through a social
and psychological landscape towards a personal and communal
resolution, on the way overcoming various obstacles relating to
the role of the subject in society. In its representation of a
certain kind of imagined social and political community; in its
creation of certain 'typical' roles for narrator, hero and reader;
in its narrative movement through conflict towards climax and
resolution; in all these ways the form of the novel exactly
rehearses, argues Anderson, the preoccupations of the imagined
nation, requiring the same leap of faith between the individual
and the large unseen community in which his/her actions and
thoughts make sense.

In this model, then, there is a fundamental link between
the novel and the nation. The former does not merely take the
latter as its theme, but is rather one of the material conditions
of possibility for the emergence of the idea of the nation. This
thesis, however, based on the influence of the medium of the
printed word on western history, would have to be modified in
any analysis of contemporary Irish fiction, appearing as it does
during a technological revolution in which print functions in
radically different ways from the early capitalist and Fordian
models examined by Anderson.

The novel as national allegory

Another link between novel and nation can be found in the work of the American Marxist theorist and critic Fredric Jameson who argues that a genre such as the novel 'is essentially a socio-symbolic message ... form is immanently and intrinsically an ideology in its own right'.[11] This means that the novel is closely connected with the ideologies of the community from which it emerges, that in fact a reciprocal relationship operates between novel and society. Changes in the ideological expectations and assumptions of a society will impinge on the kinds of novel produced in that society; similarly, formal and generic shifts in the novel will have implications for the society in which such shifts take place.

For Jameson, however, the link between novel and nation does not work the same way in all societies at all times. In culturally underdeveloped communities such as are found in the Third and post-colonial worlds, he suggests that the relations between novel and society tend to be straightforwardly *allegorical*: 'The story of the private individual destiny is always an allegory of the embattled situation of the public national project.'[12] The reason for this is that such communities are still at the stage of calibrating their social and ideological base, and have not had the opportunity to formalise all the contradictions upon which a modern society is based. For Jameson, this impoverishes both the creative and the critical processes. He criticises any system (cultural nationalism is a prime example) which comprehends the novel merely as an allegory of history, an echo of reality – any instance in which the text is written (and subsequently rewritten by the critic) 'in terms of some fundamental master code or "ultimately determining instance"' (p. 58), in this case the master code of the nation.

A more subtle method, according to Jameson, would be concerned not with discovering the 'real' meaning of the text – some kind of historical national truth encoded into the text by the author, or used by the critic to decode the text – but with analysing how a text functions to reveal the contradictions upon which society is built. Accordingly, the novel would not so much *represent* the nation, as *contain* the nation within its form, its structure, its silences. The novel does not simply import and reproduce the national reality into its form; it is, rather, a rewriting or restructuration of a prior historical or ideological *subtext*, it being always understood that the 'subtext' is not immediately present as such, not some common-sense external reality, not even the conventional narratives of history manuals, but rather must in itself always be (re)constructed after the fact. (p. 81)

The novel, therefore, is at once an effect and an articulation of the nation – a paradox whereby 'the literary work ... brings into being that very situation to which it is also, at one and the same time, a reaction' (p. 82). In this theory, the nation is neither 'history' nor 'text'; the novel should be neither an allegory nor an effect of the nation, but a complex historical articulation of the 'national unconscious'.

Whether novels produced in a society with heightened nationalist concerns are, or could be, *merely* allegorical is far from clear, however. Jameson has been criticised for failing to recognise that the novels of South America, for example, do not allegorise the societies and histories with which they engage, but offer rather 'a motley space in which different historical developments and cultures overlap'.[13] At the same time, he has been attacked for attempting to recuperate such novels in term of disabling First World concepts such as 'postmodernism' – a term which does little (it is claimed) to explain the complex generic and historical matrix out of which contemporary South American novelistic discourse has emerged. Ireland also offers an interesting test case for Jameson's theories given its historically anomalous cultural location – a decolonising *Irish* nation with an active cultural (and therefore allegorical?) impulse, alongside a highly developed *Anglo*-Irish cultural imagination alive to its own contradictions.

Howsoever, Jameson's theory of the novel as a socially symbolic act allows the retention of a fundamental political dimension to analysis without resorting to crude determinist formulations which rely on some master-narrative of national development. It thus becomes necessary to deploy a sophisticated textual criticism so that we may consider the ways in which the novel 'narrates' and gives form to the nation, without falling into the trap of saying that the nation has no reality outside the text.

The novel as resistance

The relationship between novel and nation becomes especially contentious when two countries are locked in an unequal relationship. In the case of Ireland, as with many colonial and post-colonial nations, debate persists not only over the possibility of a subordinate national culture, but also, and crucially, over what form that culture should or could take.

The novel as a form of resistance has come very much to the fore in recent years with the great vogue for post-colonialism as a cultural/critical theory. The novel, it is argued, is a primary site of cultural challenge to the narratives of the metropolitan centre. This is because culture played a crucial role in 'claiming' the non-west by narrating and making sense of it within its own colonialist terms of reference.[14] Colonialism tried to impose its version of 'reality' on the colonial relationship so that no matter what opinion was expressed, this 'reality' was always the discursive terrain upon which exchange occurred. The colonialist, therefore, has a strong investment in 'reality', but also, given the importance of culture to the colonial project, in that aesthetic system which claims to be most fully representative of reality – realism. 'Realism' is thus an important part of colonialist ideology, and the culture that disseminates it an indispensable part of any colonialist project, because it is by means of such a representative strategy that the colonial version of 'reality' remains dominant.[15]

Within any narrative of resistance, therefore, culture must also function as a crucial weapon. It is maintained by some that the novelist in a decolonising formation must also be a teacher; his/her task is to interrogate and expose the received narratives of the dominant culture, and to educate the oppressed population as to alternatives.[16] The novel is one of the principal means whereby narrative possibilities circulate in the colonial society; therefore, it is the novelist's national *duty* simultaneously to resist the 'reality' of colonialist discourse, and to propose alternative national realities which can serve as the narrative drive for decolonising discourse.

There are a number of tactics available within this overall subversive strategy. One is to encounter the imperialist novel on its own terms, by simply offering realist national narratives in place of the ones violently imposed during the process of colonisation. If Irish history itself is fractured, then the realist novel can compensate by supplying satisfying images of unity and coherence. In fact, an Irish realist tradition did emerge during the nineteenth century, offering a challenge to the version of reality disseminated by colonialist discourse and attempting to heal the radical fissures at the heart of Irish history through the construction of closed, coherent narratives. Both the tradition and the tactic have been criticised, however, in that while such texts might wish to attack colonialism, in fact they collude with colonialist discourse in as much as they reproduce certain effects – linear time, self-regulating subjects, the transparency of language – which reinforce the values and beliefs of the dominant formation. For such critics, realism is collusive, no matter what radical intentions inspire it, and it is part of colonialism's subtle cultural politics always to invite resistance precisely where it is least likely to be effective.[17]

A far more effective tactic, according to currently dominant post-colonial theory, is to refuse the representational discourse of the dominant formation, in effect to refuse colonialism's 'reality' though a variety of anti-mimetic techniques which operate at both the formal and the conceptual levels of the text. All the typical effects of the realist novel (linearity, centredness, coherence, causation, closure, above all a *metanarrative* location from which to judge the action of the story) are challenged by ones which more closely represent the reality experienced by the colonised subject (confusion, displacement, ambivalence, in effect a radical alienation from the reality promulgated by colonialist ideology). Moreover, it is not enough for decolonising novelists just to write *about* these alienating experiences; rather, they have to embody these feelings of confusion and uncertainty in their narratives, to try to make the reader experience the same sorts of emotions. The narratives and experiences considered normal and relevant under a colonialist aesthetic must be interrogated by those narratives and experiences which cultural colonialism had consigned to the margins of history. And for all these tasks, colonialism's dominant representational form – realism – is simply not adequate.

This tactic, however, brings its own problems. For one thing, a critical discourse which locates value solely *within* the text – asking: does this text collude with, or refuse, received colonial reality? – seems to overlook the impact of the contexts in which texts are consumed. Realism is not 'bad' in itself, and it would be unwise for the post-colonialist critic to write off a whole tradition of realist Irish fiction simply because within the terms of an abstract theory it is understood to collude with colonialist discourse. Such a strategy is also open to accusations of elitism, as it might be said that such a formal critique of colonial reality would only signify to a reading community already conversant with the ideology underpinning such tactics – in other words, with a fairly restricted avant-garde or academic audience. It seems clear, rather, that in different contexts, the most 'collusive' text could be read subversively, while the most 'radical' anti-colonial text could be ignored or recuperated by colonialist discourse. We might wish to suggest at this early stage that meaning, anti-colonial or otherwise, resides not *within* the text but rather in a complex set of negotiations between authorial intention, textual structure, reading context and audience resources. Any analysis of the Irish novel will have to address this matrix of interpretative factors if it is to avoid pat and misplaced judgements, both on individual texts and on whole sub-traditions.

A second and more fundamental criticism is that colonial reality can never be completely denied, as it constitutes the pre-established terrain upon which all cultural initiatives within the colonial formation must operate. A discourse of resistance which refused received realities completely would be psychotic. The tactic has to be refined, therefore, so that the decolonising subject may change from within a situation that he/she is forced to inhabit. There is no permanent location 'outside' the reality of Irish–British relations from where the decolonising novelist could posit a completely alternative narrative of Irish experience or Irish identity; novelists are thus forced to write from within colonialist reality even as they work to subvert it. This means that the resisting novelist must inhabit a dual location simultane-ously within and outwith colonial reality, reproducing that real-ity but in ways which always question its provenance, its rel-evance, its political function. The most effective post-colonial tactic according to this theory is not one which seeks to replace colonial reality with a pristine national reality which has some-how miraculously remained unscathed from colonial history, but rather 'to evolve textual strategies which continually "consume" their "own biases" at the same time as they expose and erode those of the dominant discourse'.[18]

This strategy has started to be theorised by post-colonial crit-ics in terms of hybridity, mimicry, parody and a range of other discursive devices which, it is claimed, unsettle the borders which structure traditional critical and creative practices.[19] It represents, above all, a deliberate policy of 'being difficult', being difficult at a formal level – that is, problems of reference, allu-sion, intentional ambiguity, interpretation and so on – but also 'being difficult' in the sense of a recalcitrant, trouble-making attitude towards the common sense of the colonial nexus.

The political imperative foisted onto the novelist by anti-colonial and, more lately, post-colonial criticism has not always been well received by Irish writers or critics. Many Irish novelists would simply not acknowledge the post-colonial model of politico-aesthetic discourse just described. It could indeed be argued that novelists from formerly subaltern formations who self-consciously adopt tactics of mimicry or hybridity or whatever are answering the agenda of metropolitan theories of how a post-colonial novel *should* be written, and thus complying with neo-colonialist strategies for maintaining the discursive borders between the centre and the margins.[20] However this may be, it is a good argument for not allowing theory to dominate the critical process, but using theory rather as a point, or a series of points, of departure for criticism.

The novel as carnival

Since the development of the idea of a modern Irish nation, the novel has had to compete with other cultural forms as the most effective 'narrator' of the nation. During the nineteenth century, when cultural nationalism was at its most active and most self-conscious, the novel suffered in comparison with poetry. This was partly because cultural nationalism at this stage was still influenced to a large degree by *past*-oriented culture *of* the nation which looked back to the Gaelic bardic tradition as the highpoint of Irish cultural achievement. Verse, especially epic and occasional (that is, written about specific events or people), was immediate, ritualistic, heightened, clearly *of* and *for* the nation in ways which prose fiction seemed not. Similarly, during the Second Celtic Revival around the turn of the twentieth century, it was to poetry and drama rather than prose that cultural nationalists looked to articulate the nation, cultural forms in which *how* you wrote had to answer the serious nature of *what* you were writing about.

Many Irish cultural nationalists felt that the novel, on the other hand, was inadequate to the task of representing the nation. The novel, it was felt, was a form which had emerged specifically from the concerns of British cultural history and the existence of its leisured middle class. Given the distortions of which it was capable and the kind of readership it seemed to attract, the novel was a debased cultural form wherein it was impossible to address the serious concerns of nation-building. There seemed to be something deeply contradictory in *fictional* representations of national *reality*, and there was always the danger that the message of even the most didactic novel could be lost if the reader became preoccupied with the pleasures of the narrative. At the same time, it seemed to many that Irish society was too 'thin', not subtle or developed or large enough to sustain a novelistic tradition, and when prose fiction did emerge as a form it was the short story – with its roots in the Gaelic story-telling tradition and the moral-didactic tales of the first part of the nineteenth century – rather than the novel which drew the Irish prose writer. Behind such critiques of the amorphousness of Irish history one can usually detect a nostalgia for some kind of organic, pre-lapsarian society in which the individual and the community were at ease with each other. It is arguable that Irish history never witnessed such a situation; and even if it had, it is by no means certain that a stable, 'thick' society, contrary to the standard argument, produces more or better novels.

These tendencies for drama, verse and shorter fiction, and against the novel, have continued to exercise an influence on Irish cultural debate to the present. Certain contemporary critics still argue that the typical realist novel with its coherent narrative focused on an individual hero progressing towards self-knowledge is alien to the historical contradictions out of which modern Ireland has developed. It is only when the novel is made difficult – parodied, mimicked, overlain with other forms of narrative and other genres – that it ceases to collude with the colonialist *status quo*.

This deep-seated prejudice against the novel is important now that we have come to look at the work of the Russian literary critic and philosopher of language Mikhail Bakhtin, whose theories regarding the mutual development of the novel and the nation are of seminal importance to our concerns here. Turning to his theories of language first, all western societies, claims Bakhtin, experience a struggle between two contradictory politico-cultural tendencies. On the one hand, the history of these societies reveals a tendency towards *monoglossia* – 'mono' meaning one and 'glossia' meaning language. As any society develops it will attempt to 'unify and centralise the verbalideological world' – in other words, to close down the relationship between language and meaning to the point where they appear to map onto each other in an entirely natural, organic way.[21] This movement towards centralisation and the unification of language and meaning, Bakhtin claims, is typical of the way power has traditionally operated within western societies, and its effects can be discerned in all manner of cultural and political discourses.

The nation, at least in its early stages, demonstrates just such a tendency. As it emerges in the eighteenth century, nationalism is characterised by the singularity of its vision, by the fact that it works for a monologic discourse which will convey essential national truths in an essential national language. *Future*-oriented culture *for* the nation, especially, invests in the notion of an organic link between language and society in which the very essence of the community is embodied in one particular serious, straightforward discourse. Other discourses tend to be marginalised because they cannot express the nation's sense of social, political and historical destiny. The success of the imagined community, especially when it is engaged in a colonial struggle, depends on monoglossia, on getting enough of the subjugated population speaking the same language, asking the same questions and arriving at the same answers at the same time to effect political and cultural change.

The cultural form which answers this drive towards unity and coherence is the epic. As derived from ancient Greek and Roman example, the epic encapsulates the spirit of the imagined community in a single, serious, straightforward narrative. Because it has taken as its task the prior constitution of the nation, cultural nationalism requires epic representations of the nation; it requires, that is, texts which not only represent (that is, show) the nation at the thematic level, but which also represent (that is, stand for) the unity and coherence of the nation at a formal and generic level. The problem was, however, that despite the best efforts of Irish and European scholars to discover such a text, none appeared to exist.[22] These scholars could posit the existence of an *Ur*-epic, an original text from which all Celtic mythology derived; sometimes, indeed, the land itself becomes an ideal image of the epic – in the words of the poet Seamus Heaney, a sort of manuscript which Irish people have lost the skill to read.[23] But the fragmentary nature of the medieval and early modern texts that did exist were an implicit indictment of the incoherence and dispersion of the nation. In the absence of *the* epic which would serve as the basis for cultural and political unity, therefore, Irish critical discourse from the late eighteenth century became obsessed with the identification of epic effects in other, less deserving but more amenable forms. One such form was the novel.

At the same time as cultural nationalism insists upon unity and integration as pre-requisites for full decolonisation, however, the very struggle to impose unity undermines the ideology of a single, natural, national language. In fact, Bakhtin discerns a counter-tendency which emerges alongside monoglossia, one which works to decentralise and disunify the discursive practices of any given society. A national language exists, by definition, in the fatal awareness of other languages, for beyond the borders of the imagined community there are many other languages against which the nation measures its sense of identity – a historical development Bakhtin calls *heteroglossia*. At the same time, the idea of a natural link between language and meaning is inherently flawed as there is always struggle *within* a given language for control over meaning. A particular *national* language is stratified into all manner of *social* languages – all the different ways of speaking in all the different situations that may be found in any society. All language, that is, is radically *dialogic* – active, unstable and diffused rather than fixed. For Bakhtin, language is material and historical, not ideal and universal; language use is always a process of making meaning rather than just an act of communication from within a pre-established code. From the civilisation of the Greeks to the twentieth century, the history of western culture demonstrates the ongoing struggle between these two tendencies, a struggle which emerges in a variety of cultural, political and ideological practices. This brings us back again to the question of the novel.

Each of the tendencies Bakhtin discerns in the history of western societies give rise to specific cultural forms and practices. The epic is a serious, straightforward discourse wherein the monologic tendency attempts to impose its singular vision of the world and the relationship between language and meaning. At the same time, these practices excite ironic rejoinders, laughing doubles in which serious monological discourse is parodied. This effect, moreover, is ubiquitous. As Bakhtin writes:

> It is our conviction that there never was a single straightforward genre, no single type of direct discourse – artistic, rhetorical, philosophical, religious, ordinary everyday – that did not have its own parodying and travestying double, its own comic-ironic *contre-partie*. What is more, these parodic doubles and laughing reflections of the direct word were, in some cases, just as sanctioned by tradition and just as canonized as their elevated models.[24]

For Bakhtin, literary discourse in general, and the novel specifically, developed to introduce heteroglossia into mono-logic national discourse. The novel is the inheritor of those ancient and medieval genres which had been sanctioned to combat the incomplete vision of the monoglossic epic. The novel, that is, embodies the spirit of *carnivalesque*, that time and place in a society's existence when 'normality' is temporar-ily suspended, and laughter and heteroglossia are the order of the day. Carnivalesque discourse, founded as it is on the mock-ery and menace of the circus, is a threat to the solemnity of cultural nationalism. Unlike the epic, there is no direct discourse in the novel, only dialogic, or what Bakhtin calls 'double-voiced', discourse. A novel 'quotes' from the multitude of languages available within the social, political and historical formations within which it is produced, and the author 'orchestrates' these languages into an artistic whole. But it is specifically its many-voicedness, its juxtaposition of all the high and low languages of the day, that distinguishes the novel as a genre.

Here lies the root of cultural nationalism's antipathy to the novel. In cultural nationalist discourse the novel is required to forsake its carnivalesque inheritance in order to carry out the prime nationalist directive of representing and embodying the imagined community. The novel is expected to function as a straightforward statement, an 'allegory' in Jameson's terms, on the state of the nation by an individual author, demonstrating the unity of artistic vision which will function as a cultural prerequisite for a successful political nationalism. In insisting that the novel belongs to the nation, however, cultural national-ism is forced to construe the novel in a manner which denies its dialogic, carnivalesque lineage; that is, the absolute heteroglossia identified by Bakhtin as constitutive of the novel form is cat-egorically disallowed. Cultural nationalism appropriates the novel, compelling it to perform monologic ideological tasks for which, as an essentially dialogic form, it is fundamentally unsuited. In this task, however, it can never be entirely success-ful, and even when novelists self-consciously take on the role of decolonising teacher the form of the novel will resist and exceed all such intentions. The novel, it would seem, is capable of articulating *and* resisting both cultural colonialism *and* cultural nationalism.

One of the advantages of Bakhtin's theories is that they allow us to avoid abstract and ahistorical moralising about realism and the subversive powers of anti-realism. Much post-colonial cultural theory, as we saw in the previous section, turns on the notion of disrupting imperial reality as expressed in its dominant narrative forms. It could be argued, however, that such a theory seriously overplays the homogeneity of imperial cultural discourse. The typical English novel of the nineteenth and twentieth centuries, for example, although obviously emerging from a much more secure tradition than its Irish counterpart, seldom fits the image of the stable, coherent narrative against which the disrupted, resisting narrative of the colonised subject can be measured. Like any novel, it is dialogic, multi-voiced, composed of various social and political discourses and orchestrated into a narrative by the organising voice of the author-narrator. Reading from Bakhtin, however, we can avoid the post-colonial fairy-tale which tells of the Big Bad Wolf of English realism versus the playful, subversive, anti-realist nature of Irish story-telling. Rather, the struggle between colonising and decolonising cultural discourse can be understood in terms of an economy of *centripetal* (centralising) and *centrifugal* (decentralising) tendencies, a discursive economy that is closely linked to the wider politico-historical relations between the colonial communities. Theorising in terms of historical *tendencies* rather than universal *attributes* allows for a much more flexible and sensitive criticism. Thus, the English novel might be said to be dialogic, but as part of the colonialist project to centralise and normalise the terrain of cultural exchange it is also recognisably *centripetal*, organised in such a way as to silence and control the disparate voices of which it is composed. Similarly, we can account for the *centrifugal* tendencies of Irish fiction and the emergence of a tradition of Irish modernism, and we can trace the influence of such a tradition down to the present day. At the same time, such a theory does not tie Irish novelistic discourse to a perpetual anti-realist impulse, as at certain times and from certain points of view a secure, centralising tendency will dominate.

CONCLUSION

This is the cluster of critical and theoretical concepts to be brought to bear on Irish fiction in the remainder of this book. We have looked at the rise of the nation and cultural nationalism, preparing the way for an assessment of the impact of these ideas on Irish cultural history generally and on the development of the novel particularly. We have also examined a number of theories specifically regarding the relations between the novel and the nation. From Anderson we get the idea of novel and nation as reciprocal 'imagined communities', the former functioning as a kind of material analogue for the latter. Such a theory allows us to ask questions about the self-conscious development of national identity, about the relations between novelistic hero and community, and between cultural and political discourses generally. From Jameson we get the idea of the novel as a 'socially symbolic act' which functions as a cultural eruption of the 'national unconscious' operating below the 'real' or conscious history of colonial relations. This theory constrains us to raise issues to do with literary form and its relation with the historical 'reality' to which a text ostensibly refers. Jameson also raises crucial issues for traditional critical discourse and its mission to unify authorial intention, literary form and critical interpretation; the text, he suggests, should rather be read as a site of contradiction and conflict, both in terms of its formal constitution and its critical history. From contemporary post-colonial theory we get the idea of the novel as resistance, a political strategy to disrupt, if not fully refuse, the oppositional 'reality' posited by colonial discourse. The decolonising novelist, working necessarily within colonialist terms of reference, undermines the narratives that circulate in society while indicating the possibility of different positions from which to read and write and make sense of the colonial nexus. Finally, from Bakhtin, we see the novel as a refusal of both cultural colonialism *and* cultural nationalism, the site, rather, of a conclave of the many languages and voices operating in any society, where the pretensions of *monologic* authorial discourse of whatever persuasion are countered. With his theory regarding the development of language, Bakhtin also provides us with a map of cultural history in which we may begin to trace (even if that means revising Bakhtin's own findings) the development of different stages of national form, and especially the form of the novel.

Taken together, with their many points of overlap *and* contradiction, these theories provide the critical backdrop for our analysis of the 'Irish novel'. As should already be clear, these two words are in fact in constant conversation with each other, for if the 'novel' asks questions of what it is to be 'Irish', then the word 'Irish' has always challenged any normative notion of the 'novel'.

To quote David Lloyd, and to anticipate slightly:

> We are only just beginning to forge the theoretical terms in which
> the atypicality of the Irish novel can be analysed but ... it may be
> that we are approaching a 'less coherent but in many ways more
> interesting theory of the novel'.[25]

2 FORMS

By all accounts, writing novels in and about Ireland has never been a straightforward business. This is not a pejorative judgement on the inability of Irish writing to measure up to some standard model of what the novel should be. Neither does it place an onus of enforced 'strangeness' on the Irish novel. The peculiar history of fiction writing in Ireland tells more, perhaps, about the ideology of cultural prescription than it does about any lack or anomaly in Irish history. Yet, it is still necessary to account for the peculiarities of that history if we are to trace the formal and thematic lines from which the modern Irish novel springs. What follows in the next two chapters, therefore, is not a straightforward chronological or critical account of the history of the Irish novel, of which there already exist a number of examples of varying usefulness (see 'Criticism and theory – Irish context' in the bibliography). Rather, I wish to describe very briefly the nation's novelistic tradition in terms of certain recurring themes and formal characteristics which, I shall be arguing, have significant implications for novelistic discourse at the approach of the millennium. In this way, I hope to provide a genealogy for the contemporary Irish novel, showing how it continues to engage with many traditional concerns even as it looks to renegotiate the possibilities of the novel in relation to the developing nation.

Chapter 3 will examine three of the major recurring themes of the Irish novel by way of preparation for their revisitation and reworking in the texts analysed in Part 2. In this chapter I shall look at the questions of form which have influenced the development of novelistic discourse in Ireland. All artists are constrained to negotiate a relationship between the reality they wish to represent and the means available to do so. This relationship becomes especially fraught, however, in situations (such as colonialism) where both sides of the artistic equation

– reality and representation – are thoroughly infused with considerations of power and privilege. Traditionally, for the Irish novelist to attempt to represent the nation, she/he had to engage with a discourse in which both medium and message had complex political resonances. These resonances, moreover, did not simply disappear with the changing fortunes of history. Rather, they evolved, accommodated, hybridised and sublimated themselves, so that the modern Irish novelist continues to work with them, consciously or not. In this chapter, we shall be examining the relationship between reality and representation in Irish novelistic discourse by looking at issues of authorship, narrative form and audience.

THE AUTHOR

Irish writers have been writing long prose narratives in the English language for a great variety of reasons for many years. It is only since the late eighteenth century, however, that such a practice came to be directly linked with the process of nation-forming; even then, the impulse to represent the nation constituted only one among a number of possible options animating the Irish novelist. Nevertheless, the proliferation of narratives concerning the state of Ireland and Irishness from the turn of the nineteenth century is testament to the fact that novel and nation were becoming directly linked in the contemporary imagination. But why? Given that a particular writer wishes to engage with the nation, why choose the novel as the vehicle of that engagement? If one's assumed task is to combat certain stereotypical images of Irish character, or to assess the historical and economic factors underpinning contemporary conditions, or to mobilise large numbers of people behind a certain cause or belief, why choose the novel rather than the pamphlet, the ballad, the poem, the history, the editorial or the political speech? If you do choose the novel, why write it in English, the clearest emblem in the national life of Irish defeat and English domination?

The novel, in fact, was far from an innocent or trouble-free choice for the early Irish writers, and when a novel tradition did begin to emerge it revealed traces of all these other genres in its formal make-up. For the early Irish novelist looking to represent the nation, however, there were three basic problems concerning the issue of authorship which had to be addressed.

Anthropology or fiction?

The first problem was the danger of losing focus on the primary principle of the form – narrative – in the wish to polemicise and to intervene actively in contemporary debate. Novelistic discourse, that is, was in danger of being overwhelmed by a sort of anthropological discourse in which, as part of a general decolonising programme, Irish writers used their intimate knowledge of the manners and morals of the nation to combat negative and disabling colonial representations. The novel could become the vehicle for special pleading, a showcase where the peculiarities of Irish life could be displayed with the purpose of eliciting sympathy or arousing anger. The narrative itself was of secondary importance; indeed, some Irish novelists of the nineteenth century were not averse to suspending any mimetic pretence by frequently referring to real events, places and people in their 'real', non-narrative voice. But as the narrative was manipulated to answer an extra-literary agenda – the real world of contemporary Irish–English politics – so that world was a constant threat to the narrative impulse intended to expedite the national cause. For example, whereas Maria Edgeworth managed to keep the anthropological and narrative impulses in more or less equilibrium in her exemplary novel *Castle Rackrent* (1800), by the time she came to write *The Absentee* (1812) this facility for balance appears to have deserted her, and the latter novel is quite obviously a special plea for a political settlement favoured by the author. The fictional world, that is, loses its potential to engage the reader in as much as it can be seen to be subservient to another, 'real' world; as a consequence the narrative is constantly on the verge of degeneration into melodrama and stereotype.

So, within the typical Irish novel of the nineteenth century there was a dual impulse – one towards the virtual world in which the narrative is set, and one towards the real world in which such representations are part of the key currency of colonial power. Maintaining a balance between these impulses presents the Irish novelist with a difficult and recurring problem.

Stereotypes

If the anthropological impulse becomes too strong, the novelistic character can cease to have an active role within the fictional narrative and become merely a counter in the extra-literary world of Irish–English colonial relations. As a consequence, the wish to analyse and describe Ireland can very easily fall into the trap of reproducing the stereotypes of colonialist discourse, only this time with a fragile positive emphasis. As every colonialist knew, Ireland was everything England was not, but in the hands of a writer such as Lady Morgan (Sydney Owenson), for example – author of the infamous *The Wild Irish Girl* (1806) and a number of similarly improbable Irish tales – this was precisely what was attractive, romantic and exotic about the country. In fact, the category of 'national character' which had arrived in Ireland as part of the colonial enterprise proved too strong a temptation for most Irish novelists, and if it facilitated the exploitative fictions of Lady Morgan, it has proved a persistent bane to the creativity of other writers more conscious of their responsibilities in representing the nation.

Maria Edgeworth's *Castle Rackrent* is usually hailed as the first regional novel of the British Isles, and this is true in as much as there exists a clear gap in knowledge and power between the world of the narrative and the manner in which that narrative is organised and related. But this hiatus between the *telling* of the tale and the *world* of the tale is one that troubled authors much more sympathetic to Ireland than Edgeworth. The colonial and post-colonial novelist is forced to tread a very precarious line between positive reclamation of the nation on the one hand, and stereotypical reproduction of a received, exotic otherness on the other. Moreover, despite authorial intention, these positive images are so many hostages to the fortune of an audience dispersed over time and space, for what begins its career as a positive, enabling representation can in different contexts be deployed for the most negative, disabling reasons.

The problem of representation was of course made more difficult for the early Irish novelists in that they were attempting to forge a tradition of Irish fiction in English where little existed. But the difficulty itself has persisted and emerges in the work of the post-colonial novelist. Even when the contemporary Irish writer attempts to refute colonialist stereotypes – by simply ignoring them or by showing the complexity of Irish character – something of the original force of those stereotypes remains, testament to the fact that colonialism is as much a matter of cultural representation and psychological perception as it is of politico-economic organisation. Thus, a novel such as James Stephens's *The Crock of Gold* (1912) can turn up sixty years later as the Francis Ford Coppola film *Finian's Rainbow*, metamorphosing in the process from brilliant exploration of the tradition of fantasy and magic into blatant exploitation of stage-Irishness.

Alienation

Maintaining an ironic distance on Irish life could be empowering, as in the case of Edgeworth, but it could also be a radically unsettling experience, especially for those who had a less self-conscious identification with Gaelic Catholic Ireland. Indeed, this distance between reality and representation, when experienced as a necessity rather than as a choice, could be said to be responsible for one of the principal recurring motifs of Irish artistic experience – alienation.

As part of the general decolonising discourse of cultural nationalism, the early nineteenth-century novelists self-consciously took it as their task to describe Ireland from the inside. In doing so they confirmed their organic links with the community. But that task involved a necessary act of translation – literal and metaphorical – from one way of experiencing the world into another, and with translation came loss. Most obviously, the language (English) and the form (a long prose narrative) in which the novelists chose to present their images of the community were alien to that community, and thus a clear sign of its fragility, if not its imminent loss. The early novelists wished to record and celebrate a unique Irish world, but by translating that world into the English language and into novelistic form they were at the same time implicated in its demise.

More generally, it might be argued that a culture needing, or indeed allowing, translation into a modern idiom is already lost, because the very act assumes that culture's inability to sustain itself. The modern age is one in which reality relies upon representation for its existence, and the artist, as the main broker of representation within society, is heavily implicated in that loss. To the extent that Ireland assumed a literary existence in the work of the early novelists, it began to lose its actual existence as a factor in their lived experience. Rather than functioning as confirmation of the artist's authentic links with the community, therefore, the novel could instead signal the diminution of such links. For the Irish novelist, then, representing the nation is a highly ambivalent undertaking. As well as being the practice whereby the writer confirms her/his identification with the community, it is also the location where 'authentic' Ireland is undone, becoming an effect rather than a cause, and having to rely upon artificial discourses such as the novel, and the printed word generally, for what had formerly seemed a spontaneous order of experience.

The artist, as a representative national figure, is one of the first to experience the dismantling of the organic link between the individual and the community. As the tradition grows, however, this loss can come to seem more of a burden to be resented than a breach to be healed. The guilt of being implicated in the loss of the community turns to feelings of resentment, and the paradox whereby every act *for* the nation is also an act *against* it creates a kind of artistic neurosis in which the very act of writing becomes a highly unstable practice. By the same token, special knowledge of the community can be seen as a curb on creativity rather than as the fountain from which artistic creativity springs. This accounts for the ambivalent relationship many novelists have with Ireland: drawn towards it because of their intimate knowledge on the one hand, yet exiled from it – actually or metaphorically – through guilt and fear of being overwhelmed by that knowledge. At the same time, buried deep beneath the resentment and alienation there may frequently be discerned a romantic nostalgia for the lost community.

Much of the Irish novelistic tradition is marked by this movement, from initial confirmation of the community, through subsequent recognition of its inevitable loss (and the part writing plays in that loss), and on to an attempt to heal the breach between individual and community through the construction of more and more artificial resolutions of the contradictions of Irish history, or to the invention of alternative myths of community and belonging. In an uncanny reversal of priorities, art itself comes to be seen as an alternative order of experience in the work of many novelists, a possible escape from the millstone of history. The key figure here is James Joyce, and his character Stephen Dedalus (from the novels *A Portrait of the Artist as a Young Man* [1916] and *Ulysses* [1922]) is the most fully drawn image of alienated artist in the Irish novelistic tradition; but the critic Seamus Deane is surely correct when he traces the Joycean motif of alienation to the work of early novelists such as William Carleton and, even earlier, Charles Maturin.[1] Much of the novelistic discourse of the nineteenth and twentieth centuries is characterised by the unstable economy of duty, denial and nostalgic affirmation.

These three problems of authorship which face the Irish novelist – special pleading, the reproduction of stereotypes, and the cycle of alienation and nostalgia – emerge in different ways in the contemporary novel, sometimes overtly, sometimes unconsciously, sometimes parodically, but always in ways which relate to wider developments in Irish identity. This is true also of the problems surrounding the medium in which the Irish novelist works – the novel form itself.

THE TEXT

Narrative as event

The novel was also a problematic form for the early Irish novelists in that its chief formal characteristic – an extended written narrative – was in competition with other, already established forms of story-telling operating within the cultural realm. We recall from Chapter 1 that one of the main arguments against the novel as representative of the nation was that it was an alien import incapable of doing justice to the cultural forms which reflected Ireland's peculiar social and cultural history. Irish writers with their roots in traditional communities had access to the strong oral tradition inherited from Gaelic civilisation. The narrative forms that emerged from this tradition were based around the anecdote, the tale and the sketch; related forms and figures include the street ballad, the Irish Bull (verbal paradoxes, oxymorons and contradictions seen as typical of the Irish character) and perhaps even the Joycean 'epiphany', that moment of insight when something of the nature of things is manifested.

Common to all these forms and figures is the notion that narrative is an *event*, performed by somebody for somebody in specific social and political contexts. Such a discourse differs in many important ways from the novel. For one thing, there is a strong element of *performativity* informing the narrative event. Pleasure is organised not so much around the revelations of plot but around the telling of the tale. The story-teller is not outside or above the story, as is the typical omniscient narrator of the nineteenth-century English novel, but is an active part of it, employing a wide range of skills to collapse the borders between the tale and the telling, while all the time maintaining the audience's investment in the world of the story. The audience can enjoy the tale for itself, but is also invited to participate in the narrating event, to appreciate the way in which the meaning of the tale is dependent on the personality of the mediating story-teller. The realist novel was evolved into an organic whole, requiring the writer to maintain a coherent plot over an extended period of time, and to resolve all loose ends, to close the narrative. The event, on the other hand, is based on specific encounters (which is not to say that it cannot have a complex motivation) and is not averse to including developments and exchanges extraneous to the main action. Such forms also tend to favour dialogue over narrative as the motor of plot. This adds to the atmosphere of the event, while demonstrating the writer's familiarity with the world of the tale.

We noted in the previous section that the transposition of indig-enous oral forms into written ones was an ambivalent undertaking for many Irish writers, a way of damaging the community even as one looked to preserve it. The impetus behind this transposition came by and large from Anglo-Irish-inspired cultural nationalism which, with the vogue for Celtic civilisation from the late eight-eenth century onwards, and with their increased familiarity with local cultural practices, enabled writers from the settler community to sample and reproduce the techniques of traditional story-telling. In fact, its development into specific written forms added another dimension to the possible pleasure of the narrative-as-event, as the reader's identification could now switch between the world of the plot, the moment of narration and the moment of consumption – an economy of reading providing a rich and highly sophisticated cultural experience.

Although, as a technique, narrative-as-event has been employed most successfully in the written form which in terms of length and organisation most closely resembles the traditional discourse – the short story – it is also a recurring figure in the Irish novelistic tradition.

Metafiction and the unstable novel

Another influence on the formal development of the Irish novel was the absence of a secure model of novelistic discourse generally. The novel was not always conceived as a straightforward, develop-mental narrative, nor did the disjunctive Irish novel always arise from the native penchant for anecdote, or the adaptation of tradi-tional oral techniques to literary forms. In the infancy of the genre, the often amorphous nature of Irish novelistic discourse could have more to do with the fundamentally unsettled nature of the novel as a form.

The novel also developed at quite an early stage in its evolution a metadiscursive capacity, to the extent that much of the time, narration and the novel form itself – its limitations, its social and cultural impact, its mythic potential – emerge as explicit themes. The most enduring example (at least until James Joyce's *Ulysses*) of the metanovel was produced by the expatriate Anglo-Irishman Laurence Sterne in his book *Tristram Shandy* (1759–67). So dedicated is the eponymous narrator to communicating the full story of his life that 'real' narration time begins to outstrip narrative time, producing the bizarre situation in which Tristram spends almost the whole book describing the background to his conception and birth. The narrative of Tristram's life is beset by digressions upon a multitude of subjects, and he is forced to abandon, rather than close, the story after nine volumes – a gesture that anticipates the scepticism towards the novel shown by a later Irish writer, Samuel Beckett. This text reveals, then, at the very moment when novelistic discourse was consolidating, the philosophical contradictions upon which the form is based. At the same time, *Tristram Shandy* incorporates a host of other discourses (mathematical, philosophical, religious, military, legal) and narrative techniques (autobiographical, critical, annotational, epistolary) making it, at least in Bakhtinian terms, perhaps the most typical novel in the history of the genre.

These points regarding the instability of the novel form and its own self-questioning are indeed obviously linked with the discussion of Bakhtin in Chapter 1, where it was argued that the novel is defined precisely by its unfinished, unsettled formal status, and by its ability to incorporate a multitude of discourses, genres and forms. Throughout its history, in fact, the Irish novel has demonstrated an ability to sample other forms and influences, to improvise and evolve in the light of changing circumstances, making it perhaps the most exemplary, rather than the most marginal, of novelistic traditions.

Decolonisation

Research into the history of former colonial formations has shown that the difficulties of the colonising and decolonising processes leave enduring scars upon the cultural conscience of writers from the oppressed community. In some fairly obvious ways, political struggle in and over the island has loomed large in Irish fiction. There is, for example, a subgenre of writing, evident in Irish fiction since the eighteenth century, which takes the relations between Ireland and Britain as its explicit theme. The historical novel has also been a popular option for the Irish writer, and there are many novels dealing with the important events in the island's political history.

One of the recurring aspects of this tradition, indeed one of the recurring attractions of writing about fighting, is its 'realism' – that is, the attempt to depict graphic political violence. As we shall see in Chapter 5, in recent years this tendency has been a marked feature of the plethora of novels which take the conflict in Northern Ireland as their theme. This is not to say, of course, that popular genres such as the thriller are incapable of sustaining complex novelistic visions. In *The Informer* (1925), Liam O'Flaherty used the conventions of the thriller to explore the impact of decolonisation, without reducing that struggle to private motivation or indulging in voyeuristic violence. More recently, Bernard MacLaverty's *Cal* (1983) placed realistic political detail in ironic juxtaposition with a self-conscious and recurring motif of Christian imagery. Though poles apart in some respects, the sensitive Cal and the animalistic Gypo (the eponymous 'informer') are similar in that they are both enmeshed in, and made to feel responsible for, social, political and historical contradictions beyond their control. This, these novels seem to suggest, is the ultimate violence that colonialism does to both conqueror and conquered – the psychological damage ensuing from attempts to resolve the irresolvable. This colonial heritage, moreover, can be discerned in ways less obvious than the exploration of violence – indeed, the whole of this present study is in some senses an exploration of that history.

One recurring response to the trauma of colonialism is to introduce another, third term into the equation – hence the importance of the theme of exile. This can mean, on the one hand, actual physical exile – displacement from the homeland as a matter of choice rather than as enforced emigration. The exile differs from the emigrant in that the latter – in the case of Ireland, usually the victim of colonial mismanagement or post-colonial insularity – is likely to bring all the traditional oppositions with his/her other baggage. Even if in time the condition of expatriatism reflects back on the original category of Irishness, emigration is no guarantee of the distance necessary to escape the deadly prison house of colonialist modes of thought. Neither is exile, of course, but in its willingness to introduce another voice into the Irish–English exchange, it represents the beginnings of an enabling post-colonial discourse, one in which both Irishness and Englishness can be seen for the contingent, mutually implicated categories that they are. In his actual physical exile from Ireland, as well as in his art, James Joyce offered a cosmopolitan critique of colonialism, seeing it as a parochial sideshow to the main events of human history – love, perception, death. And in less ambitious ways, novelists such as Kate O'Brien, Julia O'Faolain and Francis Stuart have used the device of the Irish subject abroad, as well as their own experiences of exile, to shed ironic light on the narrowness of the Irish–British imagination at home.

By the same token, true exile can take place without physical displacement. Exile can be an interior process of alienation from the narrow definitions of homeland which characterise post-revolutionary Irishness. When, in the first sentence of the novel, the unnamed student narrator of Flann O'Brien's *At Swim-Two-Birds* retires into the privacy of his mind with a mouthful of food, he is exiling himself from the mean spiritual and intellectual fare of post-colonial Ireland. The reader enters a realm in which Ireland is relieved from its constant oppositional status, a realm in which the nation's rich cultural inheritance will nourish rather than constrain the national subject. Indeed, there exists an entire counter-tradition of the Irish novel which can be understood as an attempt to escape the limitations of the nation's colonial heritage and the manner in which it was forced to construe the world in terms of rigidly defined, oppositional categories – Irish and English, woman and man, national and alien.

It may be the case, as Seamus Deane has argued, that Joyce's towering example has led some Irish artists to make a fetish of exile, seeing physical displacement and the elevation of art into an alternative mythology as the only valid responses to the contradictions of colonialism.[2] It may also be, as is arguably the case with Joyce, that what the exile – physical or mental – eventually discovers is the impossibility of exile. Yet that discovery in itself surely constitutes some kind of development beyond the cycle of affirmation and denial fostered under colonialism.

THE READER

For whom does the novelist write? The question of audience is of course a major consideration for any artist, both in practical terms (encompassing issues of marketing, publishing, technology, ethics, and so on) and in terms of imagining the actual reading event (the physical encounter between text and a range of possible readers). Since the Industrial Revolution, and despite the Romantic ideology of the spontaneously conceived work of art, every novelist has been constrained to consider the market and the relationship between private vision and public consumption. Every novel is thus targeted at a particular readership, although this does not constrain possible reading opportunities, or indeed the ways in which the text will actually be consumed and activated by its target audience. At the same time, every novel, like every example of human discourse, has an addressee of some sort encoded into its discourse, an ideal reading subject whom the text, as it were, brings into being. When we read novels, therefore, we are also being read by them in terms of their authorial intentions and expectations.

Writing for the coloniser

Like the other formal issues examined so far in this chapter, the category of audience is of crucial importance in societies touched by colonialism. The Irish novelistic tradition from the early eighteenth century to the present reveals a discourse in which all manner of special pleading, cultural pandering and subtle hegemonic manoeuvring is directed at an encoded English reader. Some of these considerations are entirely practical. Since the eighteenth century Britain has possessed a much stronger publishing and literary culture than Ireland, and it seems only obvious that generations of Irish novelists should turn to London when it came to bringing their work before a reading public.

But the influence of an implicit English audience can have more insidious effects. It has been argued that Ireland was invented as a response to certain British needs at a particular moment in the history of its imperial development.[3] The image of a romantic Celtic fringe was developed in the latter half of the eighteenth century as a foil for England's own pragmatic, progressive identity and to provide a space where the jaded metropolitan imagination could take occasional holidays from the rigours of the imperialist project. Novels provided one of the major locations for this invention, a discourse, as in *The Wild Irish Girl* (1806) by Lady Morgan, in which the 'Ireland' that is described is one heavily dependent upon English notions of what life in the Celtic margins *should* be – romantic, sentimental, wild and natural, capable of healing the rift between Nature and an overly refined European civilisation in danger of complete enervation.

In keeping with the split in the English imagination between reason and emotion, Ireland becomes the repository of the affective, the spontaneous, the extreme. 'Our national music', reveals Glorvina, the wild Irish girl, 'like our national character, admits of no medium in sentiment; it either sinks our spirit to despondency by its heart-breaking pathos, or elevates it to wildness by its exhilarating animation' (p. 64). It could be said in fact that the Ireland of Lady Morgan functions as a sort of English unconscious – a site where the fears and desires repressed under the pressures of the real world of capitalism and imperialist politics surface. This is a typical strategy of containment, a means of securing one's own identity by the invocation of all that is different yet uncannily familiar and attractive at the same time. History is reduced to personality and 'Ireland' becomes the quaint, exotic, romantic object of the colonial gaze.

What *The Wild Irish Girl* reveals, in fact, is the radical instability of an Irish identity founded on conflicting notions of equality and difference, and the formal problems ensuing from such a wide discrepancy between narrative and audience. Instead of Bakhtinian carnival the Irish novel can all too readily degenerate into a kind of fictional zoo – a space where the sophisticated English reader may visit to marvel at the sheer otherness of Ireland before returning once again to the security of metropolitan normality.

Writing for the post-colonial

The formal contradictions of *The Wild Irish Girl* are mirrored in Morgan's own position as a subject doubly alienated because of her hyphenated national identity, and alienated still further because of her gender. Of course, there were good reasons for Anglo-Irish novelists to play this particular game of pandering to an English audience. The reproduction of stereotypes was an effective system of demonstrating Anglo-Irish control over the recalcitrant Irish, a way of confirming leadership through intimate knowledge of Irish language, landscape and character. But the problem of audience is more acute for future-oriented cultural nationalists dedicated to the realisation of an Ireland independent of English tastes or preferences. There is always a danger that the Irish novelists will be tempted to reproduce received images of Irishness and thus repeat the cycle of misrepresentation and misrecognition. Even the most anti-colonial novel can degenerate into melodrama, a mere rehearsal of stereotypes across a well-established social and political canvas. The dearth of a sufficient native audience can also manifest itself in artistic discourse as a regret for the lost connection between the individual and society.

Lack of confidence in a domestic readership is one reason for the great flowering of Irish modernism around the turn of the twentieth century, as well as that strange blending of naturalism and self-consciousness that passes for realism in much Irish writing. Nevertheless, the doubt and decline fostered under colonialism has been interspersed with periods of cultural confidence in which, as part of a broad cultural nationalist discourse, Irish novelists were less concerned with an inevitable English readership than with a native audience independent of off-shore considerations. But just as Irish artists were discovering that they could forsake the slavish gaze towards England, they found themselves victims of probably the most draconian anti-literary measures in the 'free' world – the Censorship of Publications Act of 1929. And as these measures were endorsed by successive governments, an entire generation of novelists who should have benefited from the post-colonial dispensation found themselves castigated and their books banned. It is impossible to gauge with precision the impact of censorship on Irish writing. Most novelists, it would seem, refused to compromise – indeed, there was a certain *kudos* involved in having one's books banned by the state. We could speculate counterfactually on the Irish novels that did not appear because of censorship, but perhaps it is more useful to understand the phenomenon as indicative of a wider post-revolutionary condition in which the state's paranoia regarding its own credentials introduced a general atmosphere of malaise into every sphere of the national imagination.

Censorship eased somewhat during the 1960s with the fading of the political old guard and the coming of new times and new figures in Irish life. In recent years the appearance of a number of Irish presses producing a range of domestic literary material, as well as fundamental changes in the nation's social, economic and political life, have acted as incentives to a new generation of novelists. The Irish remain the greatest book-buying and reading public in Europe, and after seventy years of independence the Irish writer can assume the existence of a settled social basis against which to set fictions. This confidence may be observed in many ways. Approaching the end of the century, Irish novelists no longer feel constrained to locate their work in terms of self-conscious 'Irish' concerns. They offer to deal instead with a broad spectrum of human experience, and with themes which, perhaps possessing local significance, also have a wider resonance. At the same time, there is enough of a domestic audience to ensure that these novelists need not interrupt their narratives to explain the use of local forms and themes for a non-indigenous readership. Irish experiences of life in the modern world offer enough of a bridge to foreign readers – if such a bridge is required – and the nation's writers do not need the props of revolutionary history or stereotypical character or local idiom to evoke international interest. In short, the contemporary Irish novelist may take for granted the existence of a domestic audience inhabiting the same social, cultural and political milieu. Of course, this does not mean that such novels will confirm the world view of the audience that constitutes their fictional milieu – more often than not, in fact, the contrary is true.

3 THEMES

MADNESS AND DREAMS

Since the eighteenth century, the Irish cultural imagination has revealed a deep fascination with discourses of insanity, horror, fantasy, nightmare – any instance, in fact, in which 'normality' or 'reality' comes under pressure. The alternative realities produced by madness and dreams can be pathological or drug-induced, comic or tragic, central or peripheral; but the theme spans all aspects of the Irish novel from the most intellectual to the most popular. But why have madness and dreams played such important parts in Irish fiction for so long, and why do they persist into the present?

There are four major sources for the recurrence of these themes in contemporary Irish fiction – the violence of colonialism and decolonisation; the experimental possibilities afforded by an invented or rediscovered tradition of myth and magic; the nightmare of an alienated, 'Gothic' history as manifested in religious, architectural and familial discourse; and the 'unreal' or 'anti-rational' nature of literature itself. Taken together and in a wide range of possible combinations and degrees, they provide a discursive matrix in which it would have been highly unlikely for madness and dreams not to have appeared in some form or other in the cultural produce of this historical community.

Colonialism and mental health

Many commentators and critics have focused on the socio-psychological damage wrought by colonialism, and two accounts have been especially influential. In his book *The Wretched of the Earth*, the Algerian psychiatrist and political activist Frantz Fanon tried to identify the particular kinds of mental disorders which occur in a colonialist situation.[1] Fanon argued that the various factors attending colonialism and decolonisation – the constant questioning of one's identity, the context of violence, the common acceptance of social, political and cultural inequality – constitute a threat to the psychological stability of colonised subjects. Whether the passive victim of colonialist oppression or the active agent of decolonisation, the colonial subject is forced to negotiate traumatic social, cultural and political developments, and these traumas can eventually lead to crisis and breakdown of mental health. Thus, there is for Fanon a specific historical reason behind the ubiquity of madness as a theme in, and as an influence upon, the culture of colonised and post-colonial peoples.

Another figure who has focused on the psychological aspects of colonialism is the Indian writer Ashis Nandy.[2] Nandy sees colonialism as an operation which occurs principally in, and is legitimised by, the mind. This is not to deny the economic or political basis to colonialism, but merely to stress that such material processes need the support of coherent cultural and psychological systems to rationalise, indeed to idealise, what otherwise might appear to be unacceptable. As such, colonialism is one specific historical instance of the mental process whereby external phenomena are organised in ways which allow subjects and communities to enter into unequal, stratified relationships with other subjects and communities. And because colonialism occupies the mind and the imagination of the oppressed as well as the land, decolonisation can never be just a process of successful armed resistance. It would be naive, Nandy suggests, to believe that the structures of thought which characterise the specific historical phenomena of colonialism and decolonisation simply disappear at the moment when the colonial power decamps. Instead, such psychological systems persist well into the post-colonial era, producing all manner of observable effects in the individual and in society at large.

This mental dimension to colonialism is, for Nandy, its chief and most insidious characteristic, for it fosters a culture 'in which the ruled are constantly tempted to fight their rulers within the psychological limits set by the latter' (p. 3). We have encountered versions of this argument above when discussing the choice facing the decolonising novelist between operating within colonialist reality or refusing that reality and seeking to construct alternative systems of representation. In terms of the mental health of the decolonising subject, however, both these alternatives constitute a danger: resisting 'within the psychological rules' set by the rulers means that even when successful the subject remains a victim of alien modes of thought, trapped within a colonialist logic of Self and Other; refusing the consensual logic of colonialism, on the other hand, means that the subject is in constant danger of complete alienation, slipping into a madness which once again confirms the opposition between (rational) coloniser and (irrational) colonised.

Where Nandy differs significantly from Fanon is in his stress on the mental damage that colonialism does to oppressor as well as to oppressed. The 'victors' in the colonial encounter 'are ultimately shown to be camouflaged victims, at an advanced stage of psychosocial decay' (p. xvi). Domination, that is, produces mental systems and conditions which warp the dominating subject. Another danger behind the decolonising subject's wish to 'defeat' the coloniser is that one kind of victimage will be replaced by another. Nandy and Fanon are united, however, in their insistence that colonialism is produced by, and produces in turn, specific mental conditions, and while every colonial formation is obviously different, there is enough of a common basis to make these models very suggestive for an analysis of Irish cultural history.

The Gaelic tradition of fantasy and the macabre

Another factor bearing on the ubiquity of madness and dreams as themes in the Irish novel is the ancient Gaelic tradition of non-realist narrative based on legend, myth and magic. Scholars have revealed a recurring scepticism amongst early Irish artists and philosophers with regard to the material world, and a concomitant fascination with fantasy, dreams and visions. The principal location of the Gaelic otherworld tradition is the ancient Mythological Cycle based upon the exploits of the *Tuatha Dé Danann* (The Tribes of the God – or Goddess – Danu), the fairy race who held Ireland before the coming of the Gaels and who subsequently disappeared into the landscape. These tales incorporate a number of figures and forms which have proved significant in the emergence of an Irish novelistic tradition.

The poet W.B. Yeats was the key figure who worked to reintroduce the ancient narrative culture as an important aspect of modern Irish artistic discourse. Yeats functioned as a conduit between the Gaelic scholars of the nineteenth century and the poets, novelists and dramatists working in the contemporary Irish–British public sphere. After Yeats, the ancient Gaelic tradition became an important part of the Irish writer's imaginative landscape, and it became possible to incorporate elements of the tradition, as well as to experiment with its characteristic themes and forms. As one critic puts it: 'There is no doubt that the fairies and the ancient gods provided the Irish prose writer with a remarkable opportunity for experimental fiction, for breaking with the conventions of realism in pursuit of a purer sense of reality.'[3]

This 'pursuit of a purer sense of reality' is a crucial aspect of any discourse of decolonisation. As has been emphasised already, colonial reality and its attendant aesthetic discourse of realism constitute a problem for the colonised community and for the decolonising writer. The rediscovery or invention under the auspices of cultural nationalism of a tradition in which the world of the immediate senses is only one amongst many different kinds of realities affords the modern Irish writer an established means for refusing or problematising colonial reality, one that appears to emerge 'naturally' from pre-colonial times as evidence of the cultural and political validity of the nation. This latter issue – the extent to which the tradition inherited by post-Yeatsian writers was in fact an *invention* of cultural nationalist discourse of the 1890s – cannot detain us here; what we do need to recognise is that this reluctance to countenance the organisation of the world along materialist, positivist lines might appear to those with an investment in that world to be a form of madness, a perverse refusal to accept the world as it 'really' is. The image of the 'Mad Irish' has entered the collective imagination of large sections of the world, especially those with significant Irish populations, and madness can thus be seen to be caught up in a complex web in which it simultaneously resists and reinforces colonial ideology.

What are the principal figures that the modern Irish novel inherited from the Gaelic tradition? Three things are worth pointing out: visions, magic and humour.[4] Visions were an important part of the ancient Cycles and reappeared during the eighteenth century in the work of the disinherited Gaelic poets in the form of the *aisling*, a genre in which a vulnerable woman (symbol of the ancient Gaelic order) is encountered by a young man (symbol of contemporary Irish youth coming to the defence of the nation). Such a theme may be said to echo still in the many and varied uses of the dream as a motif in contemporary Irish fiction. Magic was another important aspect of the ancient tradition, leading some critics to argue that its reappearance in the work of certain novelists of the twentieth century constitutes an Irish precedent for magic realism, the fictional form so

popular and successful amongst novelists from other decolonising
formations such as Latin America and the Indian subcontinent.[5]
Finally, humour in its many different facets – wit, wordplay, the
absurd, the macabre, the grotesque – was fundamental to the
Gaelic imagination, and also a significant influence on the development of the Irish novel. For many people, indeed, humour
remains perhaps *the* predominant 'Irish' characteristic.

Irish Gothic

Madness was also a major theme of Anglo-Irish Protestant imagination and the gothic variations which emerged from its accom-
panying racial, religious and gender ideologies. Isolated amongst
an alien population, separated from the country where supposedly its first allegiance lay, confused by the contradictions of its
hyphenated identity, the culture of this community eventually
began to reflect these feelings and experiences. Gothic has been
theorised as a subconscious manifestation of Anglo-Irish guilt
and alienation, a fixation on the ways in which the past persists
in the present, as well as being caught up in a peculiarly Protestant imagination of life and death.[6] (This development also
reminds us of Nandy's point about the way in which colonialism
damages not just the colonised but all those implicated in the
violence of colonialism.) More generally, Homi Bhabha has described the principal gothic effect of 'unhomeliness' as 'a paradig-
matic colonial and post-colonial condition ... a "non-continuist"
problematic that dramatizes – in the figure of woman – the
ambivalent structure of the civil State as it draws its rather
paradoxical boundary between the private and the public
spheres'.[7] Bhabha's argument – that the colonial text's revelation
of the hidden beneath the homely relates 'to the wider disjunc-
tions of political existence' (p. 11) draws together discourses of
colonial resistance, gender and textuality in particularly revealing
and enabling ways.

The classic Irish Gothic novel, such as Charles Maturin's
Melmoth the Wanderer (1820), is characterised by a combination of
narrative complexity, emotional hysteria and the incursion of
supernatural systems on a hopelessly flawed and corrupt 'real'
world. In the gothic vision, any hope of social change in the
present is belied by the persistence of the sins of the past. The
message is that we are all victims of history, only most have not
recognised it yet. Gothic thus becomes a way of indicting the

present, allowing the novelist to offer a perspective on the immediate in terms of the metaphysical and the universal, but without
having to invest in any consoling vision or compensatory myth,
precisely because there is nothing to be done.

Dissatisfaction with the present and obsession with the
memory of the dead can degenerate into psychosis. Insanity is
never far away in the gothic novel, and as the form mutated it
brought this legacy of madness with it. Irish Gothic has evolved
in strange and unusual ways since its heyday around the turn of
the eighteenth century. The ghost of Protestant Gothic returns to
haunt many modern Irish novels, and whenever we encounter
the incursion of the past onto the present, or characters who
express alienated from their environment and begin to invest in
alternative realities, or themes of betrayal and guilt, or complex
plots in which form and content overlap in sometimes comple-
mentary, sometimes contradictory ways, then the gothic is never
too far away. The gothic vision, in fact, has attractions for any
individual or group who feel themselves alienated from the
present social organisation. As Siobhán Kilfeather writes:

> Gothic fiction enables Irish writers to address anxieties about speech
> and silence, to accuse the state and the family of psychological terror-
> ism without having to propose a program of reform. It allows women
> in particular to question why their sexuality is so often implicated in
> the violence and guilt of their fathers' experiences. It demands some
> reflection on what possibilities for change are allowed by an obses-
> sion with the memory of the dead.[8]

Literature and madness

The final source for madness as a theme in contemporary Irish
fiction has nothing to do with the *Irish* novel as such, but rather
with literature's general alienation from reality. For if there is
one area in which madness has not been silenced in western
history, it is literature.[9] Especially since the growth of Romanticism in the late eighteenth century, literature has generally been
regarded as an intense emotional response to experience, a sort of
licensed insanity with regard to 'normal' life and language.
Whereas academic discourse has tried to *understand* madness,
literary discourse has indulged and facilitated it, for despite the
historical predominance of *mimesis* – the attempt to represent
reality in art – literature is quite obviously not reality. In fact,

with its reminder of the alternative properties of language – rhyme, rhythm, pattern, sound, repetition, and so on – literature challenges the dominant philosophical tradition inherited from the ancient Greeks which insists that language is merely a form of communication referring to other things rather than a material thing in itself, possessing its own pre-discursive signifying capacities. Like madness, then, literature is implicitly dangerous because it serves as a reminder of the contingent nature of reality; and like madness it has to be closely monitored and regulated by a controlling metadiscourse purporting to 'understand' but in fact violently delimiting it. The name we give to that policing discourse is 'literary criticism'.[10]

Literature and madness, therefore, share an ambiguous relationship with western thought. With their insistence on alternative systems of meaning, they constantly threaten to expose the limitations of that thought. At the same time, they are part of the formation of discourses needed by discourses of power (such as colonialism and philosophy) to constitute themselves and the social and political formations they serve. Literature and madness, in fact, are allies. As Shoshana Felman says:

> ... by virtue of their very historical opaqueness, madness and literature have been made partners throughout history, as objects of misapprehension and denial ... between literature and madness there exists an obscure but essential kinship: a kinship entailed, precisely, by *whatever blocks them off*, by that which destines them alike to repression and disavowal. (p. 16)

As with all the issues addressed in this book, the relationship between literature and madness takes on a particular resonance in the colonial situation. That is, there are specific historical and psycho-social reasons determining the form in which madness surfaces in Irish literary texts generally and in the Irish novel particularly.

FAMILY MATTERS

At the end of John Banville's 1973 novel *Birchwood*, the narrator Gabriel Godkin wishes that he could run up to some people shouting: *'Look, I am not my father, I am something different.'*[11] Gabriel knows, however, that such a gesture would be useless, and that as a son he is doomed always to carry with him some genetic and behavioural traces of his ancestry. This image, in which the child wishes for freedom from the fate imposed through the fact of birth but is finally constrained to acknowledge the inescapable influence of the past, engages with one of the most enduring and resonant of Irish cultural obsessions – the family. Interest in the family has also fed into some of the other issues which have emerged as recurring preoccupations of the Irish cultural imagination.

The family, comprehended in the constituent terms of gender and generation, is a crucial concept for both colonising and decolonising discourse. Female iconography played an important part in Gaelic culture, and this fed into a later colonialist tradition in which the country was represented as a woman – either an old woman or a beautiful young queen, exhorting the menfolk to oppose the invader. From the late eighteenth century on, as C.L. Innes writes, 'both in English and Irish writing and representation, Ireland is frequently allegorized as a woman, and the allegories are ones in which family or gender relationships are metaphors for political and economic relationships with a male England'.[12] During the nineteenth century, the opposition between coloniser and colonised was cast in terms of the 'natural' division of the sexes, the former as the generally benign but always controlling male, the latter as the female, by turns vulnerable and predatory, attractive and dangerous. In the construction of this framework for colonial relations between Ireland and England, moreover, British colonialist discourse had the sanction of the 'apolitical' and 'disinterested' discourses of science and culture which had revealed what one influential scholar called the 'essentially feminine' nature of the Celtic race.[13] As an apologist for Irish adoption into the British 'family' wrote: 'No doubt the sensibility of the Celtic nature, its nervous exaltation, have something feminine in them [sic], and the Celt is thus peculiarly disposed to feel the spell of the feminine idiosyncrasy; he has an affinity to it; he is not far from its secret.'[14]

The nexus of colonialism and gender left a deep impression on the Irish cultural imagination. Uncritically adopting the gender division imposed by colonialism, Irish decolonisation attempted to deny its representation as 'an essentially feminine race' by reconfiguring the national division of the sexes along specific (unequal) lines. Thus, the Irish male was constructed as active, a fighter and earner, occupying the public and political realm outside the home; the Irish woman was passive, a nurturer, mainstay of the family, bastion of the domestic realm of home and hearth. In other words, nationalism imposed *within* Ireland the economy of unequal gender relations that colonialism had constructed *between* Ireland and England. This model, moreover, became enshrined in law in post-colonial Ireland, Article 41 of the Constitution stating that:

> (1.1) The State recognises the family as the natural primary and fundamental unit of Society, and as a moral institution possessing inalienable and imprescriptible rights, anterior and superior to all positive law ... (2.1) In particular, the State recognises that by her life within the home, woman gives to the State a support without which the common good cannot be achieved. (2.2) The State shall, there-fore, endeavour to ensure that mothers shall not be obliged by eco-nomic necessity to engage in labour to the neglect of their duties in the home. (3.1) The State pledges itself to guard with special care the institution of Marriage, on which the Family is founded, and to protect it against attack ... [15]

As well as rewriting a national history in which women had played a significant (if often strategic) part, such an ideal was guaranteed to produce a particular system of unequal gender relations in twentieth-century Ireland.[16] The consequences of this system are observable in obvious areas such as the organisa-tion of employment, education and healthcare, but also in a myriad of subtle resonances which have infused modern Irish culture and society. And perhaps the most significant of these resonances concerned the social and cultural representation of sex. When 'Mother Ireland' officially fused with 'Mother Church' in the Constitution of 1937, the Irishwoman's body was identi-fied as a vessel for the production of children within marriage.[17] With its uncritical reproduction of gender stereotypes received from colonialism and its close identification with the Catholic Church, the possibility of sex as non-productive pleasure became one of traditional Irish nationalism's most damaging blindspots.

Between 1960 and 1990, however, the average family size in Ireland fell from 4.6 to 2.3,[18] and this, perhaps more than any-thing else, is the most telling indication of the important changes overtaking society during this time. As passive reflection or ac-tive deconstruction, much of the fiction produced in and about modern Ireland can be analysed in terms of its engagement with the social and individual fall-out from the gender division im-posed by the post-colonial state, and the gradual (re)introduction

of sexual desire as one of the fundamental aspects of a modern
Irish identity.

The other area of familial discourse that has had an inordinate influence on the production of cultural representations of
Ireland is that of generation, something which we have already
looked at briefly under the rubric of 'Gothic'. The clash between
parents and children is a recurring trope of Irish cultural discourse under the colonial dispensation, representing a youthful
repudiation both of received narratives (English or Irish) and, by
extension, of the seemingly 'natural' mechanism whereby the
past dominates the present. Again, however, the potentially liberating force of generation is skewed by the colonial context, and
the child's rebellion against the authority of the parent inevitably
ends up re-installing the principle of authority in some other
guise or mode. In terms of Irish decolonisation the key difference, as Declan Kiberd has described matters, is not between
coloniser and colonised but between the *rebel* and the *revolutionary*. The former seeks merely to replace one particular mode of
authority with another (more authentic, more authoritative, more
real); the latter seeks to improvise versions of authority in ways
which, while remaining respectful of the burden of the past, can
respond imaginatively to the uncertainties of the future. Modern
Ireland has had more than its fair share of rebels but very few
real revolutionaries, and the period between 1916 and 1922 saw a
major victory for the former. As Kiberd writes:

> The revivalists [that is, the rebels] had won: the fathers with their
> heroes and ghosts from the past. The revolutionaries were snuffed
> out: the sons with their hopes of self-creation in the image of an
> uncertain future. Yet the revenge of the fathers was barren in almost
> every respect, since it represented a final surrender to received modes
> of thought. (p. 393)

Nevertheless, fathers and sons, mothers and daughters, past and
present – these relations and the wide range of social and cultural
situations to which they can be applied haunt modern Irish life and
art, constituting one of the fundamental aspects of the national life
with which the new fiction has found itself obliged to engage.

In terms of the novel, the place where the twin elements of
gender and generation are most effectively engaged is in James
Joyce's *Ulysses* (1922). Published at more or less the same time as
the victory of the rebels, this revolutionary text simultaneously
repudiates the gender stereotypes inherited from colonialism as

well as the pattern of generational reproduction into which Irish identity was seemingly locked. As David Lloyd has pointed out, 'where the principal organizing metaphor of Irish nationalism is that of a proper paternity, of restoring the lineage of the fathers in order to repossess the motherland, Joyce's procedures are dictated by adulteration'.[19] Adulteration – in terms of content, certainly, but also at the more fundamental levels of form and style – is a threat both to colonialism and to the nationalism which seeks to replace it, precisely because of its challenge to the discourses of gender and generation upon which established power relies. At once a refusal of the past and an assault on received gender roles, *Ulysses* offers no alternative source of authority which could harden into a social myth, unless it be the individualistic myth of self-creation. The irony is that Joyce himself has become one of the great 'father figures' of Irish art, re-inscribed into all manner of generational and gendered discourses despite the profoundly recalcitrant nature of his work. The revolutionary nature of the texts has tended to be obviated by the conservative institutional contexts in which they circulate; as such, Joyce's work has often functioned as a stultifying influence on later Irish writing, yet another voice from the past looking to dictate both the representation of the present and the organisation of the future.

THE CITY AND THE COUNTRY

The final theme of modern Irish critical and creative discourse I wish to examine here is the opposition between the city and the country. The clash between rural and urban discourses in Ireland is a version of a more widespread process that has been over-taking all western societies since the onset of the Industrial Revolution in the eighteenth century.[20] On the one hand, there is the myth of a modern civilisation evolving into a better, more exciting and rewarding way of life. On the other hand, there is the draw of the traditional community, the security of complete identification with the landscape and cultural idioms of one's immediate environment. As with so much else in modern Irish history, however, ideas concerning the city and the country are complicated by colonialism, cultural nationalism and the demands of decolonisation.

From its roots in the eighteenth century, modern Irish nationalism was concerned as much with issues of space (owner-ship of the land, landscape and identity, geography as destiny, exile, and so on) as with the temporal status of the nation (the present as a point in the ongoing narrative linking national past and future). Irish cultural nationalism during the nineteenth century developed a highly sensitive, if seldom formulated system for measuring Irishness, as if national identity was a quantifiable phenomenon. And one of the key elements of this system was the elevation of the country above the city as a signifier of Irishness. Typically of decolonising discourse, however, the pastoral myth invoked by Irish cultural nationalism owed much to the Romanticism of English writers such as William Wordsworth and later in the century Matthew Arnold, a discourse which characterised the Irish as a quaint but essentially disempowered race of peasants. Thus, the process whereby a system of (rural) values was arbitrarily positioned over and against another system of (urban) values is in fact a reflection of the colonial discourse whereby England defined itself in opposition to Ireland. The cultural revival of the late nineteenth century, as Fintan O'Toole writes, 'nationalised colonial attitudes, internalising a process which belonged to the colonial mentality and selling it back to the outside world as a reflection of Irish reality'.[21]

The authenticity sought by the nation was to be found not in the hustle and bustle of the modern city (which in the Irish context usually means Dublin or Belfast, the two biggest population centres on the island) where everything was in a state of constant flux, and where individuals were alienated from themselves as well as from each other. As cultural nationalism was emerging during the nineteenth century, Dublin was degenerating from its eighteenth-century grandeur into one of the worst European cities in terms of poverty and disease. For nationalists, this bore out the notion of the city as an alien imposition upon what remained fundamentally a land-based, knowable community. The truly national was the natural, and the natural was to be found in those relationships and systems which appeared to emerge organically from land-based life. Irish cultural nationalism thus embraced a typical pastoral myth, in which an idealised rural population of peasants and fisherfolk were represented as the true holders of the national flame.

This emphasis was taken up by the leaders of post-revolutionary Ireland and converted into one of the major sustaining myths of the nation. Such a myth, however, was problematic for a number of reasons. In the first place, the equation of 'rural' with 'real' in cultural nationalist discourse was by and large an invention of city-based individuals both in Ireland and abroad, often those who

had moved from the country and allowed nostalgia and sentimentality to colour their perspective. Pastoralism failed to acknowledge
both the complexity and the banality of Irish rural life. Country
people were invited to self-identify in terms of stereotypes which
had little purchase in what could be a difficult and frustrating
existence.[22] More insidiously, these stereotypes militated against
an acknowledgement of the immensely subtle geographical and
spatial possibilities available throughout the island. Moreover, the
pastoral myth offers a straw target which continues to deflect attention away from these difficulties and possibilities. Revisionists
criticise the dominant nationalist representation of rural Irish life
as an idyllic if primitive community, organically linked with the
landscape. Modern Ireland's infatuation with a rural past, it is
claimed, is part of the process by which an urban present is denied,
and by which Irish identity remains locked into specifically opposi-
tionalist discourses typical of colonialism. However, as Luke
Gibbons has pointed out, 'the pastoral image of the countryside
singled out for criticism – that of an organic community with an
enclosed, continuous past – is itself an urban construct, having
little or no connection with the actualities of life in what was far
from an idyllic, agrarian order'.[23] The revisionists' error, in this
reading, would be to mistake the ideology for the reality, focusing
on the pastoral myth promulgated by dominant nationalism
instead of the critical and cultural politics that have developed as a
result of the island's colonial history.

The second problem with the pastoral myth is that the nostalgia for an always declining rural order denies the validity of
urban experience, as if city-dwelling was somehow less 'Irish'
than living in a village or town-land. It was this implicit spatial
politics that partly inspired Joyce's championing of the city and
his exploration of different modes of Irishness. Even so, the
Dublin of the Celtic Revival, like the city depicted by Joyce
throughout his fiction, was hardly the unknowable society that
functioned simultaneously as pastoralism's 'other' and as such an
important part of the modernist imagination.[24] It was in fact
little more than a large village where everyone knew everyone
else, a kind of metaphor for real cities such as London, Paris and
New York. In any case, the image of the city that proved most
influential in popular cultural and novelistic terms emerged not
in Joyce's difficult texts but in the early work of the playwright
Sean O'Casey, or in the deceptive realism of a text such as *The
Charwoman's Daughter* by James Stephens. But here, however, as
O'Toole has argued (pp. 114–15), the city turned out to be a

mirror of the country, a sort of urban pastoral in which an enclosed, knowable community went through the stereotypical motions of alcohol, poverty and domestic violence.

This form of pastoralism continued to dominate the imagination of space in Ireland well into the post-colonial era. As late as 1985 O'Toole could still maintain:

> For the last hundred years, Irish culture and in particular Irish writing has been marked by this dominance of the rural over the urban, a dominance based on a false opposition of the country to the city which has been vital to the maintenance of a conservative political culture in the country. (p. 111)

However, the seemingly unstoppable growth of 'New Dublin' since the 1960s has seen the emergence of a genuine urban consciousness and the growth of a cultural imagination aiming to engage with the experiences of the large numbers of Irish people now living in the city. Finding urban life ignored, misrepresented or sentimentalised, the new Irish novelists of the 1980s set about developing forms and techniques which could adequately represent life in a city which as the end of the century approached was fast outgrowing the range of traditional images. Such a self-conscious artistic programme brought its own difficulties, however, in that it seems not to have entailed a dismantling of the 'false opposition of the country to the city' but merely a shift in emphasis from the former to the latter. The problem, as with many movements conceived in counter-mode, was that the offending opposition was maintained even as it was reversed. One could thus argue that the Dublin created by the new novelists of the 1980s, with its images of urban decay and alienation, fostered a myth as inimical to city life as the pastoral one it looked to replace.[25]

A number of specific subgenres have emerged in Irish fiction which engage with the social and political discourses just described. With regard to rural life these include the 'Big House' novel, anti-pastoral novels about the restrictions of life in farming and village communities, tales about the provincial leaving the land to live in the 'Big Smoke', novels which make use of landscape for atmospheric purposes and which explore the relations between geography, imagination and identity. With regard to the city Joyce looms large, and most novelists looking to represent the city – Irish or otherwise – have found it difficult to avoid measuring their work in relation to his seminal explorations. Even if, as already mentioned, a 'New Dublin' requires new forms, many contemporary Irish novelists appear to have got hung up on trying to write texts which either confirm or deny *Ulysses*. Joyce's potentially liberating example is thus once again compromised, with both his work and his lifestyle functioning ambivalently at best, but more often than not casting a restrictive and forbidding shadow on subsequent artistic endeavours.

It seems clear that both city and country people suffered as a result of nationalism's investment in pastoralism, which in turn was based upon the ideological opposition between the active, future-oriented coloniser and the passive, past-oriented colonised. Since the eighteenth century, the Irish novel has developed a range of forms, narratives and styles which engage with the relationship between nation and geography, from full romantic identification to a radical scepticism couched in tones of irony and parody. The new Irish novelists have inherited these discourses, finding themselves constrained to engage not only with a literary legacy but also with a present in which both city and country (as well as the imaginary line dividing them as experiences) are undergoing rapid and fundamental change.

PART 2

The novel: a piece of extended prose fiction that has something wrong with it.

Source unknown

4 RODDY DOYLE AND THE NEW IRISH FICTION

This chapter examines the work of one of the key modern Irish novelists, Roddy Doyle. It also looks at a number of other texts in terms of a range of issues raised in the analysis of Doyle's work. In this way we may begin to address some of the points broached in Part 1 regarding the new Irish fiction, its formal properties, its range of subject matters and, perhaps most importantly, the prevailing social, critical and artistic discourses regarding the relations between novel and nation in modern Ireland. Doyle's work is given a central place here not on grounds of artistic value, commercial success or thematic typicality, although it could be argued that he rates highly on all three of these criteria. Rather, a chapter organised in this way is offered as itself a fiction of sorts, a story about modern Ireland – not *the* story (as if such a thing were possible), but one version of the narrative which describes a modern European nation attempting to come to terms with rapid social, political and cultural change.

Roddy Doyle began writing in his spare time during the early 1980s when he worked as a teacher in a secondary school on the north side of Dublin. After a few false starts (including a novel with the unpromising title *Your Granny's a Hunger Striker*) he began work on *The Commitments*, the book that would become the first in the Barrytown trilogy and that would bring him to the attention of the public in Ireland and elsewhere. Unable to secure a publishing deal, Doyle and a friend took out a bank loan to print and produce the book themselves. A decade later, he is a Booker Prize-winning novelist, has scripted an acclaimed television series as well as a number of highly successful films and is certainly one of the most successful Irish writers of his generation.

Doyle has managed to bridge the divide between popular

success and critical recognition. His work has crystallised with great insight and force many of the significant themes and debates of contemporary Irish culture. *The Commitments* signalled the start of an exciting phase in the nation's cultural history, characterised by an intense re-examination of what it might mean to be Irish in the late twentieth century. Refusing to rest on the success and the originality of that first effort, however, Doyle has continued to revise the initial optimism of his early work and remains at the cutting edge of the new Irish fiction.

The unformulated remit of this discourse, as was claimed in the introduction to this book, involves an intense engagement with the social and cultural milieu from which it springs, as well as the opening up of the national narrative to a range of traditionally silenced voices from the past and the present. In the course of the five novels, Doyle engages with various personal and public discourses, developing a subtle and complex vision of modern Ireland. But if there has been one overriding theme in Doyle's work to date it is the exploration of the relations between individuals and the collectives in which they find themselves, especially that collective known as the family. His representation of life as experienced by the Rabittes, the Clarkes and the Spencers offers a range of perspectives on the ideology of the family as it operates in modern Ireland, and the serious challenges that were offered to that ideology as the 1980s slipped into the 1990s.

Doyle's work was challenging from its first appearance, because it did not fit easily into any recognisable tradition of Irish art. Any writer whose work is so firmly based in Dublin will inevitably invite comparison with James Joyce, although this is a limited critical exercise, so removed are the two novelists in context, method and intention. In its exploration of the limits of the family and the role of the individual within the community, Doyle's representation of working-class life on Dublin's northside has also been likened to the early plays of Sean O'Casey. But Doyle's artistic heritage appears to be wider and more eclectic than this. Some critics have argued that his combination of serious social comment with a comic technique has more in common with the quintessential English writer Charles Dickens than with any Irish novelistic tradition. One could also trace the influence of musical and visual culture – such as Dublin rock music, British television and American cinema – given the important part these appear to play throughout the five novels.

This uncertainty of influence and tradition reflects the complex social and cultural milieu that Doyle attempts to represent in the fictional world of Barrytown. For one thing, Ireland itself has changed and grown, and it is perhaps no longer possible to offer a single artistic vision of the nation. Along with certain other modern Dublin writers, Doyle depicts a side of Irish life that had never found its voice in the nation's fiction. Barrytown is not Ireland; indeed, it is not even Dublin. It is a fictional construction of a working-class suburb on Dublin's northside, and as such it displays many of the characteristics of the suburban phenomenon as experienced throughout large parts of the world – proximity to the city, knowledge of a rural hinterland, displacement of older communities into large population concentrations, often without adequate civic or cultural support, and so on. At the same time, alongside these extra-national tendencies there exists an irreducibly Irish element to Doyle's work, couched in the idioms, the mores and the histories of a specific local community. In fact, although the quintessential 'realist' in many ways, Doyle's work might also be described as 'postmodern' in the manner in which it juxtaposes the effects of mass international culture with a residual local culture.

Doyle's novelistic technique is tuned to this dual affiliation. Since the start of his career his work has been geared more towards 'showing' than 'telling', letting characters speak for themselves as far as possible. As a result his books are capable of achieving highly subtle effects through suggestion and narrative restraint. The reader must become an active part of the meaning-making process, filling in the gaps and making choices deliberately left by the narrator. This is one of the reasons why Doyle's books will sustain second and third readings: the active reader is always likely to make connections and discover subtle links that were missed first time. Such a technique refuses the notion of a single vision of modern Irish society. Doyle does not offer a snapshot of a stable society – a finished image of a finished reality. Rather, modern Irish society is shown to be in flux, a conclave of voices and visions – official and popular, emerging and residual, comic and tragic. As an artist looking to engage with such a society he is constrained to open meaning up rather than close it down.

In as much as this is so, Doyle's work may also be said to owe a debt to the tradition of Irish short-story writing – especially rural-based – in which great narrative economy and skill were required to capture the nuances and subtleties of community life. In fact, although working predominantly in the novel form, Doyle has had success with other genres such as the

short story, drama and screenplay. Indeed, most of the novelists dealt with in this chapter have worked in other forms, and
this raises important questions for an analysis of the modern
Irish novel: what the writer feels can be achieved in the form,
what is distinctive and appropriate to it, how it relates in
practical terms to less labour-intensive forms such as poetry
and the short story, or more labour-intensive forms such as
drama and screenplay-writing.

Doyle's work has not appeared without criticism, especially
in Ireland. Some commentators have accused him of a form of
'moral tourism', recycling stereotypes and disabling notions of
the sentimental Irish character. His work, it has been claimed,
is a form of 'pastoral' in which an idealised rural community is
transplanted into the semi-urban environment of Barrytown,
testament to the fact that a supposedly discarded ideology is
still determining the nation's artistic agenda. Doyle is also
liable to the criticism that in his drive to subvert certain
national stereotypes he merely produces new ones, and that his
work represents a glib but essentially hollow repudiation of
traditional values – in the words of one commentator, 'as negative critique become its own orthodoxy'.[1]

The readings which follow engage with all these issues. It is
worth stressing again the point made in the introduction,
however, that this critical organisation of Doyle's work is as
partial in its way as any artistic vision, and it is up to readers
to make creative use of the available materials – literary, critical and theoretical – in their construction of meaning in these
novels.

The Commitments (1987)

The Commitments is the first and, thanks to the internationally
successful Alan Parker film, most famous of the Barrytown trilogy. Doyle won awards for his part in the adaptation of his novel
for cinema, but he had a head start over most screenwriters in as
much as *The Commitments* was from the outset a very visual and
dialogue-based text. It is a novel in which scenes and exchanges
between characters take precedence over description or explanation by the narrator. It is also a short book that feels like a long
book, and while this may have something to do with the film
adaptation it is also a result of the subtlety of Doyle's writing
technique, in which he manages to create the impression of a

much larger social and cultural canvas than is actually set down on the page.

In making his readers an active part of the meaning-making process, Doyle confirms the essentially *democratic* nature of his artistic vision. His writing practice is based firmly on respect between author, reader and characters. *The Commitments* is not a first-person narrative, so we do not have the privileged or partial insights of one particular character. But neither is it a typical third-person narrative, because the narrator does not dominate the story. Rather, Doyle demands that characters be judged on their own terms. The narrator does not offer opinions on the actions or exchanges but describes them in such a way as to leave it up to the reader to decide; and in deciding, we are commenting as much on our own values and assumptions as on those of the characters. Doyle refuses to patronise or pander to the reader by telling everything about the characters or the action; by the same token, his novels insist that the reader does not adopt an ironic or patronising tone with regard to the characters or their concerns, but takes the world of the text on its own terms.

It might be claimed that there is something contradictory about a written form – the novel – which relies so heavily upon (representations of) the spoken word for its success. Especially in the Barrytown trilogy, Doyle seems to shy away from the specifically literary aspects of writing, those things which differentiate the written word from face-to-face interaction. The text is not divided into chapters, nor are the characters' words placed inside quotation marks. *The Commitments* is also very present-centred; there are few passages of retrospection or anticipation. There are no long sentences or difficult words, and few abstractions. Spelling and punctuation are altered to capture the Dublin idiom; in fact, it almost seems as if the author is embarrassed at having to write at all, and that the novelistic discourse is most successful when it masks itself.

This does not mean, however, that the writer is any less skilful; on the contrary, as one critic says of Doyle's style, 'the easier it is to read, the harder it was to write'.[2] But the form of *The Commitments* would appear to be in sympathy with the general anti-intellectual content of the story, an ethos expressed throughout the narrative to the effect that any hint of abstract thought is identified as pretentiousness and condemned from a position in which, like the soul music which constitutes the predominant motif of the book, straightforwardness and emotional honesty are valued. When Jimmy Rabbitte Jr, the manager of The Commitments, discovers that Dean the sax-player has been developing ideas about music from Channel 4 television and the *Observer* newspaper (both English and regarded as somewhat 'arty' and intellectual) both are upset and embarrassed.[3] Anti-intellectualism is something for which Doyle himself has been criticised, and there does appear to be something contradictory about the general suspicion of technique and theory characteristic of his early work, given the impressive technical achievement of his own writing practice.

Nevertheless, the democratic principle in Doyle's fiction has aided its success, both in Ireland and abroad. *The Commitments* is poised between total immersion in the local and invocation of a multinational, postmodern world. Barrytown is a community in which people know each other, and life in the neighbourhood is ordered along familiar social, cultural and geographical lines. At the same time, as that life has changed in recent years, so have its terms of reference. Much of the experience of working-class life on housing estates on the edge of a big city like Dublin cannot be explained with reference to Ireland or Irishness. The cultural discourses regularly encountered by Barrytown dwellers, for example – the music, sport, television, radio, cinema and literature – are derived in large part from Great Britain and the United States. This also helps to explain the novel's appeal for audiences from widely different national and social backgrounds. It demonstrates the same accommodation between the local and the general, between the residual and the culturally aggressive, experienced by most of its potential audience – even those, for example, from the United States and Europe, social formations which are by and large responsible for the erosion of traditional local cultures.

The specific Irish dimension to the narrative should not be underestimated, however. Many of the references would only register with a reader familiar with the customs and idioms of modern Dublin. For example, the 'crack' referred to throughout the book is not the drug so popular in America, but an anglicised version of the Gaelic word '*craic*' which refers to the fun to be had on social occasions when music, conversation and drink combine. Or again, when the band are discussing Jimmy's idea that they should all wear 'monkey suits' (tuxedos) Derek the bass-player says 'I'd be scarleh' (p. 39). This is Dublin pronunciation of the word 'scarlet', referring to the reddening of the cheeks with embarrassment. It is not possible to know what a British or American reader, or one for whom English was a second language, would make of these local references and terms, but it is a measure of the writer's skill that he manages to incorporate such a large measure of local detail alongside a comic vision that has proved to have such a wide appeal.

In one sense, Ireland is evoked with reference to traditional political discourses. In a direct reference to the 'Troubles' in Northern Ireland, Joey the Lips's explanation for returning home is to bring music to the Irish Brothers who, he believes, 'wouldn't be shooting the asses off each other if they had soul' (p. 27). More significantly, in his elucidation of soul music as 'the politics o' the people', Jimmy Jr evokes a discourse of class at odds with the nationalist and racialist agendas which have dominated the Irish political arena since the nineteenth century. He criticises English art-school music as 'bourgeois' (p. 12), and 'the way their stuff, their songs like, are aimed at gits like themselves. Wankers with funny haircuts. An' rich das. – An' fuck all else to do all day 'cept prickin' around with synths' (p. 10). Finally he puts his finger on it:

> – The Irish are the niggers of Europe, lads.
> They nearly gasped: it was so true.
> – An' Dubliners are the niggers of Ireland. The culchies have fuckin' everythin'. An' the northside Dubliners are the niggers o' Dublin. Say it loud, I'm black an' I'm proud. (p. 13)

Here, racial, national and class discourses combine to form a complex economy in which meaning moves between the local ('culchies', that is, people from rural areas, and 'northside Dubliners', traditionally more working-class than those south of the River Liffey) and a much wider set of cultural references ('niggers' – a crucial word for black politics in the United States).

Above all, however, *The Commitments* is a joyful novel, intended to entertain. It is also a novel about fulfilment, about the possibility of exceeding expectations and realising potential. And this, perhaps, is the main reason for its wide appeal, as its evocation of stardom through popular music is a dream with which many young people in the modern world can identify. It is also an 'adult' book, however, in so far as it refuses to sink into sentimentality. Despite its evocation of the power of youth and the ubiquity of dreams of success, *The Commitments* remains true to the world of late twentieth-century working-class life.

The Snapper (1990)

Each novel in the Barrytown trilogy stands on its own, although there is an obvious intertextual element to the series. In *The Snapper*, the Rabbitte family, which had been peripheral to the action in *The Commitments*, becomes the centre of attention. Sharon, the eldest daughter, is pregnant, and although receiving the support of her family, is unwilling to reveal the identity of the father. The action centres around the developing relationship between Sharon and her father Jimmy Sr, and the Barrytown community's reaction to her condition, especially when it is discovered that the father of her expected baby is a local family man.

It is with *The Snapper* that the themes of family and gender begin to take on the significant implications that they will have throughout the rest of Doyle's work. Once again, the author is extremely subtle in his representation of the relations between the different members of the family and the ways in which identity is negotiated in terms of gender, class and culture. In a long passage near the beginning of the novel (pp. 161–8) we see the development of a family scene, as the parents Jimmy Sr and Veronica are gradually joined by the children, Jimmy Jr, Darren, the twins Linda and Tracy with the puppy who will become Larrygogan (the name of a disc-jockey on Irish radio), and finally Sharon. The only one missing is the mysterious Leslie, whose absence sounds a note of disharmony that will become louder as Doyle's exploration of the limits of the family group develops. But in what is essentially a 'feel-good' book, Jimmy Sr's later comment that 'We're some family all the same, wha' (p. 337) strikes the keynote.

The discerning reader soon learns that Jimmy Sr is immature, needing to be humoured and coaxed, while the real adults coping with the unexpected pregnancy are the women, Sharon and Veronica. Jimmy's frankly old-fashioned views on what constitutes proper male behaviour are challenged when he begins to take an interest in Sharon's condition. As he becomes more and more involved, Jimmy Sr is forced to review his assumptions regarding his role as a father, and the role of men in Irish society generally. The late 1980s saw the development of a number of attempts by men throughout the western world to reclaim some of the ground lost under sustained feminist pressure – the 'Men's Movement', the 'New Man' so beloved of the advertisement industry, the 'White Guys' movement in the United States – and Jimmy Sr is in some ways part of this. He learns to cry, to shoulder responsibility, and to appreciate the miracle of pregnancy; he discovers sexual foreplay; altogether, 'He was a changed man, a new man' (p. 320). Other men in the text, such as his drinking buddies, remain trapped within the narrow limits of traditional Irish masculinity. Again, the narrative does not make judgements, even when Jimmy Sr goes somewhat over the top in his attempts at self-reform. Nevertheless, he does offer at the end of the novel the seeds of a new model of Irish manhood and fatherhood, one who has at least begun to acknowledge a feminine dimension to his identity.

The Snapper is once again a dialogue-based text, beginning and ending with spoken words rather than the narrator's reflections or opinions. Doyle displays great skill in the economy with which he introduces characters and relationships, making small details and dialogue do the narrative work for him. Like *The Commitments*, this is somewhat of a fairy-tale, but whereas the earlier book was celebrated for its youthful, joyous anarchy, *The Snapper* has been criticised for trading in disabling stereotypes of Dublin life and the prevailing ethos of 'gas' (a Dublin variation on 'the crack'). This 'feel-good factor' – attractive to some, banal and irresponsible to others – is encapsulated at the end of the novel. As Sharon lies in hospital recovering from labour, she decides that her baby will be named 'Georgina' as an ironic reference to the father George Burgess, and as a gesture of defiance to the Barrytown community which had taken her pregnancy as matter for public discussion and glib moralising. So tickled is she by this decision that she becomes quite animated, and is addressed by another new mother from an adjoining bed:

– Ah, said the woman. – Were yeh cryin'?
– No, said Sharon. – I was laughin'. (p. 340)

This, however, is the last time in Doyle's fiction that comedy will triumph so easily and so unproblematically over tragedy.

The Van (1991)

The Barrytown trilogy is completed by *The Van*, in many ways a different book from the first two in the series. Although still very readable, it is considerably longer than either *The Commitments* or

The Snapper – an indication perhaps of Doyle's growing confidence with the form. It is also a much darker story, telling of Jimmy Sr's unemployment and the pressure this brings to bear on his sense of self, as well as his relations with friends and family. In this way it anticipates many of the themes that were to dominate his subsequent work.

The Van shifts focus from the experiences of young adults to the peculiar problems facing adults in the working-class community of Barrytown. The novel is an exploration of Jimmy Sr's fragile identity, and especially his sense of masculinity. Much of the ground gained in *The Snapper* is lost when the staples of life – work, family and friends – begin to change beyond Jimmy Sr's ability to control them. Finding himself without work, he looks for ways to fill up the long hours at home, gamely trying to take more responsibility and improve himself. *The Van* tells a familiar post-industrial tale of the banal horrors of unemployment in which an old-fashioned, strongly masculine work ethic is exposed by the whims of multinational capitalism. The earlier part of the book details in extremely subtle ways the physical, social and psychological changes experienced by the jobless working-class man, as Jimmy Sr becomes an outsider on his own life, passive object rather than active agent. For example, the romanticism of Jimmy Sr's library book (*The Man in the Iron Mask*) and Darren's homework (the poetry of Gerard Manley Hopkins) is ironically juxtaposed to the enforced poverty and loss of self-respect which accompanies loss of work. Frustration and resentment grow despite Jimmy Sr's attempts to retain his humour, and Doyle depicts with merciless precision the private fall-out from large developments in the public sphere.

Once again the house and family are presented, at least in the early part of the novel, as microcosms of the larger community, as well as bulwarks against it. Nevertheless, a major part of Jimmy Sr's sense of self is being slowly eroded, and as he waits for something to happen, tensions in the Rabbitte household begin to surface. The twins are growing wild. Sharon cries in her room for no apparent reason, and Jimmy Sr does not know how to cope. He feels guilty about Leslie's anti-social tendencies and his lack of commitment to the family. More seriously for Jimmy Sr's sense of male respect, he has to accept cash presents from Jimmy Jr, while in one of the most biting exchanges in the narrative Darren deliberately challenges his father's traditional role as provider and mainstay of the family:

– What abou' you? said Darren to his da. – Look at the state o' you.
Jimmy Sr looked at Darren. Darren was looking back at him, waiting
for a reaction. Jimmy Sr wasn't going to take that from him, not for
another couple of years.
He pointed his fork at Darren.
– Don't you forget who paid for tha' dinner in front of you, son,
righ'.
– I know who paid for it, said Darren. – The state. (p. 440)

This exchange takes place in the middle of another family scene,
but one which functions as a grim rejoinder to earlier and lighter
ones. It emerges that the whole family is experiencing severe
pressure in the fall-out from Jimmy Sr's unemployment. In the
strand of respectable working-class culture with which he identifies, reliance on the state is tantamount to failure, and Darren's
comment cuts to the bone. The relationship between Jimmy Sr
and his youngest son is in fact one of the most subtle aspects of
the novel, tracing a complex emotional economy of respect,
pride, shame and jealousy. Darren is too old not to notice what is
happening to his father, yet not old enough (unlike Jimmy Jr) to
understand what unemployment really means in terms of loss of
control and confidence. The text sets out the generational gap
starkly: as Darren is receiving news of his acceptance to university, his father wakes to a hangover and the recurring suspicion
that he is 'a useless cunt' (p. 601).

When Jimmy Sr's best friend Bimbo is also laid off, the two men
decide to use the severance money to set up business with a fast-
food van, and from here to the end of the novel focus remains on the
relationship between the two men. Irish working-class manhood is
revealed to be based upon an elaborate system of rituals and codes –
alcohol, slagging (teasing and banter), the crack and, perhaps most
importantly, sport. In his exploration of soccer as theme and symbol of Barrytown life, Doyle taps into a wider discourse in which
sport is understood to play a major role in the functioning of
post-industrial societies in the west. *The Van* is set at a time when
the Republic of Ireland football team had been performing particularly well, and the action of the narrative is set during the summer
of 1990 when the national team reached the quarter finals of the
World Cup in Italy, on the way beating Romania in a tense penalty
shoot-out watched by a large proportion of the population. Events
such as this constitute key moments in the community's sense of
itself, while in terms of the novel it represents the last moment of
unselfconscious friendship between the central male characters.

As Jimmy Sr and Bimbo begin to realise that friendship and business do not mix, the former also finds his familial commitments are being compromised, especially when he finds himself attracted to his sons' girlfriends and more than interested in another friend's tales of extra-marital sex. These narrative strands are linked when the two friends decide to have 'a night on the batter' to resurrect their friendship and to reconfirm their masculinity. But the night is a disaster, Jimmy Sr's failed attempt at an illicit engagement leaves him feeling more hopeless than ever, and he and Bimbo become even more estranged. The novel ends with the destruction of the van in an attempt to save the friendship, and Jimmy Sr's literal return to the family embrace. But there are no comic resolutions or ironic triumphs. Jimmy Sr is still unemployed, and his relations with friends and family have been perhaps permanently damaged.

The Journey Home (1990) by Dermot Bolger

Doyle's depiction of a city and a community less than at ease with itself in *The Van* should be seen as part of a wider impulse that was making itself felt in Irish cultural politics during the 1980s and 1990s. In the Barrytown trilogy Doyle gave a voice to a section of society traditionally rendered silent by a post-independence ideology which insisted that Ireland was essentially a rural and agricultural country, and that urban society was an alien subculture with no place in the national imagination. This ideology persisted into the era of the 'New Dublin' – the late twentieth-century city of huge housing estates filled with displaced, resentful populations. In his insistence on the validity of the new Dublin, Doyle's work can be linked with another figure – the publisher, poet, playwright and novelist Dermot Bolger.

Bolger's *The Journey Home* has been described as 'perhaps the first great novel of the new generation' and 'certainly the most significant odyssey through Dublin since Joyce'.[4] But the city depicted in this novel is far removed from the one made famous by the Joyce canon. *The Journey Home* is one of the key texts of a style that briefly came to be known in Irish critical discourse as 'Northside Realism' (albeit much to the chagrin of Bolger and the other artists involved). In this style, the gritty and garish world of Dublin in the 1990s is described in a form of 'poetic realism', a mixture of the quotidian and the elevated which mirrors the blending of international culture into local topography characterising the postmodern world. Dublin is depicted as a typical large European city, with sex, drugs and rock 'n' roll as its new cultural currency. The romance of Saturday night is always haunted by the bleak epiphanies of the Sunday morning hangover as post-nationalist Dublin proves itself to be a difficult and dangerous inheritance.

Part of this inheritance involves the formation of identity in relation to place. Whereas Doyle set his books in the fictional, albeit typical, area of Barrytown, Bolger maps a much more literal city, describing an urban landscape familiar to many readers of Irish fiction and to most Irish people. But if the geography is local, the actions described – lust, prostitution, hypocrisy, corruption – are all part of a much wider condition for which the new Dublin is seemingly not prepared. *The Journey Home* is thus as much anthropological and polemical as novelistic in its orientation, constructed by its author to shock a complacent Irish bourgeoisie with its angry portrayal of a disaffected, betrayed Irish generation.

The Journey Home depicts the squalid machinations and alienation which characterise life in post-colonial Ireland. The novel is made up of a number of interconnected narrative layers, each written in a peculiar style and from a particular perspective. The story of Hano's escape with Cait/Katie after the murder of the corrupt businessman Pascal Plunkett is a journey through a modern nightmare towards the only place that he can now think of as home, an old woman's cottage somewhere in the dark hinterland away from the city. Such a quest adds to the archetypal, fairy-tale status of the narrative. In another strand, Hano relates how he came to undertake such a journey, his meeting and growing relationship with Shay and Cait/Katie and their fatal involvement with the Plunkett family. It is Shay who introduces Hano to what Bolger has described elsewhere as 'the hidden underbelly of our capital city'.[5]

Far below, Dublin was moving towards the violent crescendo of its Friday night, taking to the twentieth century like an aborigine to whiskey. Studded punks pissed openly on corners. Glue sniffers stumbled into each other, coats over their arms as they tried to pick pockets. Addicts stalked rich-looking tourists. Stolen cars zigzagged through the distant grey estates where pensioners prayed anxiously behind bolted doors, listening for the smash of glass. In the new disco bars children were queuing, girls of fourteen shoving their way up for last drinks at the bar. (p. 35)

Finally, there is a poetic discourse running throughout the narrative, marked typographically in italics, in which Shay laments from the grave the freedom he never knew, while simultaneously indicting the forces that combined to take his life. For it becomes clear that in *The Journey Home* neither the old nor the new Ireland offers any consolation. The nationalist shibboleths have degenerated into grotesque caricatures and empty tokens. Power resides with the Plunketts because of their ability to exploit a false past and a corrupt present. Hano, Shay and Cait, on the other hand, are haunted by their lack of agency, by the way in which all their social, economic and emotional options seem to be mapped out for them in advance. The message of the novel is that the new Ireland, like the old Ireland, means dispossession and displacement for the majority of the population. And as with all narratives of the dispossessed, home is lost, the journey is all.

The Journey Home is perhaps more important for what it represents than for what it is – an angry novel indicting the community out of which it emerged. To the extent that his discourse *is* didactic and interventionist, however, Bolger falls prey to some of the formal problems confronting earlier Irish novelists, many of whom were more interested in articulating a special plea for Ireland than with constructing an engaging narrative. There is, for example, a marked discrepancy between the Dublin idiom of characters in the novel and the dignified poetic language in which they are described – a discrepancy that at certain points in the narrative becomes embarrassing. The effectiveness of *The Journey Home*, and indeed many of Bolger's novels, suffers as a consequence.

Neither can the author entirely escape the accusation that to create the impression of young, alienated Dublin he has exaggerated the significance of the old ideological guard of priests, teachers and politicians.[6] One could argue that Bolger's representation of Dublin as a sordid, unfriendly city unable to sustain its modern inhabitants actually feeds into, rather than undermines, the notion of rural Ireland as the real Ireland. Much of Bolger's energy, in fact, seems to be given over to the production of what the American film-maker Sam Goldwyn famously called 'new clichés' – in this case, the post-colonial clichés of a country having to reassess its entire ideological constitution as it confronts the terrors and excitements of life in the late twentieth century. At the same time, for all its new-found cosmopolitanism and its one-time reputation as heroin capital of Europe, Dublin is not London or New York or Los Angeles. But as the nation plunged headlong into the postmodern world after decades of post-colonial lethargy, there was bound to be confusion over what was worth hanging onto and what needed jettisoning. In *The Journey Home*, Bolger not only described this dilemma, but formally, and perhaps unwittingly, re-enacted it.

Paddy Clarke Ha Ha Ha (1993)

Bolger and Doyle, like many of the most innovative and challenging of contemporary Irish novelists, grew up during the 1960s, when Ireland was undergoing an intense renegotiation of its identity and role in the world. From being a backward-looking and isolationist nation, Ireland moved to embrace the modern world – socially, economically, culturally. The pace of these changes, given the long years of stagnation which preceded them, seemed all the more unsettling to many Irish people. The world, if not turned upside down, was certainly revolving faster than it had for many years and while some welcomed the belated onset of the twentieth century, others feared the consequences of the clash between established practices and what had traditionally been represented as 'alien' ideas.

It is in just such a world that Doyle's Booker Prize-winning *Paddy Clarke Ha Ha Ha* is set. In 1968 the Barrytown which Doyle presented as an established 1980s community in the trilogy is itself in the process of formation. Paddy and his gang roam a strange world of green fields, new houses, unfinished roads; they inhabit a borderland between the city and the countryside, the residual and the emergent. Paddy's imagination is fired by American television shows and British football teams; at the same time, these discourses are in dialogue with older, well-established socio-cultural references – religion, the Gaelic language, national history. And this textual dialogue is a microcosm of the changes being negotiated in the wider national community, itself the site of competing narratives of national identity.

Once again, the family is the focus of attention. But if we saw the institution coming under pressure in *The Van*, here we see it cracking and falling part. The dysfunctional family is a symptom of an increasingly disjointed society, for the confusion Paddy feels with the onset of his parents' break-up is anticipated by the confusion already confronting him at the social and cultural levels. George Best's autograph is not his autograph (p. 134), and it is with shock and bitterness that Paddy first begins to appreciate the gap between representation and reality. A similar gap appears between what his parents should do, according to the rules of the community, and what they really do. 'It didn't make sense' (p. 191) Paddy says; and it is precisely this lack of sense with which he is going to have to come to terms as he watches his family disintegrate. What Paddy is in the process of learning is the essentially adult skill for survival, entailing the acceptance of contradiction where once there had been only accord. He both loves and hates his father, so too his mother and his little brother Sinbad, and it is this paradox which turns his world from a securely based adventure into a process of constant emotional improvisation.

Paddy's experience moves from sufficiency to inadequacy. 'We owned Barrytown, the whole lot of it. It went on forever. It was a country' (p. 150). Such feelings of possession and belonging give way as the novel proceeds to ones of displacement and isolation. If Barrytown, like Ireland, was a country, then like Ireland in the 1960s it was soon to have the myth of national possession and self-sufficiency shattered. The fields and cows disappear, newer and bigger gangs take over, and Paddy finds himself boycotted by his former friends because of the social stigma attached to the break-up of his family.

Recognising contradiction as the basis of society is traumatic enough. The trauma is exacerbated when contradiction is thrust upon the individual too soon – as with the children of dysfunctional families – and even more so when the individual lives in a society that is in mass denial regarding the fragility of the family, one of its most sacred institutions. Contradiction, moreover, implicates everyone. In a society that does not officially recognise the failure of marriage, frustration and violence will surface despite, or perhaps because of, communal repression. Thus, the easy-going class comedian David Geraghty is intimidated into striking Paddy with his crutch, much to his own distress (p. 271). Nothing is stated openly, but the reader is left to infer the emotional and psychological damage done as a result of this peaceful individual getting caught up in the community's hidden agenda of violence.

Nothing communicates the movement from certainty to contradiction, from comedy to tragedy, so well as the title of the novel. Offering itself initially as another variation on the comic Dublin family theme which Doyle had found so effective in the Barrytown trilogy, it is only at the end of the book that the reader discovers the pathos and the cruelty underlying the phrase, 'Paddy Clarke, Ha Ha Ha'. The text, in fact, warrants a second reading in the light of this tragic eventuality, for with the knowledge that there is no happy ending waiting to be pulled like a Rabbitte from the author's bag, much of the earlier comedy takes on a darker edge.

The ability of a text to continue to resonate within the reader's imagination is a sure sign of a writer's command of his craft, and it must be said that as well as offering a timely and provocative vision of Ireland's recent history, *Paddy Clarke Ha Ha Ha* is also an impressive technical achievement. With an alert eye for period detail and the vision of childhood, Doyle convinces the reader that the story is being narrated by a ten-year-old boy. At the same time, he manages to depict the unfolding of the family break-up and Paddy's emotional passage through confusion, guilt and bitterness with consummate skill. Much of the comedy and tragedy comes from our privileged adult insight into Paddy's childish perceptions, but the narrative never poses the question of the process of narration itself – the extent of symbolic detail, the use of figurative language, plotting, structure, and so on. The story is all, and it is this lack of narratorial self-consciousness and Doyle's characteristic respect for his characters and his readers that make for such a successful novel.

The Butcher Boy (1992) by Patrick McCabe

Patrick McCabe is from the same generation as Bolger and Doyle, and shares many of the same concerns. If *The Journey Home* and *Paddy Clarke Ha Ha Ha* were part of the process whereby a young, highly educated, post-nationalist community began to interrogate the discourses which had structured modern Ireland, as well as their own lives, McCabe's *The Butcher Boy* is the text wherein those discourses are most fully and most wickedly indicted.

There are in fact many similarities between Doyle's Booker Prize winner and McCabe's book which, despite the appearance of the critically acclaimed (and even blacker) *The Dead School* in 1995, remains his most famous and successful work to date. Both are set in the 1960s, although *The Butcher Boy* depicts an Ireland at the beginning of the decade yet to emerge from the complacency of post-independence. Both stories are narrated by young males, and one of the shared themes is the dangerous discrepancy between physical, psychological and emotional maturity. Both concern the relations between the individual and the widening network of social and cultural institutions which the individual must negotiate – family, friendship, community, church, authority.

There are also significant differences between the two texts, however, both in vision and style. This is not the city or the suburbs, but the rural slums of small-town Ireland, with the Brady family as its white trash. This is a world beset on every side by institutions of one kind or another, those 'houses of a hundred windows' which crop up throughout the story to curtail the freedom which Francie believes he once possessed, and which in his arrested mental state he so desperately desires to recapture: the orphanage to which his father and Uncle Alo were sent as children; the 'garage' (hospital) to which his mother goes for her depression; the borstal where Francie is sent after his first attack on the Nugents; the boarding school which consolidates the betrayal of Joe and from which Francie is excluded; and of course the institution for the criminally insane to which he is eventually sent and from where he narrates his story. This is a community which does not need a communist nuclear attack to turn it into a wasteland; it is already moribund, inhabited by morally bankrupt authority figures and spiritually broken people entertaining the ghosts of their dead dreams. Such a community, so at odds with the official pastoral ideology of modern Ireland, finds the hero it deserves in Francie Brady, for as well as being the agent of evil and resentful revenge, Francie is also a scape-goat for this community, the empty, innocent vessel into which all its repressions and vices are poured.

To say the Brady family is 'dysfunctional' would be to under-state the case. Hearing Da say to Ma: 'God's curse the fucking day I ever set eyes on you!' (p. 7) is hardly the help young Francie needs to develop into a well-adjusted young man. Because of his mother's suicide, Francie has not been able to experience the gradual separation from her that would allow him to mature emotionally and psychologically. This leaves him stranded at a particularly susceptible age between childhood and adolescence, but still fundamentally in thrall to the image of his mother. The remainder of the book becomes a search by Francie to find objects and relationships capable of replacing the replete identity he experienced with his mother; but as this was only ever an imaginary relationship anyway, all such attempts are doomed. Alo, Mary and the good old days, his parents' sojourn in the Bundoran guesthouse 'Over The Waves', his own childhood adventures with Joe, all are slipping further and further away from an increasingly unsatisfactory present. At one point early in the novel, Francie's father looks in vain for a pattern in the whiskey he has spilt on the floor after his denouncement of Alo and the cursing of his wife (p. 36); and it is essentially this same practice which Francie engages in when he tries to make all the disparate voices battling in his head conform to some kind of coherent narrative that will explain how things got so bad, how the past slipped away, and how, most significantly, the past is a sentimental invention by those marooned in the present.

But Francie never makes the move (which is thrust upon Paddy) from being the object of others' narratives to being the subject of his own; he never, that is, finds his own voice, so his world degenerates into ceaseless role-playing – local roles, such as the Bogman and Francie Brady Not A Bad Bastard Any More, and more exotic roles gleaned from popular culture, such as Algernon Carruthers and the various Hollywood heroes. He quotes all, but is none, of these characters. The ringing in his head which starts to overtake him towards the end of the story represents the increasingly unmanageable clash of all these voices. Francie confronts the perfidy of discourse and the gap that always exists between representation and reality, but unlike Paddy he cannot breach that gap, and his identity begins to crumple under the strain.

Having taken the shards from all the broken dreams with which he is surrounded and put them back together in a warped mirror of reality, what is revealed to Francie is the culpability of the Nugent family, and especially Mrs Nugent, in the failure of the present to live up to the past. The Nugents are returned exiles from England. As a well-off, middle-class family with experience of the wider world, less than pleased with the rural idiocy to which they have returned, the Nugents anticipate the new Ireland which economic and ideological change was beginning to make possible. Francie is his father's son in so far as he resents the material success of the Nugent family and the courage they have displayed in making a life, rather than having one imposed upon them by circumstances and community expectations. The text would seem to suggest that there are, however, deeper and darker reasons behind Francie's targeting of Mrs Nugent as the source of all his family's woes. The author appears to take delight in rehearsing all the constituents of a classic Oedipal breakdown – a brutal father, mother fixation, repression, displacement, good breasts and bad breasts, the whole gamut, in fact, of psychoanalytical discourse as it has filtered down into the popular imagination. But the text operates first and foremost as a compelling narrative of the disintegration of a mind, and the reader is not compelled to follow the subliminal narrative to enjoy the book. This ability to function on a number of levels at once doubtless contributed to the critical and popular success of *The Butcher Boy*.

The Woman Who Walked Into Doors (1996)

After the massive success of *Paddy Clarke Ha Ha Ha* Doyle left teaching to concentrate on writing full-time. His work has revealed a growing intensity and seriousness, and an unwillingness merely to reproduce the successful early packages. Instead Doyle is interested in stretching himself as a writer both formally and conceptually, as well as testing the limits of novelistic discourse generally. Alarmed by the prospect of a 'Roddy Doyle industry' he has resisted the celebrity status which normally accompanies success, recognising perhaps that celebrity is one of the ways in which Irish society accommodates its artists while robbing them of any radical edge. That Doyle wishes to maintain that edge is evident from the appearance of *The Woman Who Walked Into Doors*, his most ambitious novel to date.

The question of the role of women in Irish society had not been fully addressed in Doyle's earlier work. It could be argued that although Jimmy Rabbitte Jr is the main character in what is otherwise an ensemble piece, it is the Commitmentette Imelda Quirke who has the most influence on the action of the first novel, for she it is who holds the band together through lust, and who is indirectly responsible for breaking up the band when for a joke she tells Joey the Lips that she is going to have his baby (p. 136). It seems clear, also, that Veronica, the mother of the Rabbitte family, has a story to tell, despite remaining on the edges of the action throughout the trilogy. Her voice, however, is lost amongst the more insistent voices of her children and her husband. 'You never knew with Veronica', thinks Jimmy Sr in *The Van* (p. 407); she is, like Paddy Clarke's mother, a missing chapter of Doyle's ongoing book of the nation.

Doyle began to write this chapter, however, with *Family*, a four-part television series produced for Irish and British television, screened in 1994. *Family* became an immediate 'event' of Irish cultural history, exciting intense debate and polarising

opinions amongst both the public and the professional cultural
critics. It was a highly topical intervention, as questions regarding the traditional role and function of the family had been much
to the fore for over a decade, in the form of referenda on divorce
and abortion, and in a number of public scandals regarding authority figures from church and politics. *Family* was a hard-
hitting slice-of-life drama, filmed in a deliberately anti-narrative,
documentary style. Characteristically of Doyle, it offered no
judgements on the highly sensitive subjects of urban poverty and
domestic violence; it did, however, insist that Irish society confront a series of problems which it had been ignoring since the
formation of the state. Paula's narrative is an anatomy of terror, a
word often used in Ireland but seldom outside the sphere of the
Northern conflict. And in this insistence upon the centrality of
the world of domestic politics, Doyle joins with those who recognise the personal alongside the public as the terrain upon which
issues of Irish identity and destiny are worked out.

   The Woman Who Walked Into Doors grew out of *Family*, and
indeed shares some scenes with it. It is narrated by Paula
Spencer, the wife and mother from the television series, as she
tries to make sense of her life with and without her husband,
the brutal Charlo. Doyle has said that the novel was written
partly as a response to the many people who said that in
reality Paula would never have married Charlo in the first
place, or that she should have left immediately on finding out
what kind of a man he was. But such, he suggests, are simp-
listic readings of domestic violence from those unfamiliar with
its day-to-day dynamics. Instead Doyle tries to show, through
Paula's words and point of view, the contradictions thrown up
by the act of violence, the guilt, self-hatred and victimage
which she has to combat as well as Charlo's physical assaults.
For along with Charlo's fully believable threats of pursuit and
murder, Paula also finds herself confronted with a society in
massive denial about sexual abuse of all kinds. This is the
same society that has convinced Paula she is worthless. Doctors
and nurses look through her or blame her condition on drink.
Her father and mother say nothing, one overcome by spite and
jealousy, the other by fear. Most insidiously, the voice of the
community – represented in italics at various points throughout the text (pp. 171, 185) – constantly undermines Paula's
position by feeding the belief that she is to blame for Charlo's
assaults and that such behaviour is normal in society anyway.

   The title refers to one of the standard excuses used by

battered women to explain their injuries, but as the novel develops, the image of the door takes on a more symbolic resonance. It is a way in and a way out. The door curtails her freedom, as in the story of the little girl who got trapped in a discarded fridge and smothered after she pulled the door shut (p. 150). The door is also the mark of Paula's own space after she throws Charlo out: 'I couldn't go through the door, so I fucked him through it instead' (p. 214). The image of the door thus represents the threshold between self-control and subjection, and at the end of the book Paula is half in and half out – like Charlo's death sprawl, hanging from the getaway car which he could not drive – reclaiming her role as mother and home-maker but still dependent on alcohol to carry on.

Thus the book ends, although not the story, and Doyle leaves it up to the reader to decide which way Paula might go. There is a strong case for either side. *The Woman Who Walked Into Doors* maintains for the most part Doyle's subtlety of technique and the respect for reader and character shown in earlier novels. 'Her name is Sally' (p. 203) Paula writes of the baby she lost as a result of one of Charlo's beatings, and the alert reader learns more of Paula's agony from this short sentence than from reams of sociological analysis or descriptive prose.

'Writes' rather than 'says' or 'thinks', for unlike the earlier works, which had remained unencumbered by any self-consciousness regarding the form of the narrative, this novel possesses a definite and recurring *meta*narrative element. Paula's sister Carmel accuses her of 'rewriting history' (p. 56) and while such an act is understandable on a metaphorical level as part of Paula's need to take control of her life by placing it in some kind of narrative order, it is the actual 'writing' aspect that may seem anomalous here. We have already remarked the symbolism of the door, a sustained literary device which has no precedence in the Doyle canon. And the 'literary' recurs throughout the text, as Paula makes reference to the moment of writing: 'It kills me writing that and reading it – *I could never afford good shoes for my kids*' (p. 10); or, '(I haven't been drinking, by the way)' (p. 170) as she writes in one aside. She also deliberates on the discrepancy between real life and the language she must use to represent it – 'I choose one word and end up telling a different story. I end up making it up instead of just telling it' (p. 184). Unlike the previous novels, the text is organised into chapters, and it uses typographical and stylistic devices such as italics and parentheses to indicate different levels of discourse.

In all these ways, the text draws attention to itself, to its textuality, to its status as a written document. But written by whom? Are we being asked to believe that Paula has become a professional novelist, with the structural and organisational skills required to produce a text like *The Woman Who Walked Into Doors*? Such a question could also have been asked of Paddy Clarke – a ten-year-old narrating a Booker Prize winner? – but nowhere in that book was attention drawn to the narrative moment itself. I would suggest that Doyle's introduction of a metadiscursive aspect here is a way of defamiliarising the narrative, not in order to alienate the reader from Paula's plight, but rather to highlight the issues of authority and responsibility which are the actual themes of the novel. In effect, the text is asking the reader a series of questions. Can language describe violence? How does literature relate to the 'real'? Can a person tell the story of his or her own life? How reliant are notions of identity and character on textual devices? Can a man tell a woman's story? It is indicative of Doyle's skill that when he employs formal defamiliarising techniques – which can seem so hollow in the hands of modish postmodernists – the effect is to heighten rather than mitigate the message of his novel.

The Woman Who Walked Into Doors may be read in terms of its author's ongoing exploration of the role of the family in modern Irish life. It is also a story about a woman written by a man, and – whether fortuitous or calculated – ties in with the resurgence of women's issues that has overtaken Irish cultural debate since the early 1980s. But precisely because he is an established writer, and a male, and has a history of writing novels about other aspects of modern Irish life, Doyle's book circulates and functions in very different ways to similar texts written by Irish women. Doyle himself has remarked on the difference in marketing between his own 'woman's story' and a number of similar texts appearing around the same time – *The Maid's Tale* (1994) by Kathleen Ferguson, *Another Alice* (1996) by Lia Mills, and *Mother of Pearl* (1996) by Mary Morrissey. Soft-focus covers and flyleaf blurbs are just one way of ensuring that these texts can be contained under the disabling rubric of 'women's issues'. But, as one critic has put it:

> isolating women into a single category has the self-defeating effect of further marginalising them from the literary mainstream. If their claims to be given an equal place alongside their male peers are to be

taken seriously, women writers must be pushed into the flood, there to sink or swim on their own merits.[7]

In the remainder of this chapter I wish to look at these three debut novels which deal with aspects of women's experience in modern Ireland. These texts are considered here rather than in the later chapter on marginal voices ('Borderlands') because such a critical organisation of material would be guilty of reproducing the same conditions and assumptions that helped to marginalise Irish women in the first place. It is true that these novels are given 'special' status within this chapter itself, but their inclusion here is intended to reflect back on all that has been said so far regarding the nature of Irish identity and the changes affecting modern Irish society. In the same way that Paula Spencer's story reveals itself not as an addendum to the national story but as one of its central voices, so these three texts should be seen as central to the critical narrative offered here, demanding a reconsideration of the history of 'Irishness', 'woman' and the relations between these categories.

The Maid's Tale (1994) by Kathleen Ferguson

The Maid's Tale tells the story of Brigid Keen, a woman in her fifties who has spent the greater part of her life as a housekeeper in the service of a Catholic priest, the appropriately named Father Patrick Mann. Like Paula Spencer, Brigid narrates her own story, and although of a different age and background, she also tells a tale of official complacence and culpability, of socially sanctioned abuses of power and enforced silence. Crucially, like Paula, she also tells of strategies of resistance on the part of the dispossessed.

Brigid's father killed her mother in one of his periodic fits of rage and is forced to accept incarceration in the local mental hospital to avoid imprisonment. Brigid is raised with her brother and sister in an orphanage run by Sisters of Mercy in Derry. Then, while still little more than a child, she is given over into a life of virtual slavery for the local clergy. Brigid's relationship with Father Mann is virtually a marriage, as she makes clear in asides and comments throughout the narrative. Marriages in the novel are suspect enough, unequal battlegrounds for the frustrated and the disappointed. But this 'marriage' does not even have the dubious compensations of a physical dimension, and

Brigid's repressed desires emerge in dreams and fantasies which she does not understand. Father Mann is revealed as a jealous, manipulative man who from being a friendly young novice soon learns to use his position to get his own way with Brigid and to deny her a voice. He practices a form of psychological and linguistic violence on her, bringing the force of his education and social standing to bear when sense and reason will not answer. Despite this, Brigid loves him, and even more so after he is struck down with Alzheimer's disease – a physical and psychological extension of the spiritual malady to which he has already succumbed.

The Maid's Tale is a bitter indictment of unaccountable institutional power, and of the corrupting force such power has on the lives of individuals and whole societies. The theme of the unfortunate Father Green's first sermon after he has been pressganged into the priesthood is especially ironic – 'We must die to ourselves before we can come alive in the Lord' (p. 76). Religion in this form becomes a denial rather than an affirmation of identity, a negative rather than a positive force. The organised Church is depicted as a rotten institution, encouraging emotional cowardice amongst those who through socialisation or education feel compelled to embrace its tenets. Rather than operating as a healing force in society, religion has destroyed the power of love. Men in the novel are angry and frustrated, women are emotionally crippled and physically frustrated, and discord and misunderstanding characterise the relations between the sexes (p. 160). Like *The Butcher Boy*, this novel is awash with institutions for the physically, psychologically and emotionally stricken. Irish society itself, it appears, is a form of institution for curtailing freedom, with the Catholic clergy as its warders.

Although officially silenced from birth because of her gender, Brigid resists in any way she can. Men have dominated her life, her imagination and her desire. But she develops a healthy scepticism in the face of the rituals employed by patriarchal institutions such as the Catholic Church to maintain their moral hegemony. She devours the symbols of the body and blood of Christ in ways which subvert the disabling ideology into which such symbols are locked, taking a body-oriented, libidinous pleasure from gobbling up the hosts (p. 9) and getting drunk on the altar wine (p. 186). As her life with Father Mann starts to disintegrate, Brigid realises how she has been abused and manipulated throughout her life, how her faith was betrayed and how she has paid for crimes that occurred as a result of that flawed ideology. It is ironic that it takes a man, the violently anti-clerical Tim who in other circumstances might have been Brigid's lover, to put his finger on it: 'Your Catholic Church, with its man-God, expects a woman to keep her mouth shut. To keep her mouth shut and serve. And that's what you've been doing all these years – all these years you could've been living a full life for y'rsell' (p. 189).

As Brigid realises towards the end of the narrative, however, the real sin of the Catholic Church is that it duped her into thinking in the same, manipulative ways that it encouraged amongst its own agents and adherents. 'The fact is', she says, 'I used Father just the same way he used me' (p. 193). It is not clear what kind of future Brigid is escaping to, but the very action of leaving after a life of servitude and silence is itself a positive gesture. All the male figures in her life have abused or manipulated her for their own ends – her father, Tim, Father Mann, Bishop Cleary, God – now she must learn to be her own 'master'.

The novel shows Brigid becoming her own author, in effect her own god. Rather than having her life described in terms of other people or institutions, she tells her own story in her own words, thus reclaiming the sense of self which the Church had insisted she sacrifice. *The Maid's Tale* is written in the form of an oral history, and Brigid's resistance to patriarchal ideology is supported by the control she exerts over her own narrative. Telling the story of her life is an enabling act for Brigid, a way of affirming identity in the present. She insists on ordering her own life, allowing space to certain things while omitting others, employing her own idiom and her own perspectives to combat the weight of institutional discourse. The narrative ethos is one of the spoken rather than the written word. Brigid does not try to pretend that her version is objective or uninfluenced by her position in the present. This narrative is alive, and the reader is invoked throughout and invited to take an active part in the narrative process.

At the same time, this sort of oral, amateur ethos is a way of exposing the authority of those in society who rely on privilege and education rather than moral example for their authority. This is shown early in the novel when Brigid describes her reaction to Tim's diatribe against the Catholic Church:

I didn't like the sound of this at all, as you can imagine. It wasn't the old Tim I was used to listening to. Though, looking back now, I see there was some truth in what he says. Derry people, women in particular, made a wild lot of the clergy – and still do. A Derry woman or man wouldn't pass a priest in the street without salute. (p. 15)

In this passage, the anti-narrative gesture is linked to the anti-authoritarian gesture; for just as the narration here exposes the contingent nature of all narrative ('as you can imagine', 'looking back now', 'and still do'), so the 'salute' which signifies the laity's acknowledgement of the clergy's traditional moral authority is revealed as calcified custom, a formulaic response indicating fear rather than respect or acknowledgement of moral authority.

Mother of Pearl (1996) by Mary Morrissey

Like many of the writers examined in this chapter, Mary Morrissey gravitated to the novel form from the short story (her collection *A Lazy Eye* was published in 1993), and the influence of the latter is evident in her debut novel. In *Mother of Pearl* Morrissey stitches together three interrelated stories which with a little work could probably have stood on their own. Taken as a whole, however, the narrative operates as a sort of neo-gothic myth, drawing together themes of desire, guilt and identity in a grim indictment of modern Ireland.

Part 1 of the novel concerns the kidnapping of a baby by a childless couple, Irene and Stanley, themselves victims of the family institution. Irene's father spends most of his time on a lighthouse away from his hated wife and family, and all that follows in the way of betrayal and disappointment stems from this initial loss of the father figure. Opening in a tuberculosis sanatorium, the physical disease from which Irene suffers operates as a metaphor for the disease-racking Irish society – namely, its inability to produce forms of identity capable of meeting the community's spiritual and physical needs. Stanley is forced to sever the links with his mother on her death, but so confused are his emotional and physical desires in the wake of this trauma that he is rendered sexually impotent. To stave off the social stigma of childlessness Irene invents a phantom baby named Pearl, but when this no longer suffices she steals Baby Spain from a hospital, telling Stanley that the child has been fathered by an old acquaintance. Part 2 finds the kidnapped baby's real father and mother, Rita and Mel Spain, likewise caught up in a complex web of desire and guilt. At first Rita does not want Baby

Spain, but so consumed with guilt is she after it is stolen that she bargains with supernatural forces to take Mel if only she can have the baby back. Mel is indeed 'taken', murdered in a botched sectarian assassination after Rita has had another baby, Stella, by her Italian dancing master. In Part 3 Pearl (now named Mary) has returned to her lawful family, but the past refuses to lie down, and in her desire to rid herself of the fantasies and guilt of the past she self-aborts during pregnancy.

The word 'neo-gothic' was used above to describe this novel and this seems appropriate. Such a labyrinthine tale of desire, guilt and sin, of ghostly doubles and grim Faustian pacts, as well as the genealogical/generational structure underpinning the narrative, certainly recalls some of the dominant tropes of the gothic tradition. The themes are elemental, but the plot is intricate and subtle. Madness in one form or another underpins all three subplots, the warped logic of a warped society dominated by the past. The action throughout is governed by the influence of 'phantoms' on the living, and by the inability of people to come to terms with their social and familial inheritances. The imaginary Pearl 'haunts' Irene and Stanley (p. 57); Rita becomes a 'ghost' as soon as she marries Mel Spain (p. 103); Mary destroys the living baby she is carrying 'for a phantom, a wilful sprite, a demon, perhaps' (p. 216). Most typical of the gothic, however, is the theme of identity and loss of identity which recurs throughout. All the characters in the text are unstable, having to improvise versions of themselves in response to socially determined discourses of desire. All are victims to an extent, but Mary it is who, in a horrific act of atonement in which she is part Eve, part Jesus, takes the weight of accumulated guilt upon herself. With her multiple identity – Baby Spain, Pearl, Hazel-Mary, Moll – she represents the nexus of so many desires and fantasies that finally she feels compelled to erase the past and start over. 'I am a *tabula rasa*', she says, 'born again, with my history excised, cut out of me' (p. 216).

Like the character of Mary, however, one could argue that *Mother of Pearl* takes too much upon itself and is finally overcome by the weight of all the discourses it attempts to represent. There appears to be something self-conscious and deliberate about both plotting and style, the inevitability with which desire excites guilt, and the heavy symbolism (such as the sea/ship metaphor that runs throughout all three parts, the biblical passages on motherhood, and the fairy-tale dimension to the naming of characters). There is also a vague and half-hearted attempt to link issues of familial dysfunction to sectarian strife in Northern Ireland, where the action is apparently set. This, however, is at odds with the otherwise unspecified nature of the narrative, engaged as it is with parable and myth rather than geography and history. By the end of the text, the narrative is operating on so many levels that something is in danger of getting lost – the story. Mary is a fairy-tale figure, a Catholic, a reincarnation of Rita's 'real' lost Baby Spain, a mother, a wife, Eve, Jesus – in fact, too many things for even the most complex novelistic character to sustain. The plot becomes an exercise in trigonometry, and while we might admire its cleverness, its ability to engage at the elemental level of story has been compromised.

Mother of Pearl is concerned with the impingement of repressed fantasy and disappointed desire on the real world of work and family. Despite its formal shortcomings, it is part of the process whereby modern Ireland is attempting to come to terms with itself, identifying the ideological roots out of which the nation has grown and measuring the distance it has come.

Another Alice (1996) by Lia Mills

'This is not me' (p. 1) thinks eponymous Alice Morrissey at the outset of this powerful novel. Along with the title, this short sentence immediately signals that here is a book concerned with the struggle for identity and with different levels of experience. In fact, *Another Alice* touches upon most of the themes signalled throughout this book as central concerns of the new Irish fiction – the family, madness, dreams, gender and nation – pulling them together into an ultimately enabling vision of the role of women in modern Ireland. This makes Mills's debut novel perhaps the most typical book of the latest generation of Irish novelists and, as such, a fitting text with which to finish this exploration of the new Irish fiction.

The action is set in the same period as all the other texts examined so far in this chapter, the present and recent past, and the story is one of a desperately unhappy woman learning to come to terms with her past and with the strategies she was forced to adopt to survive a severely traumatic experience. At the outset of the text, Alice is in therapy and it quickly emerges that she is at a crisis point in her life. As a child she had been abused by her father, but so traumatic were the experiences that she has repressed them. At the moment of the assault, Alice leaves herself behind and looks on dispassionately as her body is violated and her innocence corrupted. Thus is born her refusal to identify with an Alice so obviously ruined, and thus are planted the seeds of all her future problems. For, true to the psycho-analytic theory which provides the metanarrative basis for *Another Alice*, the repressed memories return to haunt Alice in the form of a dream. Locked into the traumas of her childhood, fearful of adopting a self which might be hurt again, she cannot develop a normal healthy personality and as a consequence remains a stranger to herself. Reality is the place where danger and hurt reside, so she prefers the world of dreams, or even madness. The dream motif throughout the narrative is closely linked with Alice's difficulty in coping with reality; while in her childhood, the fantasy worlds of spy adventure and ancient Gaelic myth offer relatively harmless escapes, when she moves on to the more adult compensations of sex, drugs and alcohol she is a danger to herself and everyone within her range of influence.

As Alice tries to cure herself by talking through her night-mares and eventually naming the cause of all her problems, so the text itself is looking for its own cure – the 'meaning' of the book. The form of the text mirrors the underlying psycho-analytical metanarrative in that the text/patient must narrate a story to the reader/analyst before the story can be closed/cured. The narrative is complex, shifting between different times and different voices. Alice is in fact looking for a story form that will make sense of her life. The present constantly interrupts the past, which moves closer to the present as the story progresses. When the two coalesce, the story will end. But so intense is the reality that there is a danger that the story will never end; as the climax approaches, language itself seems in-capable of bearing the burden, shifting from narrative and communication towards rhythm and rhyme (p. 348).

Different themes emerge in relation to Alice's trauma – guilt, shame, feelings of complicity and self-hatred, and most centrally an inability to love. So traumatised is Alice by her ordeals that she is in danger of transferring all these feelings onto her daugh-ter Holly, thus perpetuating the cycle of guilt and shame precipi-tated by her father's assaults. Initially, Holly is merely another strategy to refuse reality rather than face up to it. Alice watches herself playing the role of mother rather than engaging with the reality wherein she has been so damaged. The past, rather than offering an enabling narrative of origins and genealogy, weighs upon the present, stunting the emotional growth as well as the actual physical health of those caught in its gaze. 'You've no one to blame but yourself' (p. 328) Alice says to Holly after striking her, immediately realising that she is forcing her child to accept guilt for something which was not her fault, just as Alice herself felt guilt for becoming a victim of her father's assaults. As her therapist Ruth points out, guilt is a cycle that will return to destroy Holly's life if Alice does not acknowledge the hateful reality underpinning the dream.

The dream was a strategy automatically invented by Alice to cope with a traumatic reality, but it has in its turn placed a spell over Alice's future, refusing to let the past go and tainting the present with the repressed nightmare. 'She's in a constant dream' (p. 82) her mother says at an early point in the narrative, and it is precisely her inability to realise that the dream is in fact a distorted reality that keeps her in thrall to the past, preventing her from living in the present. The dream was merely a device she used to cope with a horrific reality, stepping outside herself so that she did not have to identify with her own defiled and guilty body. In conversation with Ruth, Alice finally realises the way power works to convince the victim of her own guilt. The strategies Alice developed to cope have in their turn become the very things which prevent her from ending the story and thus moving on, not cured of the past but able to recognise and deal with the ways in which it affects her present. Narration brings knowledge, and with knowledge comes the possibility of intervention and change rather than slavish return to the dream as some sort of compensation for an unsatisfactory reality.

Alice's story is linked to the wider experience of Irish women and indeed to general issues of power, gender and identity. Throughout the course of the narrative, Mills makes reference to a number of key texts and images in the history of women's subjugation. Two such images are that of 'the madwoman in the attic' (p. 183) and 'the woman in the wall' (pp. 260, 339), both either experienced or invoked by Alice as she negotiates the road towards self-knowledge. But the central myth which Mills accesses and deconstructs is that of *Alice in Wonderland*, the story of a young girl moving through a bizarre dreamscape as she tries to find her way back to reality. And as with all fairy-tales, names are crucial. As she lies in hospital after the birth of the baby she has decided to call Holly, Alice ponders the significance of names:

Her own was deceptive. It seemed innocent enough, but Alice knew what it really meant. It meant someone stuck in a nightmare, trapped

> in a world of shape shifters. A world full of menace. And then the
> polite fiction that the madness had been a dream, the lie that de-
> manded that she wash her hands and go demurely in for tea. (p. 168)

Thus she offers an alternative reading of the fairy-tale, one that
sees the underside of the official version, just as she represents
the hidden underside of an Irish society in denial about abuses of
all kinds.

Another Alice can be criticised on a number of levels. The
psychoanalytic discourse appears to be dictating the narrative
at every level. But literature is not psychoanalysis, and often
the characters seem to be merely miming the classic Freudian
narrative of trauma, repression, dysfunction and cure. The first
edition of *Another Alice* would also certainly have benefited
from more incisive editing as well as more courageous marketing and design. Perhaps most significantly the question of culpability is fudged; blaming pathology rather than culture or
society for her father's behaviour avoids the issue of agency
and the degree to which Irish history is itself implicated in
Alice's betrayal. However, *Another Alice* is a novel that works
first and foremost at the level of story, relating in frequently
harrowing detail a story that had to be told. At the same time,
in its overall positive structure, and in the way it reveals the
present learning to cope with the past, Mills's novel offers a
powerful myth for modern Ireland, a country currently negotiating the fall-out from its youthful traumas, repressions and
dreams. For Ireland itself has been changed by Alice's experiences. As she drives aimlessly away into the countryside with
Holly at the end of the book, Alice realises that the landscape,
or at least her relationship with it, has been altered.

> She turned the car south and headed down the coast. Soon they had
> left the city behind. An ache of love caught in her chest. The whole
> country seemed to stretch out in front of them. Limitless. The road
> was a leafy tunnel and then they burst out into the open again,
> mountains all around them, the sea shining on their left. (p. 392)

The land is reborn along with Alice, for the perspective she has
achieved is a vision for the nation as well as for the individual.
   Thus ends also this brief critical narrative of one strand of the
new Irish fiction. As mentioned above, it is appropriate that this
chapter should finish with a novel which engages with issues of
identity and nation, criticising as well as caring for the new

Ireland and its continuing negotiations with past, present and future. For the novel is perhaps the principal location for these negotiations, a form in which the many competing narratives of national identity can enter into a dialogue difficult to imagine, never mind organise, in other social, cultural and political spheres.

APPENDIX:
AN INTERVIEW WITH
RODDY DOYLE,
16 SEPTEMBER 1996

GS Are there any traditions – literary, cultural, social – that you are conscious of writing within or against?

RD No. I suppose when I've finished a book I begin to put it in context and begin to wonder what it is. But as I'm doing it I'm not aware of tradition. When I was writing *The Commitments* I thought I was doing something a bit fresh, but I wasn't really consciously knocking on doors or kicking at tradition. It just felt right as I was writing it and if I hadn't written *The Commitments* first I wouldn't have written the others in the way I did. Towards the end of writing *The Woman Who Walked Into Doors* when I was looking for some sort of shape for the narrative I was thinking of *Black Water* by Joyce Carol Oates – but that's not a tradition, it's a book. In the book I'm writing at the moment the narrator is a very old man. Now, we could spend the rest of the day listing off novels narrated by old men looking back. But I'm not trying to find myself a little niche in that tradition. It's just coincidence, and the fact that there's already a huge body of such work doesn't put me off in any way. I've read many of them but I won't be delving into them again to see if I can rob them. I'm a writer who reads as I write, I don't have a problem reading other people's work. I know a lot of people say they don't read fiction when they're writing, which would be miserable for me because I tend to write five days a week all the time. So when I'm working on a book, other individual books come to mind. Again, when I was writing *The Snapper*, it was partially inspired by Doris Lessing's book *A Proper Marriage*, the description of pregnancy and that, but again I wasn't trying to latch onto whatever tradition she comes from. It was just that individual section of that individual book I found stayed in my head a long time.

GS *The Commitments* is a very short book but gives the impression of a very large social and cultural canvas. You seem to make suggestions and hints which leave room for different kinds of reading.

RD *The Commitments* is only 33,000 words, very short. But yes, I've always liked to leave gaps. I still like to drop hints, an adjective just left on its own or something like that. I've always done it, but I've been more aware of it in the last few books which are written in the first person, and just trying to decide how reliable is the narrator and how much are they willing to tell. There's as much meaning in what they don't say very often as what they do say, and I just like to leave those gaps because I've always felt as a reader I only get worked up when I know I'm being asked to be involved in this thing. That's why I find that in some nineteenth-century writing, while I admire it, there's just too much there. It's not that the book is too long, but you're not being allowed to make your own mind up. You're not being allowed to add any sort of physical detail, because it's all there in too much detail. I prefer to be more pared down. At one point, for example, in *The Woman Who Walked Into Doors* Paula says of the baby she miscarried after a beating from Charlo, 'Her name is Sally'. Now, when I'm writing I don't think of people's reading habits, because I think an awful lot of people read just before they fall asleep. And if you have that in your mind all the time you couldn't write a little passage like that because they're not going to notice it very often. So you just have to write, for want of a better phrase, as *purely* as possible, you don't allow outside considerations to interfere. I think there are four lines in that little passage, and I think quite reasonably I could have made a lot more of it. I could have gone into detail of the actual physical act that led to the miscarriage, but it felt like a far better piece because it seems to convey the pain and presence of it, and the fact that it's something that never goes away. The use of the 'is', the fact of the name 'Sally' and that Sally somewhere or other is still there, a whole life that's gone missing.

GS Some of the references in your books seem to be very international, but some of them are so steeped in Dublin culture that

I wonder what people from Europe and America, and even Britain, will make of them.

RD Well, we would pick up without thinking about it a novel set in the deep south of America, or somewhere we've never been. Chances are it's going to be riddled with product names, with references to American culture that we don't know, and the odd piece of jargon or slang that we don't understand. And that's part of the enjoyment of it, I find. I don't see why the educated person in Tennessee shouldn't feel the same way about reading a novel set in Dublin or Liverpool or Glasgow or wherever. All my stories have a universal quality – like grief, birth and so on – but they're solidly founded on a couple of square miles of Dublin. I think people actually do enjoy that. It's a problem in translation, although I think the translators actually seem to enjoy the challenge of trying to capture what makes it particular. But I think they have the universal quality to lean against when they need support.

GS Perhaps this collapse of the gap between the local and universal makes your work 'postmodern', then?

RD Well, I think that because geographical distance seems to be a lot less relevant than it used to be that what we think is exclusive to our little zone in a lot of cases isn't. It's also interesting that what you think is particular Dublin slang isn't at all. I've noticed the word 'gaff' for house, which I thought was strictly Dublin, used in plays set in Liverpool, and I've heard it used in Glasgow. It's interesting to see how once a slang word becomes public how it starts reappearing all over the place. When I stopped teaching three years ago, to herald for myself the launching of my new career as a full-time writer, I accepted a lot of invitations. *Paddy Clarke Ha Ha Ha* was being published in a lot of countries, and I did a lot of travelling in the first nine months – Australia, Japan, Germany, places I'd never been to before. And what really was hammered home to me was how many people of different ages, different genders, race, religious background saw themselves in *Paddy Clarke*. It was quite astonishing – a black man in California saying 'I'm in that book. That's me.' One of the things that won him immediately was the use of the word 'Mammy' because he didn't realise that it was used outside his own Afro-American heritage. Then there was a part Aboriginal woman of about fifty in Melbourne who gave me a boomerang, and she'd seen herself in the book as well. She remembered playing on building sites. I think if you grew up before the '70s there was a building site within striking distance of wherever you lived, because they were building everywhere. Whereas Irish kids growing up today, if they read *Paddy Clarke* in ten years time they won't recognise an awful lot of it, because it's a different place. The building site which we took for granted won't be there, because most kids are living in built-up areas, and there's no room for anything else. It's as much to do with the traffic as anything else. As ten-year-olds they won't have had the feeling of just being able to walk out of the house, disappear for the day and come back. It'll be a different world completely.

GS There seem to have been a lot of Irish novels recently looking at issues of childhood and the recent past.

RD There were several reasons why I decided to use my own childhood to inspire me, although it's not my own story. Having finished *The Van* I wanted to do something very different. And when my eldest child was born I found myself thinking about my own childhood. It's probably a particularly male thing, we bring a new person into the world and start thinking about ourselves! But I just had this rush, and I began to think about my own parents as parents, and I'd find myself humming little snatches of nursery rhymes. So I decided to use that rush of memories to get going on a book and see if anything came out of it. I suppose that's probably a very common thing, not necessarily linked to the birth of one's children, but it seems such a rich area to think back on. One of the most enjoyable parts of *Paddy Clarke* was that it invited me to look at the world from a child's point of view, which was very funny. I was trying to capture the insatiable curiosity, and the refusal to accept the adult pecking order – what's important and what's trivial, what's vital and what isn't. But since I've been travelling people have been giving me a lot of books told from a child's perspective, set in different parts of the world. I actually now have at home quite a big body of work by men writing about childhood.

GS In the Irish context, could it be that these books are part of the process whereby the country is starting to reflect on its own recent history, and how it got to be the way it is?

RD There could be that, because I think an awful lot of us of between thirty and forty or forty-five are looking around and thinking, 'God, it's not the same place I grew up in'. I actually like what I see, generally, in most cases it's fine. But I do regret that my children won't have the same freedom. And it's not the bogey man out there. It's as much to do with the huge amount of cars. In *Paddy Clarke Ha Ha Ha* the rules of the game of football played on the street were bent to facilitate cars going by, because it was such a rare event. You couldn't possibly play on most streets now with any continuity. So I suppose a lot of people, including writers, around this age are looking around and thinking, 'Jesus Christ, we're living in a different country'. For anybody living in Ireland, particularly in the last five years, it's not just an economic thing. It's cultural, religious, social, every aspect. You should bring your passport to bed with you because you're going to wake up in a different place. In November we voted for divorce. Eight years previously it seemed like a very slim possibility that there would ever be a change of mind because it was so heavily defeated the first time. Something like fifteen people out of every hundred in that eight-year spell changed their minds, which is like a revolution really, a quiet one maybe but it's there. And then there is the changing attitude towards religion, because of the behaviour of priests, and the way the Catholic Church has handled the child abuse scandals. And then there was Bishop Casey, and the horror stories coming from the orphanages, and so on. And it was all building up, there was almost a daily event. It's extraordinary, really. Suddenly without noticing it, Ireland has some of the most liberal homosexual laws. Dublin especially. I love Dublin and wouldn't want to live anywhere else but it's sometimes hard to grasp that the place you live in is the place you grew up in, it seems so different at times.

GS What do you think is distinctive about the novel as a form?

RD Well, with the novel every word counts. That's probably true of fiction generally, it may be more true of the short story, I don't know. What isn't enjoyable about writing for the screen is the fact that words don't matter all that much. It should be well written, but if you're writing down a brief instruction for the cast it doesn't have to be literature. 'He enters the room' is quite adequate. It's up to the actor to make the most of that, or hopefully he will just enter the room. And a lot of attention must be given to dialogue and to linking the scenes and making complete things out of them. But with the novel you're creating an entire world and every word counts. You're putting in a word too many or taking out a word too many, and you're linking one sentence onto the next. What you're doing is creating a world that stands by itself. Whereas when you're writing a screenplay you're just making a foundation and then other people will build the house on top of it. With the novel you're building the house. Every tiny word, every comma, what seems like a casual decision – they're all important. And also you've got the rhythm to contend with. When you're writing for the screen it's a different type of rhythm, it's about linking scenes. Whereas when you're writing a novel the rhythm is in many ways as important as it is in poetry, because if the sentences don't have that rhythm the reading breaks down. And then there's the broader rhythm of the story itself. You want the dialogue to seem to have some sort of a basis in reality but if you record the average conversation and then try to transcribe it it will have absolutely no rhythm whatsoever. Not on paper anyway, because if you try to include body language and stuff like that it all breaks down. So you would have to start honing it to make it fit onto the page. And that's what I find so satisfying about the novel, sometimes frustrating but generally engrossing. Every word is absolutely vital. I love writing a sentence and seeing at the end, 'Where does that leave me now? Do I go on and write another one now, and what will that add to what I've just written, and what are the consequences in terms of what I've done in the last couple of weeks? Has this sentence negated what I wrote two weeks ago?' If you're doing a script that sort of question is quite mechanical. Finally trying to explain it is actually quite difficult. It's just creating this insulated world on paper. You create on a page some sort of a frame and you look at the page and there's still little holes in the frame and with words and punctuation you start filling the holes and each word is a little bulb that goes into the hole and the whole thing hopefully will light up. The fascination of a script is different. It's the anticipation of seeing it done, whereas the novel is just there on the day. I've just finished a script based on Liam O'Flaherty's novel *Famine* and I spent a long time working on that alone and I just found that the day was a bit hollow. It wasn't as engrossing, whereas working on the novel is far more fulfilling, although I'm going to have to do an awful lot of research and reading for the one I'm working on at the moment and it's years down the way. I'm sure at some point in the next few years I'm going to be saying 'Jesus, I wish I'd never started this thing. Why couldn't I have just rewritten *The Commitments*?'

GS Do you think there's something contradictory about employing so much dialogue in a form that's supposed to be narrative-based?

RD I've always been drawn towards work that has a lot of dialogue in it, like Flannery O'Connor, that dialogue that seems immediately to bring you somewhere specific. One of the ironies about America is that it's such a vast place but it seems to be full of tiny little places, and O'Connor wrote about tiny little places. One of the joys of reading Elmore Leonard is the dialogue, it's so alive, and a lot of the better American crime writers bring the characters alive by the way they speak. I think probably in terms of the amount of dialogue on the page, there's less in my later books because they're written in the first person, so in many ways they are monologues. But I think what started me on the road was *The Commitments*, in which you had a big gang of people together and it really didn't matter who said what very often. That was part of the fun, trying to figure out who's speaking. Being young and being from Dublin, none of them ever shut their mouths and I didn't want to interrupt the narrative by describing each in graphic detail. Many people did that anyway. Years before the film ever came out I remember reading more than one reference in reviews about 'The blond bombshell, Imelda Quirke'. There's no reference to hair colour whatsoever in the novel. That was the reviewer telling a lot more about himself than the character or the author.

GS Although it turned out she was blond in the movie.

RD Yes, well that tells you a lot about Alan Parker.

GS Speaking of Imelda leads on to a question I wanted to ask about your representation of women. I think Imelda is a much more important character than she initially appears. She holds the band together through lust, and she precipitates the break-up when for a joke she tells Joey the Lips that she's going to have his baby and he then disappears. It's like an undercurrent, a story that's not being told, and I suppose the same could be said of Veronica and Paddy's mother, before Paula comes and insists on telling her story.

RD I suppose it's increasing familiarity, but I always felt that the women characters in my books, starting with the Commitmentettes, and then Veronica and Sharon, while they conform to a certain extent to what is expected of them, at the same time they refuse in many ways to conform. So, yes, Imelda was this beautiful woman that they were all goggle-eyed at, and she was aware of it, but at the same time she wouldn't answer to that Miss Ireland kind of behaviour or demeanour. The language of the Commitmentettes is as coarse and as courageous as the lads, in fact more so. They're far more at home with themselves. The lads refused to accept her freedom to sleep with whoever she wanted, and so there was the inevitable sexual jealously. With the case of *The Snapper*, there's a certain sad inevitability that Sharon becomes pregnant. Anyone who's familiar with Dublin generally, but particularly working-class Dublin, would say that the shock is that she was twenty *before* she became pregnant, there's so many very young mothers floating around. But having become pregnant, she makes an achievement of it and refuses to conform to her father's version of what's going on. She forces him to change his mind, she lies so strongly and so wholeheartedly that everybody has to conform. And that's her strength. She does fall into the trap of one in every three young women in Dublin or whatever the figure is, but then climbs out of that trap and makes a personal triumph out of the whole thing. Veronica is the typical housewife in many ways, but again, she's doing Leaving Cert. subjects in *The Van* which is a very big thing for a working-class woman of that age to do – to admit that there's a need and then to go off and fill that need. And then the triumph of actually succeeding, and suddenly the awareness at that age that one is intelligent. I could never have written *The Woman Who Walked Into Doors* as a first book, but I suppose all these thing that have been at the back of my mind came together there. In an earlier play I'd done called *War* about a pub quiz team, it didn't really work, because inevitably all the action and humour was in the pub scenes. But there were quieter scenes in between with the husband and wife, and basically she was a good deal brighter than him, she had more information, she would have been far more useful on any quiz team but nobody noticed, and she was stuck at home. But it didn't quite work on stage. I think it was asking too much of lighting or something, and I was never happy with it. Then the opportunity came to do *Family*, and as I was doing that I felt there was a book there. I was very happy with *Family* but having written about a ten-year-old boy I wanted the challenge of getting into the head of the woman, something I felt would be even more difficult.

GS The family seems to be the predominant theme of your work so far.

RD Well, if you're familiar with Ireland you'll know that it's hard to get away from it. It's not there so much in *The Commitments*, which in many ways is about people escaping the family, that period of the late teens when you've got that freedom and you're experimenting with drink and stuff, and you suddenly realise there's nobody looking over your shoulder. But yes, the family is inevitable. A lot of people in Dublin tend to live with their parents a long time. In America you realise that people leave home a good deal earlier because they go to college or whatever, they're always on the move, they never seem to settle. And they find the idea that I live about two miles from where I grew up quite strange, and I have no intention of going anywhere else, that I'm quite happy there and that I've got as much as I need. It's just part and parcel of the Irish package, really. So you think: young woman becomes pregnant, she lives at home, therefore she has to tell her parents, it's going to be a working-class family, a lot of kids. Suddenly it's as much about the family as it is about her. Now the new book I'm working on at the moment, in the early stages the narrator is talking about his mother and father but then he's off, a loner. He will marry but essentially it will not be about his marriage or family, and part of his uniqueness in the Irish context is that he's kicked off the notion of family and just followed his nose all his life.

GS *The Woman Who Walked Into Doors* struck me as being much more *literary* than the earlier books, in the sense that it employs obvious symbolism – the door, for example – and in the way that the status of the text is an issue, the fact that it's written by Paula, and she discusses her worries over language and narrative and so on.

RD That's what I saw, that's what I visualised at first – her sitting at the kitchen table writing. And she's a 38-year-old woman whereas Paddy Clarke is a ten-year-old boy, and she would see these symbols. I wanted them to come from her, I didn't want them to be too literary or whatever. She's an intelligent woman, although she wouldn't be particularly well read. She grew up like most of us with a movie and television culture. In a poor household maybe one of the most stable things there is the video machine, whereas you'll find things missing that in a middle-class context would be hard to understand. The book is more 'literary', if you want to use that word, in so far as I was aware that she was writing it. I always visualised her sitting down, actually as I did the first time I did with a copybook and a pen, and gradually growing in confidence. At first I was going to start it off as if she was writing for the first time, and she was going to start at the beginning and tell her story in the old traditional A, B, C, D linear way. But I abandoned that pretty quickly because I thought that however well meant and however accurate it was also going to be incredibly tedious. So, I changed the structure of the book, and I abandoned to a certain extent this idea of her becoming gradually more confident as she goes into the writing. I do think it's still there, there are hints like when she says 'I'm not so sure I'm stupid anymore' about half-way through the book. But it was partly to do with the particular woman who was writing this story. It wouldn't have fitted *Paddy Clarke Ha Ha Ha*, you would have been thinking this isn't a ten-year-old boy. In the book I'm working on at the moment the narrator is a very old man and there's a certain circular quality to it, he keeps coming back to things all the time, and I expect that when it's finished it will be quite 'literary'.

GS Still, *The Woman Who Walked Into Doors* is a very good book for someone writing for the first time. Paula is balancing her own childhood and the early years with Charlo and the present, and having to maintain the rhythm of those three strands.

RD Well, I felt that by starting off in the recent past and then going to the distant past, and then you had the build-up of her marriage and the courting and so on, I felt that the reader would know this woman very quickly. It's not like you now know the woman on page 322 – we're leading somewhere but we don't know where. So almost immediately, in the first thirty pages, you would have a good idea of the woman as she is now. So it seemed to me a good way of achieving it. It wouldn't have worked with *Paddy Clarke*, because he wouldn't have had that distance, although there are hints in that book. The story meanders for the first two-thirds, and people might like it but still be wondering what it's about. And that was deliberate as well. There are strong links between each individual segment, but it's not linear at all. I didn't want to make it too obvious, but it's more to do with a subject or a colour or something that leads him off on a tangent to another thing but is really tied in. The big difference between writing *Paddy Clarke* and the first three novels was the amount of time spent on editing, on putting it all together. With the other three it was a question of paring it down and throwing away stuff, whereas with *Paddy Clarke* it was a question of taking out all the pieces and putting them together and trying to find a proper structure for it.

GS The last two novels seem to have put paid to the 'Roddy Doyle' effect that was building up around the Barrytown trilogy.

RD I have to have the freedom of not worrying too much about what kind of preconceived notions people bring to the books. The response to *Family* and *The Woman Who Walked Into Doors* has been what I imagine Woody Allen has to go through all the time: it's very good, Woody, but we loved the early stuff. It's not that I've abandoned comedy or whatever, it's just that you commit yourself to writing on a certain topic or about a certain human being, and once you have a clear picture of what they're like then they bring the tone with them. There's no room for set pieces in Paula's story. They are there to an extent but should not be the be-all and end-all. It's not written for laughs nor should it ever be. When I'm writing a book it is the entire world and I'm not going to start slipping in little references to my previous work. I would be open to the idea of going back to characters. For example, I like the idea of somewhere along the line going back to Paula when she is six years older and I'm six years older, Ireland will have changed dramatically, and there'll be plenty of material there to wonder what has happened to her. It would inevitably be a very different book because she's already told her story up to 1993, although that story is deliberately left open. All the books are unended in a way, although not because I intend going back; they're complete books, they're finished, but I like the idea of the reader wondering what's going on. I still get letters from people asking what happened to Sinbad – I tell them he's currently working for the Department of Fisheries! I suppose because it's written in the first person and the age is the same they assume it's me. I got a letter from someone saying 'I hope your life is happier now'.

GS In other interviews you've talked about other novels in relation to *The Woman Who Walked Into Doors*, such as Mary Morrissey's *Mother of Pearl*, Kathleen Ferguson's *The Maid's Tale* and *Another Alice* by Lia Mills.

RD Yes, they were all such powerful books. I suppose that a lot of people who keep an eye on the reviews and know what's coming out would have read those three novels within eighteen months or a year. Each book left a strong impression on me, they were all very impressive, but taken together there seemed to be something happening. I didn't think of them intellectually at all, I was just blasted by them, especially *Another Alice*. I did feel it could have done with a much better cover, although I think they're bringing out a better edition and it'll get a British publication and the bigger readership it deserves.

GS You've also talked elsewhere about Robert MacLiam Wilson's latest book *Eureka Street*, which is a sort of satire. Do you think satire is all that's left after comedy and tragedy?

RD Couldn't tell you. I actually never sat down to write comedy *per se*. If it's there, fine, but I didn't feel I was bound by its rules, no more than tragedy. And I think if you have comedy at one end of the pitch and tragedy at the other end I think the best stuff is somewhere in the middle. I am the Ruud Gullit of Irish fiction! I enjoy satire in *Private Eye* in tiny chunks, but the problem is that it's dated the minute you write it. If you're lucky that's also its strength. Also, when you're writing satire there has to be anger, and if there's enough then it can be very good. But if there isn't enough anger what comes across very often is smugness and a sense of superiority which I don't enjoy at all. If you're writing a book that's meant to be satirical it has its permanence, it's on the shelf, and it's not a throwaway thing like *Private Eye*. It's a huge investment of time and emotion. If you are raging against the world and can sustain that rage, and the anger clashes with the humour and the absurdity, then it can be very good. But if you are just looking down on the world and basically sneering then you have to be really special to sustain that and get away with it.

GS One of the major criticisms of your work is that it's a form of urban pastoral, like O'Casey's plays, recycling stereotypes and hanging onto worn-out notions of the sentimental Irish character but just transporting them from a rural setting to the semi-urban one of Barrytown.

RD First of all, it becomes more difficult to generalise when you have five books on the shelf. Perhaps if you take one book in isolation, maybe *The Snapper*, you could make that comment and find chunks of the book which fit that theory. But if you're going to say that in the context of *Paddy Clarke Ha Ha Ha* and *The Woman Who Walked Into Doors*, and indeed *The Van*, then it's nonsense, it just doesn't stand up to examination in any way. You can pick and choose your points, and I would not go out of my way to avoid that criticism; in other words, if there is sentimentality it's because essentially I think people are decent, for want of a better word. One of the things that welds people together is mutual affection and sentimental moments. For example, football. Looked at from the outside, people might wonder what's going on, but what seems like utter stupidity – grown men crying over a football match – can be very important. So, I don't think that criticism has much validity. Sean O'Casey wrote plays, so inevitably people pick up my novels with all their dialogue and think, 'Oh, thinly disguised plays', which is just ignorance really. They're not aware of the difference in writing a novel and a play, they think that somehow because a novel has a lot of dialogue it's not really a novel. Another problem is that a lot of the criticism comes from very close to home. I've read one reviewer condemning my work for having too much dialogue, a couple of weeks later writing a review of Manuel Puig's *Eternal Curse on the Reader of These Pages*, a fascinating book. But no criticism whatsoever from the same reviewer that the entire thing is dialogue, that there's not one descriptive passage in the book. But because it's Latin American and further away from home, it's acceptable. I've been accused of writing books for the British market because of the stereotypical depiction of stupid Paddies, but again it doesn't stand up to analysis. The idea that I'm at home doing that is so ridiculous and so absurd it's not even insulting. Probably you can make a general statement and find your evidence quite easily, but that is to ignore the reality.

GS Perhaps a more subtle criticism then concerns the short-lived phenomenon of 'Northside Realism' – that image of Dublin that was emerging around the turn of the decade with horses and high rises and so on as a sort of harsh rejoinder to the soft-focused tourist images. Some critics claim that such images very quickly became as hackneyed and as disabling as those they were looking to critique.

RD I would agree. I am partially to blame for the image of the horse because I wrote one reference into the screenplay for *The Commitments* because that's one visual thing we take for granted in parts of Dublin that is not a common sight in other cities as far as I know. But then the horse became central in *Into the West*, which I had nothing to do with. I suppose anybody putting a horse into anything visual or literary in the future is on dangerous ground. I think that one image became far too used. But part of *The Commitments* and my books and maybe Dermot Bolger's early books was just an insistence that this world exists. One of the very strong criticisms that was voiced against *The Commitments*, particularly the film, was about the image it was giving, as if this was some sort of valid excuse, that somehow we were tampering with the tourist industry. Once you've made your point – that this world exists – then you can take it for granted and start either ignoring it or building on it and writing something different. And I think that's probably what went on at the time. There was a very strong feeling, from what I could make out, from the younger Dublin people that the world as they knew it was not there. And to an extent it's still the case. Listen to how often you'll hear a strong Dublin accent on the radio or television – very rare, and usually only in parody. You don't get the real thing. There's still a gap. I got a variation on the same thing when *Family* was broadcast, this huge blanket refusal to accept that these things could happen. One theory in a newspaper said that basically the BBC wanted to cover this area but not on their own front step so they got me, gobshite that I am, to set it in Dublin. Wonderful!

GS Finally, how do you react to academic analyses of your novels and to becoming a 'studied' writer?

RD Mixed feelings. I do an awful lot of interviews with third-level students, either I answer their post or more conveniently if they're in Dublin I meet them. Particularly European students for some reason, Italians and Germans. And I answer a lot of letters from American students, and an Irish guy did his MA on me two years ago. It's very flattering, on one level, and I quite enjoy the idea of it being studied at third level because there's a certain freedom, if I remember it right. It's quite exciting because there's a sort of an unpredictability about it all, and students seem to have a fresh way of looking at the books which is encouraging. Somebody from outside Ireland will see it all completely different. But I do have mixed feelings about the books being studied at second level, as I recall it as a teacher. In Ireland the examination system was based on cramming towards the end, and I don't see how any book can survive in the affections of anybody once you realise that essentially you're not being asked to enjoy the book or to study the way it's written. You'll be asked questions about the characters, and you're going to have to come up with four good adjectives to describe the character and then it all gets very tedious. There was debate as to whether *The Snapper* and *Paddy Clarke Ha Ha Ha* should be on the Leaving Cert. syllabus. Eventually it was decided against, and I was quite happy with that. As far as I know, judging from the requests I get to visit schools and the letters I get from students, *Paddy Clarke* and *The Snapper* are found in transition year courses which seems to me to be their natural home in that there's no exam pressure there, the students have a certain freedom and they can read the books and enjoy them, if they do enjoy them. But I can't go around slapping embargoes, and saying 'No, you're not to use my book that way or this way'. I believe *Paddy Clarke* is studied in some English schools at second level, I don't know what happens to it and I'm not particularly interested in pursuing it, because I find that after a while once a book is up and running and it's finished that's the way I feel about it. I have a certain amount of affection for it but I don't want to follow its career. I'm bored after a while and want to get on. There's quite a lot of requests for the plays I did in the 1980s and I just say 'No, no, no', for the simple reason that it would be a monumental chore following them around, keeping an eye on the productions, and also it's just so boring. I feel professionally I've come an awful long way since then and I just want to keep going. I don't want to rehash the old stuff even though I suppose it could be financially very rewarding. But you have to balance it up, and I'm already making a reasonably good living so I'm not particularly interested in following the dollar.

5 THE NOVEL AND THE NORTH

Few people with access to the western media in the last thirty years can have remained unaware of the ongoing conflict in Northern Ireland. Christened the 'Troubles' in official discourse, and by and large uncritically adapted as such by the media, this conflict has been characterised as a protracted sectarian struggle between rival religious communities possessing deep yet problematic ties with the British and Southern Irish states. I do not have the space here to engage with the finer points of Northern Irish politics, although some impression of the complexity of the issues at stake will hopefully emerge during this chapter.

In justification of the inclusion here of material dealing with what is officially part of the British political, and thus cultural, apparatus, however, I would suggest that it is not possible to consider the kinds of fiction that are emerging in the different parts of Ireland in isolation from each other. Even for that section of the community which disdains links with the rest of the island, the experience of life in Northern Ireland since the 1960s has necessitated the development of different kinds of identity – British certainly, but Irish also – and this in turn impacts upon many of the other issues with which this book is concerned. As many of the novelists whose work is included in this chapter would no doubt point out, the cultural and critical imagination continues to play a crucial role in Northern Ireland, not only as an alternative to politics and violence, but also 'in consolidating, legitimising and indeed popularising the dominant perception of the conflict',[1] as well as testing the assumptions and characteristic modes of thought upon which these discourses rely. In this chapter, therefore, we shall be concerned with the question of how the emergence of a modern novelistic tradition dealing with the 'Troubles' engages with the wider political and cultural issues bearing on the constitution of modern Irish identity. Such a manoeuvre should not be seen as some kind of critical Republicanism in which a discrete Northern tradition is absorbed into an inclusive cultural national formation, but rather as part of the exploration of the limits of modern Irish identity, as well as an exposition of the limitations of any narrowly defined cultural or political tradition.

Modern Northern Ireland has not always been well served by its novelists, or indeed by those foreign writers attracted to the 'novel opportunity' provided by the 'Troubles'. As Glenn Patterson has said, the fictional representations of Northern Ireland appeared to get stuck about 1972.[2] The subgenre of the 'Troubles Thriller', for example, tends towards melodrama and a sort of voyeuristic violence in which stock characters and images are recycled in more or less disabling ways. Political violence provides an opportunity to wheel out what have become the stereotypes of the 'Troubles' – the terrorist godfather, the conscientious gunman, the *femme fatale*, the reluctant agent, and so on – in texts which, whatever their complexity of plot, invariably eschew historical explanation in favour of individual intervention and psychological motivation. For example, the publisher's blurb on the back cover of Gerald Seymour's *Field of Blood* (1985) reads:

> TWO MEN ARE TRAPPED BY GENERATIONS OF HATRED ... Sean Pius McAnally had sworn his oath to the IRA. But he quit and went south – until they came for him, made him fire the deadly rocket one last, horrific time. But then he played his final card and most terrifying role – Supergrass. David Ferris, the young British Lieutenant, hadn't wanted to join the Army. But a cruel twist of fate put him in the front line of a brutally tense war of nerves – the pawn in a knife-edged game where the stakes were the entire command of the Belfast IRA. For these two men, enmeshed in Ulster's centuries of turmoil, this was to become their FIELD OF BLOOD.

Here, it is not the 'generations of hatred' or the 'centuries of turmoil' that is at issue. The relations between the different elements in the Northern Ireland conflict are merely the occasion for violence, providing the fixed backdrop against which the personal melodrama will be played out. The reader is offered an archetypal struggle between well-established stereotypes, presented in tones designed to appeal to the most lurid and voyeuristic instincts. The language promises the thrill of violent confrontation ('deadly', 'horrific', 'terrifying', 'brutally', 'knife-edged', 'field of blood'), while trafficking in the most clichéd of concepts and images ('hadn't wanted to join the Army', 'a cruel twist of fate', 'tense war of nerves'). In a recurring metaphor, conflict in Northern Ireland is seen as a dangerous playground, reducing complex political problems to a set of ahistorical, laddish exchanges.[3] As an English journeyman novelist with an eye for the market, one can appreciate Seymour's identification of a convenient context for his populist fictions, even if it is not a very helpful development; it is less easy, however, to understand the attraction for so many Irish writers of a discourse so heavily dependent upon such disabling stereotypes.

Alongside the exploitative 'Troubles Thriller', there is also a tradition which focuses upon the complex reciprocal relations between the personal and the political. But such a tradition brings its own problems. The critic Joe Cleary describes the particular formal constitution of post-'Troubles' Northern Irish fiction in this way:

> these narratives represent a strange amalgam of romance and domestic fiction in which a political tale of the 'national romance' kind and an antipolitical tale of escape into domestic privacy are often combined or overlapped – with the former usually being superseded, overwritten, or finally being cancelled out by the latter ... the 'national romance' swerves into a domestic novel where the sexual union of the lovers, rather than serving as a celebratory metaphor for some anticipated political union, can be achieved only by renouncing politics altogether. (p. 241)

What Cleary is alluding to here are the familiar narrative tropes of 'love-across-the-barricades', in which a Catholic–Protestant romance functions as a metaphor for the healing required throughout the wider community, and the 'domestic fiction', in which the private, feminised realm of love and desire offers an escape from the public, masculine realm of political abstraction. But such a cultural model is culpable, as the above extract suggests, on three related counts. Firstly, it colludes with the disabling division of society along gender lines, thus supporting the same essentialist interpretation of cultural phenomena which structures racial and sectarian discourse. Secondly, such an artistic vision denies the political dimension to the 'Troubles' by relocating the roots of conflict in an individual psychosexual domain 'anterior to, and thus more important than' (p. 240) any collective political discourse. And thirdly, the fusion of national romance and domestic desire colludes with the 'internal conflict' model of the 'Troubles', a model which 'privileges sectarian psychology as the key to the conflict in a way that isolates sectarianism from the wider history and structure of the British and Irish state system' (p. 246). Such fictions (one of Cleary's examples is Bernard MacLaverty's *Cal* published in 1983) are typically revisionist in that they 'assume that a reciprocated embrace across the divide is no longer credible and the only solution imaginable is of a more "tragic" kind, whereby one party to the conflict – the nationalist – must finally learn to accept what he had earlier thought to change' (p. 253).

Despite Cleary's critique of the kinds of fiction being produced in and about Northern Ireland, however, many writers have sensed a need to challenge the received forms of 'Troubles' narrative, and to develop new languages and new perspectives as a contribution to the imagination of change. Resenting the 'representational onus' placed upon them by the tragedy of Northern Ireland, a species of 'prodigal' novelist emerged, defined by Eve Patten like this:

> Highly conscious of the charged political context from which they emerge and of the received patterns of writing with which their own texts engage, each of these writers has subjected the heavy contingency of Northern Ireland literature to a series of rearguard tactics, in order to renegotiate its terms of representation.[4]

These novelists are concerned not only with mapping out lines of individual desire and conflict against the background of sectarian division – a task by and large inherited from an earlier tradition of Northern Irish fiction – but also with examining the ways in which cultural representations impact on the received realities of life in Northern Ireland.

In practical terms, this means engaging with the two defining characteristics of Northern Irish fiction: the realism of the thriller tradition and the 'novelistic obligation to offer a consensual (and usually apolitical) liberal humanist comment on the predicament' (p. 31) which informs the hybrid national romance/domestic fiction tradition. Even as these characteristics are engaged, however, they are displaced and defamiliarised through a variety of strategies, the most important of which is the introduction of a degree of *distance* into the novelistic vision. Distance can be physical (as with the introduction of geographical perspectives from the rest of the British Isles, Europe and beyond) or discursive (as for example with the use of irony, parody and other defamiliarising devices). Above all, such a strategy represents 'the rejection of a literary convention which pandered to the isolation of Northern Ireland as a stagnant and erratic phenomenon' (p. 46). As Patten goes on to point out, however, the 'prodigal' vision is essentially irregular and refractory, and any attempt to formalise it as a tradition may be to curb its effectiveness as a challenge to the dominant narratives.

The remainder of this chapter offers a series of textual analyses which engage with the different kinds of Northern Irish fiction described above – realist thriller, national romance, domestic and prodigal fiction. None of the novels included provide perfect examples – fiction, like criticism, is not book-keeping – but all include individual moments as well as larger narrative threads and trends which are identifiable in terms of these different models. These analyses also attempt to engage with the texts in terms of the theoretical, formal and thematic discourses described in Part 1. Again, such readings are not intended as thesis-led or definitive in any way, but as points of departure for your own explorations.

Hidden Symptoms (1986) by Deirdre Madden

Deirdre Madden's first novel offers a bleak unrelenting vision of life in Northern Ireland, couched in the Catholic myth of redemption through suffering. The story concerns a group of young people who have been born into the 'Troubles', and it details the different strategies they have developed to cope with the violence of the society in which they live. The three main characters, Theresa, Robert and Kate, are all seriously unhappy, emotionally fragile and intellectually confused. Although this might seem to stem from personal reasons in each case it can be traced back to the violent situations in which they find themselves.

Theresa's brother Francis has been the victim of a random sectarian attack, captured, tortured and murdered. Theresa is having difficulty in coming to terms with grief and also in reconciling her religious faith with her brother's seemingly casual slaughter. She displaces her anger onto those with whom she comes into contact, and at the same time develops bitter theories regarding the fatal malevolence of the material world and all its effects. Robert has cut himself off emotionally from his roots and his family, attempting to remake his identity through intellectual abstractions. He copes with violence by refusing to engage with it. Kate has latched onto Robert and Theresa as replacements for her 'dead' father and her hostile mother, only to have her world thrown into turmoil by the reappearance of her father and his new family.

This is a novel about knowledge and perception rather than action. The major characters are members of Belfast's educated elite attempting to understand the horrific violence in their community in terms of abstract notions. The same is true of the novel itself, which does not attempt to grapple with the mechanics of violence, but is concerned instead with the underlying causes, the 'hidden symptoms' of which physical violence is just the effect. Such intellectualising, when it refuses to acknowledge the inscrutable mystery of God's design, is shown to be an effete response to the brute fact of violence. Robert's attempts to ignore the violence or Theresa's attempts to understand it are essentially wilful refusals of God's inscrutable higher design, bringing only unhappiness and frustration. This is made clear in the flashback sequences, when Francis and Theresa contemplate the glories of Rome. Art ultimately obstructs what it stands for, which, as Francis says, 'is infinitely more beautiful and which cannot be destroyed' (p. 54). What is hidden is what is real, what is tangible to the senses is meaningless. Thus sectarian conflict, personal relations and religious belief are pulled together in one conceit. Having once comprehended the presence of these hidden symptoms, the real world holds no attractions for Francis, and dropping out of university is just a prelude to dropping out of life.

What the novel gradually reveals is the way in which politically motivated violence obviates love and understanding at the personal level. In such a society, everyone is guilty, everyone is a victim of one kind or another. 'It was as if the act of murder was so dreadful that the person who committed it had forfeited his humanity and had been reduced to the level of pure evil. He had dragged the whole world down with him: everyone was guilty' (p. 44). In such a world of immutable opposites and banal evil there is no relief, only pain and suffering and the hope that God will reconcile what humankind cannot. The themes of madness and dreams which pervade the text are part of the invocation of another world, another plane of existence upon which the 'real' issues are being fought out. This is the realm of the spirit where God's love is the ruling factor. But so opaque is this realm that Theresa cannot penetrate its logic – the logic that allowed for the murder of Francis – and she is thus left with grief over his death as well as bitterness at her own inability to comprehend God's love. This is also why Francis, although dead before the narrative begins, emerges as the most important figure. The quiet, intense contemplation of God's will that he represents is offered as a counter to the hollow intellectual life represented by the other main characters. And for all Robert's embarrassment at their working-class outlook, only his sister and her family are closer to that life, and therefore emerge as ultimately more worthy within the moral economy of the narrative. The novel seems to suggest that the family is one of the few positive echoes of God's universal vision, and to the extent that he learns to need his family, Robert is reclaimed from his own spiritual emptiness.

The hollowness of life is revealed in the recurring imagery of depths and surfaces that appear throughout the novel. As he gazes at his shadowy reflection in a window, Robert 'wished that he could stop being himself and become that double so that he could be dissolved into nothingness when the morning came' (p. 88). At the end of the novel, Theresa also acknowledges the same spiritual longing to cast off the physical world and embrace the reality beneath:

> Who was that person? ... How long would it be, she wondered, until she could go beyond reflections? For how long would she have to continue claiming the face in the mirror as her own? When would there be an end to shadows cast upon glass? (p. 141)

The novel thus reveals itself as an exploration of the classic philosophical dilemma of body versus mind, with the Northern Irish conflict as the occasion rather than the theme of this exploration, a mere backdrop to the contemplation of some higher inscrutable design.

Thus understood, *Hidden Symptoms* is a deeply conservative and reactionary novel. Although dealing with one of the major issues ostensibly underpinning the strife in Northern Ireland – religion – it does so in terms of an essentially religious view of the situation. The form of the novel is thus curtailed and compromised by its subject matter. Individual insight is won at the expense of any larger political vision, and these intelligent, sensitive individuals engage with the 'Troubles' only to emerge with perspectives that are essentially apolitical and ahistorical. The religious approach is revealed to possess its own complexities and subtleties beyond the purview of the real world, which is condemned as an unchanging and intractable conflict between fixed, finished tribal identities, mere shadows of the real drama being played out at the spiritual level. Within the terms of the novel, the real issue is the existence or non-existence of God. The tragedy of Francis's death can be explained with reference to blind faith – the 'truth' that Theresa invokes towards the end of the novel – or the atheism embraced by Robert as a defence against the possibility of a malignant metaphysical order.

The problem is not that no solution is offered, but that within the world constructed by the novel no solution is imaginable. The sectarian divide is just a ghostly Platonic echo of a barely discernible metaphysical order which humans presume to know at their peril. Within the terms of this discourse there is no possibility of change and development; rather, the human world is merely a reflex of timeless, ineluctable forces too great for contemplation, too mysterious for understanding, the 'hidden symptoms' which underlie the merely phenomenal world of sectarian conflict. As such, *Hidden Symptoms* represents a special plea on behalf of the religious life. The world of the mind is culpable because it presumes to comprehend the will of God. The world of the body is also culpable, although less so because it at least is in touch with Nature, God's reflex on earth. The world of the spirit – embraced by Francis, recognised and resisted by Theresa, refused by Robert, confirmed, albeit unknowingly, by his sister's family – this is the only way forward in the face of the incomprehensible violence which is the human fate.

Resurrection Man (1994) by Eoin McNamee

Eoin McNamee's debut novel *Resurrection Man* is caught in much the same bind as *Hidden Symptoms*, although this time the 'truth' behind sectarian violence in Northern Ireland is not God's mysterious design but a sort of existential longing for non-being and a postmodern scepticism towards any kind personal or political identity. The narrative is centred on Victor Kelly, leader of the 'Resurrection Men', a Unionist paramilitary cell taking its gangland moniker from a band of nineteenth-century graverobbers. Kelly is a Protestant who in his youth has been stigmatised because of his Catholic-sounding surname. Names are indeed of great importance in the sectarian culture of Northern Ireland, and McNamee exploits this emphasis throughout the novel. Kelly attempts to compensate for his youthful exclusion from the Unionist family by embracing sectarian violence with a will that is shocking, and all the more so when one realises that this story is based upon a series of real events that occurred in Belfast in the mid-1970s.

Other narrative threads are supplied by Victor's parents, Dorcas and James, the journalists Ryan and Coppinger and Victor's sometime girlfriend Heather, with the sinister Billy McClure lurking behind everything. But although there is a coherent narrative concerning the interaction of these and other characters, the discourse operates just as much through atmosphere and emotion as through action and dialogue. The text is in fact organised around this dual trajectory of action and reflection, building up a complex narrative grammar of graphic violence and cold contemplation. The action leaps disconcertingly between past, present and future, constantly disrupting any developmental impetus to the story. Likewise, novelistic discourse mixes with other genres such as documentary, *film noir*, philosophy and crime thriller, making it difficult to settle into one consistent reading position from which to make sense of the narrative. All the characters remain enigmatic; the more information we receive about motivation and desire, the more difficult it is to say anything for certain about them. In all these ways the novel resists any straightforward reading, attempting to insinuate at a formal level the problem of alienation which would appear to be the text's major theme.

On one level, Kelly's violence is explicable with reference to the familiar tale of family dysfunction and generational resentment. But the major tropes for understanding and describing violence in this novel are narrative and language itself. These are the fundamental concepts used by humans to make sense of the world, but when the world itself stops making sense then these devices are thrown into crisis. In the world of the novel, the conflict in Northern Ireland represents a war over language, over individual words and names. 'The root of the tongue had been severed. New languages would have to be invented' (p. 16) is the comment after the first murder has been discovered, thus providing a moment when subject matter and narrative coalesce. Lacking any sense of self, Kelly adapts the roles he has learned from popular culture, such as that of the Hollywood gangster, and it is according to these half-digested images that he operates. All the characters, in fact, feel as if they are going through the motions of an obscure drama acted out before an invisible audience, performing parts not written for them. Flaps, one of Kelly's victims, makes an 'unconvincing corpse' (p. 166); his mother Dorcas 'thought of herself like a mother's story in a magazine of a dogged hunt through an uncaring world but in the end victorious' (p. 224); while Heather feels 'like a character in a strange tale' (p. 233).

With the themes of language and role-playing, however,

comes the theme of madness, of speaking in a language that no one else understands, of complete alienation from any sense of self or community. It is just such a language that Kelly speaks when he introduces into the sectarian conflict the technique of torturing and slaughtering randomly selected victims; and it is just such alienation he feels when, under the weight of drugs and dreams he cannot control, his own deluded self-image begins to crumble into paranoia. 'The dynamics of madness' (p. 97) comes to replace the normal dynamics of communication and rationality to which even sectarianism nominally subscribes.

But who or what is to blame for all this? The answer, it seems, is the city itself, which 'had decided to devise personality for them, assign roles, a script to accompany a season of coming evil'. (p. 159) Violence is the condition-zero of the city, its architecture a map of strife and enmity. Naming its streets and estates is part of Kelly's education into violence, and he is an avid pupil of all the city has to teach him by way of sectarian history. 'He felt the city become a diagram of violence centred about him. Victor got a grip on the names.' (p. 11) Evil, unchanging and elemental, is built into the architecture and the landscape; according to the moral economy of the novel, Kelly is just more honest than most in his acknowledgement of this.

In a sense, then, the novel is about its own possibility, the possibility of a language that can communicate the reality of politically motivated, savagely executed violence. And from this unimaginable violence a fundamental politico-aesthetic point begins to emerge, first noted by the journalists Coppinger and Ryan as they try to gain perspective on the atmosphere which the new reign of violence has brought to the city: 'Both of them were experiencing difficulty in defining their jobs ... Each time Coppinger wrote up a killing he felt that the report acquired implications which he had not put there. It hinted at something covert, unexplained, dissatisfying.' (p. 83) Language, it seems, has taken on a life of its own, exceeding authorial intention. Likewise, once it is introduced into any discourse as a possibility, violence possesses the ability to exceed any 'intention' couched in political or cultural terms, to take on a life in and for itself. All it needs, the novel suggests, is someone like Kelly to take violence to its extreme, logical end – the logic of random, brutal, indiscriminate chaos.

Sectarianism, then, is just a convenient handle upon which to hang our need for violence, its occasion rather than its cause. Violence is a symptom of life, especially of modern life in which to be human is to be inauthentic, to lack will or agency, to lack,

crucially, the ability to change except through ever more fundamental destruction. Humans cannot build, because there is basically nothing to build with or upon. They cannot change because
there is no self or identity there to change; they can only move
between a series of inauthentic personas, going through the
motions of a violent drama encoded into the human psyche at an
impossibly elemental level. In this sense, Kelly's violence is completely logical, constituting the most human response to the
illegitimacy of the modern human condition.

In so far as this is the case, *Resurrection Man* reveals itself as
another reactionary response to the 'Troubles', interested not in
sectarianism (nor indeed in the more significant agendas of state
sovereignty which underpin sectarianism in Northern Ireland)
but in some inscrutable darkness at the heart of the self. The
local matters only in so far as it can be incorporated into a larger
existential overview, as some sort of evidence for the human
condition. Of course, it is not the place of McNamee, nor of any
novelist, to formulate solutions which have evaded political and
diplomatic specialists. As was suggested in the introduction to
this chapter, however, rather than providing an existentialist
gloss to the Unionist–Nationalist stand-off, the novelistic imagination in Northern Ireland must surely be concerned with developing new languages and new perspectives, precisely to break out
of the orthodoxies which have fed and sustained the conflict.

Divorcing Jack (1995) by Colin Bateman

From an early point in the 'Troubles' the sordid and violent world
of paramilitary struggle lent itself to a particular kind of popular
fiction – the action thriller, characterised by complexity of plot,
rapidity of pace and the interaction of stereotypical characters in
stock situations. Then, the cease-fires called by Republican and
Unionist paramilitaries in 1993 and 1994 brought the possibility of
different kinds of perspective on sectarian violence and religious
bigotry. One such perspective was comedy, and in his debut novel
Colin Bateman manages to introduce a comic perspective into the
thriller format to produce perhaps the first 'comedy thriller' dealing with the 'Troubles'. Written at a breathless pace, incorporating
sharp dialogue and simplicity of structure alongside a frequently
surreal plot, *Divorcing Jack* nevertheless displays an intimacy with
the routines of life in a sectarian society, as well as possessing its
own quite specific political agenda. Such a combination of formal

and conceptual factors signals Bateman's engagement with a strand
of 'postmodern thriller' that has become popular in the United
States of America since the 1970s, while also marking *Divorcing
Jack* as a new departure in Northern Irish fiction.

The plot of *Divorcing Jack* is complex, involving infidelity,
murder, blackmail and double-cross. The narrator Dan Starkey is
a hard-drinking, wise-cracking Belfast journalist whose extra-
marital affairs get him involved with Brinn, a politician with
cross-sectional support on the cusp of winning an election that
would lead to a different kind of state – a 'Northern Irish Hong
Kong' (p. 88). Brinn's peace-making credentials are based upon
his survival of a bomb attack in the early days of the 'Troubles'
and his willingness to forgive those responsible. Unknown to all
but some shady secret service types and his former IRA colleague
Cow Pat Coogan, however, is the fact that rather than being
simply injured by the bomb, Brinn – or 'O'Brinn' as he was then
– was in fact planting it. Under the influence of alcohol he
confesses this to an aide – the father of Starkey's lover Margaret
– who subsequently attempts to sell a recording of the conversation. A tape of the music of Dvořák overlain with Brinn's
drunken confession provides the key to the action, as Starkey
mistakes Margaret's identification of the composer, and thus the
location of the precious tape, for the words 'Divorce Jack'.

As it samples different kinds of popular cultural modes, it is not
initially clear what kind of a novel this is, or indeed what kind of
reader it expects. It does appear, however, that cinema is one of the
strongest influences on *Divorcing Jack*, and especially the work of
the American film director Quentin Tarantino – responsible for
films such as *Reservoir Dogs* and *Pulp Fiction* – in which comedy,
popular cultural allusion and stylistic violence provide the key-
notes. As with Tarantino's films, the pleasure of the text is organised in the first instance around the shock of the violence and the
intermingling of genres. In the scenes concerning the death of
Parker the CIA agent, for example, we move from a sort of 'buddy
movie' to the horror of casual murder to the surrealism of a nun-
o-gram's last-second rescue of Starkey and his wife Patricia. Subsequently, pleasure comes from anticipation and postponement, from
the knowledge that having once occurred, casual violence might
descend at any moment from any direction.

The text's comedy, however, is deployed to vindicate a quite
specific and very serious political line. As he makes clear, Starkey
has no great commitment to his Protestant heritage unless and
until it comes under pressure from Republicanism. When he

perceives this to be the case, the message is a repudiation of nationalist pretensions to unification, or indeed of any political settlement denying the Ulster Protestant tradition. An early exchange with Parker makes Starkey's understated though fully committed affiliations clear:

> 'And stick to calling it Northern Ireland, although you'll hear variations. If you're a Loyalist you'll call it Ulster, if you're a Nationalist you call it the North of Ireland or the Six Counties, if you're the British Government you call it the Province.'
> 'And what do you call it, Mr Starkey?'
> 'Home.' (p. 46)

Sometimes, in fact, this political message threatens to overcome the narrative. Starkey's voice often slips into a journalistic discourse in which he hectors the reader on some extra-narrative point concerning (his perception of) the realities of life in Northern Ireland. In fact, the line between fiction and reality is transgressed throughout in a disarmingly casual and frank manner. Dan Starkey, like Colin Bateman, is a young journalist with novelistic aspirations who writes a satirical column for an Ulster newspaper, and the novelist clearly enjoys the opportunity to play with reality; hence, parties, personalities and events are evoked alongside familiar types, landscapes and situations, with everything finally subject to the bizarre logics of coincidence and conspiracy. We have seen that such a collapsing of the barriers between narrative and reality can be subversive, but in what is otherwise a story-based thriller, this strategy can sometimes be an irritation.

The underlying message of the text would appear to be twofold. First, there has to be a space within the imagination of Northern Ireland for non-bigoted, politically sceptical, Protestant atheists. In this respect, Bateman's novel can be seen as part of the process whereby the Protestant Unionist tradition is attempting to break free of its image as a narrow reactionary culture and reveal itself instead as a complex and subtle modern identity. Secondly, the novel seems to insist that violence has by and large ceased to be a matter of ideology in Northern Ireland, and that like the gangster films and thrillers which are inscribed into the text at both formal and thematic levels, violence is now just a matter of business. These messages, moreover, are quite obviously linked, for if *Divorcing Jack* is innovative in its introduction of the techniques of postmodern thriller to the context of

Northern Ireland, it is entirely typical in its imagination of a world in which violence is endemic and change is impossible. As Brinn and Coogan square up to each other in the novel's climax, the inevitability of the violence is confirmed, for what Starkey describes is not a strategic confrontation between ideological opponents, but a playground game transferred to the political and economic sphere, with guns and bombs instead of sticks and stones, and women as disposable pawns (p. 261).

Burning Your Own (1988) by Glenn Patterson

Glenn Patterson is one of the 'prodigal novelists' described by Eve Patten. In his first novel Patterson is concerned with interrogating the narratives, languages and symbols which sustain the division in Northern Irish society, especially as mediated through cultural discourse, as well as imagining new contexts of exchange and interaction. Through the experiences of ten-year-old Mal Martin during the Summer of 1969, the period which saw the rekindling of sectarian violence in Northern Ireland, Patterson is able to test some of the most deeply held convictions of the working-class Protestant community from which he comes, exposing its limitations and contradictions even as he highlights the reasons behind its continued attraction.

The Martin family has moved to the predominantly Protestant Larkview estate because of Mr Martin's failed business. As a new boy in the area, Mal is worried about how he will fit in, but soon begins to adopt the rituals of a typical Protestant working-class boy – football, smoking, masturbation and, most importantly, inculcation into the sectarian division of society. The latter is harmless in times of peace, but in times of crisis its basis in rituals of belonging and violent exclusion is revealed. And Mal's world is indeed infused with crisis – not only the beginning in earnest of sustained political violence in Northern Ireland, but also his parents' marriage, the sabotage of the centrepole for the bonfire to celebrate the beginning of the Twelfth Celebrations, and the first stirrings of his own sexuality. All add to his feelings of unease, all are connected and 'read' each other. Even his name is a problem – his father suspects that it has a Catholic ring to it, and it constitutes one of the many points over which he and Mal's mother argue in the opening sections of the book. But perhaps the major crisis confronting the confused Mal concerns the nature of his friendship with the 'mad Taig bastard' (p. 8), Francy Hagan.

The real theme of Patterson's novel is in fact the classic tension between individual and community. The narrative develops a sense of community based upon the characters from the estate, Mal's friends and family, the landscape itself and the Twelfth Bonfire which constitutes the central event of the story. The centrepole for the bonfire represents the heart (or perhaps the phallus) of the community, the symbol around which it organises its sense of identity. As they gaze upon the bonfire the community is named family by family, and in this way Patterson acknowledges the attraction of belonging, of feeling part of a securely based community equal with its location and its identity (p. 91). The downside of communitarian ideology is the curtailment of individual freedom. Like his Dublin contemporary Paddy Clarke, Mal is losing his capacity for childish wonder as he gradually becomes socialised into the contradictions of adulthood and the dull, unquestioned, inflexible certainties of sectarian identity.

It is precisely this sense of wonder that Francy Hagan seems able to supply, representing as he apparently does the exotic individualism of the outsider. 'That's what I want too. To be afraid of no one and answer to no one' (p. 227), says the impressionable Mal. Francy offers a radical rejoinder to the myth of social and environmental identification, exposing the stupidity of a system whereby 'All you can ever be sure is that whatever the other sort likes you're supposed to hate' (p. 217). His dump domain represents an alternative space where affiliation is to the self and to the truth, and where the oppositionalism endemic to the outside world is replaced by a sort of archaeological imagination interested in the traces and layers of other stories to be found beneath and throughout the currently dominant sectarian story. The nature of narrative itself, in fact, emerges as an important theme of the text. Mal wonders 'had he ever remembered punching his father at all, or remembered only his father's retelling' (p. 27); or, 'He had read once (or had someone told him? – he couldn't remember)' (p. 450). These issues of memory and truth reflect upon the wider social uses of narrative, problematising at the level of the individual the narrative effects around which tribal identities and sectarian conflict are organised.

There is a classic dilemma confronting the innocent Mal, then: the 'satisfaction' of being part of the team preparing for the bonfire or the ambiguous freedom experienced by Francy who has apparently cast off all his communitarian affiliations and embraced instead the essential truth of the human condition – isolation. But truth, of course, is relative, and even the arch-individualist Francy cannot step outside history. His destruction of the centrepole, which on one level can be seen as a blow for the individual against the community, is in fact read as an act of Catholic sabotage against the Protestant community. The kind of extreme individualism Mal imagined he found in Francy is not in fact available. All narratives, even those of exile into the self, are ultimately contingent, as Francy realises when he is drawn back into the tribalism which ends the book. When he does strike back, it is in the name of the Catholic community and his family – in other words in terms of the community with which he identifies, despite himself. In a final gesture which captures the dilemma of identification and de-identification, Francy destroys both Orange Sash and Tricolour, supreme tokens of the rival communities, thus refusing the very communitarian ideology for which he will shortly give his life (pp. 247–8).

The real lesson learned by Mal is that of the necessity for perspective, such as is offered in the moonlanding, or of the kind gained when he looks over the city from his uncle's house. Perspective is what allows identification to be considered in its spatial and temporal particularity. In the way that the human imagination of the moon is a function of its relationship with the earth, or that individual city streets are part of the identity of the whole city, so the individual is revealed to be fully implicated in the community, which is itself ultimately an effect of the sum of its parts. *Burning Your Own* sets up a series of binary oppositions, only to reveal the implication of each individual element in its other. The text details the 'absolute' necessity for severing the line stretching from community to individual if the latter's full potential is to be realised, while at the same time demonstrating the 'absolute' impossibility of denying the community. 'Absolutism' of any kind is in fact revealed as the root of the problem.

In *Burning Your Own* many things are left unanswered or unclear. Even the kiss Mal gives to Francy at the end can be read as *both/either* insistence on a larger non-bigoted vision *and/or* Judas kiss of betrayal (p. 231). This is a deliberate strategy on Patterson's part, for in making the reader work to discover *meanings* rather than serving up one author-intended *meaning*, he is refusing the notion of a single vision of life in Northern Ireland or a single explanation of the violence that has permeated the society since the late 1960s. Uncertainty connotes change, and change gives the lie to the narratives of identity upon which sectarianism and its unchanging codes of behaviour and attitude are based. Francy's comment on the multi-divided affiliations of life in Northern Ireland seems appropriate: 'Sure, who the fuck knows what anything means? They tell you one thing one day and something else altogether the next. Fucking beans means Heinz now' (p. 217).

Fat Lad (1992) by Glenn Patterson

Patterson's second novel continues his fictional archaeology of the contradictions and compensations of modern Northern Irish Protestant identity. *Fat Lad* explores the relations between the private and the public spheres, not in order to deny political discourse or to channel it off into an apolitical discourse of sexuality, but rather to reveal the discourses of desire under-pinning the political imagination in Northern Ireland, as well as the overdetermination of discourses of domesticity in contexts of politically organised violence.

Set in the early 1990s, Drew Linden is a twenty-something expatriate working for a successful chain of bookstores in England. Suddenly he gets the 'opportunity' to return temporarily to work in his home city of Belfast. Once home, Drew renews links with his family while commencing casual affairs with the go-getting Kay and her enigmatic cousin Anna. Another narrative strand describes Drew's family history, a tale which is also a sort of history of Protestant Northern Ireland in the twentieth century – ship-building, gun-running, World War One, riots in the 1930s, World War Two – and which reflects ironically on Drew's perceptions and actions in the present. The narrative is deliberately disconcerting in the manner in which it leaps from period to period, from charac-ter to character and from discourse to discourse. Most significantly, focus is not maintained on Drew throughout but rather weaves between episodes and perspectives from the lives of other charac-ters, especially family members such as his sister, father and grand-mother. In decentering the narrative in this way, the novel problematises the notion of a single, linear sense of self which can interact with the world. *Fat Lad* in fact represents a conclave of discourses in which past, present and future talk to each other in a manner signally unlike the different social and political discourses of contemporary Northern Ireland, characterised precisely by their unwillingness to converse.

The city to which Drew returns is one desperately trying to re-imagine itself as part of cosmopolitan Europe. The music he hears walking the streets offers 'a symphony for any city, summer 1990' (p. 209). As the narrative moves between past and present, Drew attempts to discover how this new 'buzzing' Belfast emerged out of the city known by his parents and grandparents. For as becomes clear, this city-character cannot so easily step outside its own history. Behind the high street with its facade of glamour and success, the secrets of sectarianism still lurk. Drew is also hiding a secret, the resentment he feels towards his father for unexplained beatings received as a young boy. He displaces his subsequent guilt from the domestic to the public sphere, taking the full weight of the 'Troubles' on his shoulders 'and all because, long ago, he had learnt to blame himself for having been born in the first place' (p. 127).

Like many of his contemporaries, Drew resents the political imperative foisted upon him by fate, the way in which being born in Northern Ireland has seemingly doomed him to question his identity forever. Identitarian politics of the sort practised by both Nationalists and Unionists are based upon the mystique of heroic failure, as Drew notes when he invents a composite image of Irish politics based upon the 1916 Rising and the sinking of the Titanic: 'A Dublin-born schoolteacher delivering the Proclamation of the Republic from the deck of a foundering Belfast-built ship' (p. 46). The image of his grandmother's goldfish also functions as a symbol of heroic failure and the sectarian mentality – only a three-second memory could keep the goldfish from insanity as it ceaselessly follows its own tail around and around the confined space of the bowl.

In *Fat Lad* Patterson introduces new perspectives, stressing the connections (as well as the differences) to the larger communities over the border and across the water, and indeed beyond in Europe. These borders are never denied, as if to explain the 'problem' in terms of the fatal sectarian propensities of rival communities. Rather, there is always the possibility of change, of leaving and arriving – to Dublin, Manchester, Paris. Links with the south are explored when Drew indulges his obsession with the mysterious Anna and follows her to Dublin. As well as confirming the difference between North and South, Anna's story captures in stark detail the ineluctable nexus of sex and politics while providing Drew with yet one more thing about which to feel guilty. But more importantly, the existence of these borders points to the state interests which are at stake in the conflict, the implication of larger (though frequently covert) agendas of sovereignty and security in the maintenance of the 'immutable' tribal fiction which sustains the 'Troubles'.

Fat Lad represents, then, a reluctant search for roots, a sort of narrative cure for the guilt which is threatening to overcome Drew's present. But it is also a parable on the politics of exile: what is left behind, what is brought back, the possibility of returning, the possibility of ever really leaving, and, most importantly, how the experience of another perspective alters the exile's relationship with past, present and future. Drew thinks in literary terms much of the time; like a critic, he is no longer submerged in the metaphors and plot lines of the community narrative but is able to 'read' it from a location outside the text, noting its points of connection, its absences and its inability to posit itself as a naturally occurring, always ended but neverending story of Protestant identity. Just as the critic remains essentially implicated in the text, however, so his English girlfriend Melanie comes to suspect that Drew's

> pose of ironic detachment only masked an obsession with origins as unsound in its way as anything that the extremists in all their blinkered bigotry could conjure up, and that the Ex-Pats had become just a name to gather under to drink Guinness and feel the tragedy of their birth. (p. 216)

Above all, Patterson insists that life in Northern Ireland cannot simply be a question of obsessively demarcated histories and communities whose only contact points are violent rituals of identity and otherness. Life, he suggests, cannot and does not work that way. Rather, like *Fat Lad*, all the minor stories are part of a larger unfinished story of Northern Ireland. Family history ranges alongside the politics of exile, which interacts with late capitalism and metadiscursive musings on the role of fiction and narrative, and all these discourses converse within the confines of the novel, offering no trite answers or systems of ordering but an ultimately enabling image of human interdependence. As Drew thinks to himself towards the end of the novel:

> But it was like trying to hold a pattern in a kaleidoscope, one tiny chip slipped and the whole configuration changed ... The heart of the matter was that there was no heart of the matter; or else many millions of hearts. (p. 248)

Ripley Bogle (1989) by Robert MacLiam Wilson

For all that they try to question the complacent assumptions and complicit discourses upon which traditional Northern Irish fiction relies, *Burning Your Own* and *Fat Lad* retain recognisable links with that tradition, its subject matter and its dominant forms. The same cannot be said of the first novel by Patterson's contemporary and fellow 'prodigal' Robert MacLiam Wilson. *Ripley Bogle* should be regarded as one of the most precocious debuts of any Irish writer. Set in London over four June days and nights sometime in the late 1980s, the novel constitutes an angry indictment of Thatcherite Britain as well as a scathing attack on the calcified and disabling discourses of identity foisted onto young Irish people by their forebears, living and dead.

Duality of vision and the inertia resulting from a decayed moral order constitute the novel's main themes. Bogle's cultural inheritance mirrors his own experiences and the general perspective of the text as a whole, caught between specifically English and Irish ways of seeing, and moving towards a cynical, albeit impotent, repudiation of both. At first, Bogle describes his Catholic Republican upbringing in Belfast, upon which he quickly turns his back, or rather from which he is rapidly ejected. He had tried to exist as a sort of composite identity – 'Ripley Irish British Bogle' – made up from the constituent parts of the Northern Irish community (p. 14). But the contradictions of this identity are too much, something to which the surrounding violence testifies. He does not even have the family to fall back on, describing his own as 'the usual list of subhuman Gaelic scumbuckets' (p. 7). Throughout the novel, in fact, Irishness of any kind is repudiated:

> We Irish, we're all fucking idiots. No other people can rival us for the senseless sentimentality in which we wallow. Us and Ulster. The God-beloved fucking Irish, as they'd like to think. As a people we're a shambles, as a nation – a disgrace; as a culture we're a bore ... individually we're often repellent ... all that old Irishness crap promoted by Americans and professors of English Literature. (p. 160)

At the same time, his background provides him with an intimate knowledge of those discourses of belonging and identity which exist at one end of his scale of options.

Having rejected Irishness, England provides no answers either. It is as if despite the claims to non-affiliation, Bogle has been permanently marked by his youth and background, and there is no true escape from it, either physical or psychological. England and exile, the traditional answers to the contradictions of Irish identity, have failed also. In Cambridge he finds a cohort of Thatcher's privileged children desperately looking for some authenticity (of the kind they suppose he has left behind in Belfast) to fill their hollow lives, while as a tramp in London he discovers at sordidly close quarters the darkness at the heart of modern civilisation.

So cultural hybridity, rather than offering Bogle a positive and enabling set of options, actually robs him of any power other than that of indicting both sides and adopting a spurious position above (or rather, below) and beyond the real world. He has sampled both, in Belfast, Cambridge and London, has intimate knowledge of both, and disdains both. Bogle decides to opt out of history, not to start again but to retreat into some state of non-being. This leaves him, literally, with nowhere to go, except to a deeper form of exile from the 'acceptable' world of the 1980s into the underworld of the drop-outs and discarded humanity living in the cracks of what passes for 'normal' modern life.

This search for alternative perspective is built into the very structure of the novel, taking the form of a parodic discourse which samples but offers no investment in any of the received novelistic reactions to the 'Troubles'. The novel rehearses the three standard tropes of traditional Northern Irish fiction: the involvement of Bogle's friend Maurice in paramilitary activities (thriller); his 'love-across-the-barricades' with the middle-class Protestant Deirdre (national romance); and his exile to Cambridge and affair with the English rose Laura (domestic fiction). As it turns out, however, *Ripley Bogle* turns out to be a 'fiction' in more than one sense, for these narrative tropes are exploded, revealed at the end of the narrative as an elaborate set of lies. The truth is far from the story of sexual success and proud disdain for the rat race that Bogle would have us believe in the earlier parts of the narrative; it is, rather, a story of guilt, cowardice, betrayal and failure.

Bogle, moreover, is an unreliable narrator who parodies his own unreliability, always remaining one step ahead of the interpretative game. The novel contains a metanarrative strand which constantly reminds the reader of the constructed nature of this, and any other, narrative (p. 247). *Ripley Bogle* offers itself initially as a sort of Victorian *Bildungsroman*, but sets up (in both senses) this model of fiction only to disappoint at the end. Eventually the text moves towards closure, but not of the traditional Victorian kind where all the loose strands are pulled together and the narrator-hero emerges with self-knowledge to effect social and psychological healing. Such a hero has no place in the 1980s, the text suggests, no more than the practice of living one's life according to any received narrative of identity, be it literary or political. Instead, Bogle reaches a point of physical and linguistic exhaustion: 'Where will I find the words I need?' (p. 270). All he can do is continue to go through the motions, and parody such pseudo-explanations as can be found in the terms of an exhausted nationalism: 'The world did me wrong by making me an Irishman ... It's Ireland's fault, not mine' (p. 272).

Even cynicism, however, may be seen to possess its own agenda, and in *Ripley Bogle* MacLiam Wilson finds himself siding with those who deny any political dimension to violence in Northern Ireland. Bogle's opinion of the men who murdered Maurice – 'They weren't really terrorists, these men. They weren't political, idealistic. They were crooks, thugs – they were just bad boys' (p. 254) – is typical of those with an interest in depoliticising the situation in the North by transferring the political imperative onto the paramilitaries and then denying that imperative when armed struggle inevitably degenerates into organised crime. 'Political', however, surely connotes something more subtle, and indeed it seems that in *Ripley Bogle* both character and text remain caught up in the narratives which are ostensibly denied. The image MacLiam Wilson presents of the Irish is far from flattering, and this is part of the process whereby he refuses the various disabling and stereotypical versions of Irishness disseminated by British and American interests. For all that, with his acerbic charm and unwillingness to conform, Bogle can be recaptured by those stereotypical discourses and understood as *the* most typical Irishman precisely to the degree that he disdains 'typicality'. Likewise the narrative, while offering to expose the danger of received narratives, also operates as a sort of compendium of the fall-out from colonialism and continued state-orchestrated conflict – violence, familial dysfunction, madness, nightmares, self-alienation, amorality.

Give Them Stones (1987) by Mary Beckett

Give Them Stones offers another example of the confessional realism encountered in *The Maid's Tale*, and the style and tone of these two novels are in fact very similar. Beckett's novel concerns the fate of Catholic women in Northern Ireland since the foundation of the state, and how the organisation of the staples of life – time, money, space, personality, personal expression, and so on – interconnect with the sectarian organisation of that state. Anticipating Patterson's work, the novel maps out a family history that is also a history of the province, as the story throws into mutual relief the private, the public and the political. The novel weaves a complex web of different political discourses – sectarian, class and gender – but the one overriding consideration throughout is the role of the individual in relation to the family, and the role of the latter as intermediary between the individual and the larger social and political networks which claim the individual's allegiance.

Martha Murtagh lives in a Catholic area of Belfast with her parents, her grandmother, her sister Mary Brigid and her brother Danny. Martha's father is a strong but sympathetic figure, and she enjoys a special relationship with him although having to vie with the other females in the family for his attention. Martha's envy of her mother, in fact, remains with her until the end of the narrative and colours their relationship throughout. When her father is interned during the war as an IRA suspect and thus removed from the family, however, Martha loses his influence and begins to develop the feelings of hurt and disappointment which haunt her story. These feelings are compounded when she is left behind with her maiden aunts after the family takes shelter in their country cottage to escape the Belfast blitz.

When Martha's father emerges from internment a sick and broken man, the familial tensions which had been present but submerged from the outset of the narrative surface. Despite constant claims to the contrary, Martha clearly envies her sister the opportunity she has grasped to gain an education and thus increase her chances of escaping the grind of working-class Catholic life in Belfast. Later, when Mary Brigid makes a good match with Brendan, Martha is simultaneously jealous of their happiness and ashamed of her own meanness of spirit. Her own marriage to Dermot is purely expedient, indifference turning to attraction at the moment she sees the kitchen, and especially the oven, she will inherit with the match. Even her mother recognises Martha's mercenary approach to family and marriage, indeed to all her interpersonal relations (p.125). But the most damning indictment comes from Patrick, her eldest son. When she voices her concerns over his loss of faith, he says: 'You're not pretending to be worried about me? ... That'd be a bit of a change. You never had any time for us all our lives, not one of us. All you cared about was your baking and your shop' (p. 139).

This last point alludes to the strategy Martha adopts as defence against the erosion of her sense of self. 'Are you a Republican?' asks an army officer from the local barracks, to which Martha replies, 'I am a home baker' (p. 123). And later she sulks: 'If I am not baking bread I am nobody and nothing' (p. 147). Baking, therefore, is the one thing that she can call her own, the one means she has to express herself as well as to assert her independence. In essence, what Martha is (successfully) striving for is a room of her own – that is, a space in which she can interrogate and challenge through self-expression the discourses into which she has been born and which constitute the limits of her identity. In her tendency to over-compensate for her own compromised independence, however, she loses sight of the benefits, and indeed the necessity, of the family as a buffer between individual and community.

Familial strife takes place against the background of larger social and political struggles, and the two are in fact linked in the metaphors used to describe breakdown in the community. When James Callaghan visits Northern Ireland to sympathise with the Catholics but insists that the Stormont government must stay, Martha explains it thus: 'It was like saying the wicked step-mother had treated the orphans very badly but she was still to be left in charge' (p. 121). In fact, Martha makes no bones about her nationalist sympathies, but when she does try to describe these feelings her own voice fades and the prose adopts the style and tone of popular nationalist discourse:

> I'd look off down Belfast Lough with the ships in it and the shipyard with the gantries and over to the hills in Co. Down and Bangor with the yachts in front of it and I'd think wouldn't it be lovely if it was really our own country that we could be proud in, instead of being kept in cramped little streets with no jobs for the men and sneered at by the people who deprived us. It was as if we were all in a prison looking out at a beautiful world we'd never walk free in. (p. 18)

Later again she thinks: 'I used to imagine myself in court saying all kinds of grand things about freedom and a united Ireland and then being a martyr in gaol' (p. 70) .

What Martha learns, however, is the distance between the rhetoric of nationalism and the exigencies of sectarian violence, a knowledge for which she must pay with her business and home. At the same time, she gives voice to some of the more subtle points of Northern Irish politics usually lost on a discourse constructed in terms of black and white oppositions. Criticising the modern IRA, she says they were 'supposed to be getting a united Ireland, not fighting Protestants' (p. 119). And after the murder of thirteen Catholics civilians by an army unit in Derry in 1972 on what came to be known as Bloody Sunday, Martha lays the blame on the British state rather than on the Protestant community who 'were just handy people to blame' (p. 131). Throughout, in fact, it is England rather than the more obvious Unionist community that bears the brunt of her hatred (p. 141). Again, however, insight fades into rhetoric:

> The IRA would never hurt ordinary people – only the system they were going to pull down. And the border would disappear and we'd all be one united country with our government giving fair play to everyone and the Catholics wouldn't be despised any more and we could have a bit of confidence in ourselves. (p. 131)

Martha's basically joyless and morbid outlook is directly attributable to her status as a doubly second-class citizen (Catholic and female) in a state organised along sectarian and patriarchal lines. The loss of her father leads to unfinished emotional business with her mother and the rest of her family, and she thus becomes over-reliant on her own resources and obstinate in her suspicions of any relations whatsoever. What the story slowly reveals, in fact, is that Martha is far from the straightforward character/narrator she would have us believe, and that the single-mindedness she has developed to compensate for the hurt felt at being 'rejected' by her family has determined relations with her own husband and children. Familial and interpersonal relations, moreover, are themselves caught up in the web of sectarian and gender politics. Despite this, the novel ends on a positive note, with Dermot proving himself a capable and responsible husband, and Martha preparing to re-open her bakery business in proper commercial premises. These thematic and formal discourses coalesce at the end of the novel as Martha acknowledges her limitations as narrator and partner: 'After all, maybe I don't always face the truth about myself either' (p. 152).

Death and Nightingales (1992) by Eugene McCabe

It is remarkable how few modern Northern Irish novels concern any period except the present and the recent past, or any location other than Belfast.[5] *Death and Nightingales* is exceptional in both cases, set towards the end of the last century in rural County Fermanagh. This is not a 'thin' rural society, moreover, but one explicitly connected to the wider national and international world, and certainly dynamic enough to sustain the complex narrative that unfolds. Although this novel deals with similar issues of the interconnection between public and private discourses that have been traced throughout this chapter, it does so in ways that refuse the idea of Northern Ireland as a society fatally divided along irreversible sectarian lines.

The main action of the novel takes place over one day in May 1883. Beth Winters is a 25-year-old Catholic woman living on a farm with her Protestant 'father' Billy. In another version of the 'national romance', Billy married Catherine Maguire only to find that she was already pregnant with Beth, presumably by a Catholic. After the death of Catherine, Beth becomes the object of Billy's ambivalent feelings, especially during the regular drinking bouts into which he escapes both to deaden loss and indulge bitterness. He strikes Beth from his will so that no stranger will inherit the land that has been in his family for generations, yet at the same time he loves her both for herself and for the link she provides with Catherine. However, Beth nurses her own resentment against Billy, both for the death of her mother and the dispossession of her race. She becomes intrigued with Liam Ward, a returned emigrant with whom she plans to elope. Ward, however, is a liar who is planning to murder Beth for the money they have plotted to steal from Billy. When Beth learns of this she murders Ward by upsetting the boat in which he is taking her to shelter on an island, knowing that he cannot swim. The novel ends with Billy and the pregnant Beth alone on the island, emotionally irresolved and 'cangled both to treachery' (p. 231).

The novel begins with a dream that segues into reality, and this motif continues throughout the book. The narrative in fact is haunted by dreams, madness and death, and this fact, as well as the text's engagement with more material issues relating to

paternity and inheritance, places it clearly within the gothic tradition, even as the author looks to extend the possibilities of that
tradition. The action turns upon a classic gothic image: two men
in a wood at night digging a shallow grave for a woman they
intend to murder and rob. And as with classic gothic, the uncanny and the real exist in ambiguous relation to each other,
constituting an undecidable exchange of priorities that is brilliantly caught in the title of the novel. Beth thinks: 'A dream is a
dream is a dream ... it's nothing; and the more she told herself it
was nothing the more it seemed like something' (p. 78). As the
famous Irish philosopher Bishop Berkeley once said, the Irish
'are apt to think something and nothing are near neighbours';
and it is precisely the constant movement between nothing and
something, between nightmare and history, which colours the
atmosphere of the narrative as well as providing its dominant
symbol.

But how does this symbol relate to the question of Northern
Ireland? It seems clear that this tale of love and betrayal reso-
nates along a number of interconnecting narrative levels. There
is a clear historical dimension; Catherine claims she is of the old
Irish Catholic aristocracy whereas Billy Winters is descended
from the New English colonisers who came to Ireland in the
wake of the Cromwellian wars of the 1640s. Religion is also very
important; as his lawyer says when Billy is altering his will so as
to exclude Beth: 'She could marry one of her own. Did we cross
the sea and fight for that? Have we wrought here three hundred
years to have it taken from us that way?' (p. 51) Billy works with
his Catholic neighbours and retainers but has little respect for
what he sees as their barbarous beliefs and customs. Despite his
attempts to socialise with his foreman Mickey Dolphin there is a
deep rift between them which has as much to do with religion as
it has with social privilege. Both religion and history, moreover,
are locked into the discourse of political espionage running
through the text, revealing the complex institutional machinations which have fed the cycle of sectarian hatred in Ireland.

Beneath these merely cultural and historical layers, however,
the characters are caught up in a more fundamental narrative of
which they are only partially aware. Before sectarian history,
there is a deeper natural history built into the very landscape of
the surrounding countryside. Before organised religion, there is a
popular religion based upon agricultural rituals and deeply
embedded folk symbols. Before contemporary Irish politics and
its obsession with ownership of the land, there is an elemental

politics in which the land figures as fundamental regulator of human experience. In fact, the narrative works to reveal the profound infiltration of history by geography, not lessening the onus upon the subject to act *in* history but demanding that such actions be placed in alternative perspectives and temporalities, especially in the context of a society caught up in historically sanctioned violence.

As nightmare and reality circle in an undecidable dance of priorities, so also do history and geography. This theme, moreover, is born out at a formal level. The narrative operates on the interface between an ethereal realm dominated by dreams and nature, and the real world of politics and sectarian manoeuvring, linking real events and people – Parnell, Percy French, the Phoenix Park murders – with fictional ones, thus unsettling and indeed connecting in complex ways the borders between reality and fiction. The narrative is made up of a number of different discourses, without the benefit of one finally dominant voice. Focalisation slips from characters to character, depending on the economy of information demanded by the plot. There are letters, official reports, free indirect discourse and streams of consciousness alongside normal third-person narration. Although Beth might be seen as the main character, the focus shifts from her point of view to that of Billy, Ward and whoever happens to be in the scene. The uncertainty is such that at the climax of the novel, when the tensions between Beth and Billy are finally aired, it is not possible to know where the reader's allegiance is intended to lie (p. 171).

Death and Nightingales is a parable on the development of a sectarian society which misrecognises itself as fatally riven when in fact it is fundamentally enmeshed. 'I will always hate you', says the young Catholic woman to the old Protestant man; 'I will always love you, Beth Winters', he replies (p. 231). Thus, the question posed at the end of this novel is essentially the same one facing the opposing communities in Northern Ireland: how can we carry on, given the cycle of enmity and dependence into which we are locked?

Involved (1995) by Kate O'Riordan

Kate O'Riordan's first novel offers itself as a variation on the model described in the introduction to this chapter, engaging with both the 'love-across-the-barricades' national romance and

the notion of a feminine realm of domestic desire as alternative
to a patriarchal politics. The double twist provided by O'Riordan
in *Involved* is that the 'national romance' discourse is not contained within the artificial geographical borders of Northern
Ireland, thus refusing the official fiction of a fatal sectarianism at
the root of the conflict; while the domestic discourse of love and
sex is shown to offer no respite from an all-pervading political
discourse, thus collapsing the false opposition between the sexual
and political realms. At the same time, if the domestic is politi-
cised, then the desire at the heart of the political must also be
revealed, and O'Riordan is thus forced to fall back on the notion
of a perverse sexual psychology as the ultimate cause of violence.

Set in the period just before the cease-fires, Danny (Belfast,
Catholic, working class) and Kitty (Cork, Protestant, middle
class) meet and fall in love while at university in Dublin. As well
as being 'involved' with Kitty, however, Danny is also 'involved'
with the paramilitary activities of his brother Eamon, and the
action turns on the different connotations of this word. Danny
feels the lure of what the critic Edna Longley calls 'Cathleen-
Anorexia' – an insidious ideological vision which characterises
'Irish nationalism as archetypally female' and which simultaneously 'gives it a mythic pedigree and exonerates it from aggressive and oppressive intent'.[6] Against this, Kitty tries to activate
an alternative feminine logic, one based on a flexible, nomadic
notion of identity, and the search for personal authenticity rather
than the constant reconfirmation of collective sincerity. Later,
the lovers move to London in an attempt to escape the malignant
influence of Belfast. But whereas Kitty, in the wake of her
father's death and the revelation of her mother's enmity, manages
to cut the umbilical cord tying her to home, Danny remains
under the influence of his family and thus trapped within the
imagination of the 'Troubles'.

The 'national romance' in this text has evolved to the stage
where the damaging rift is no longer imagined in terms of the
conflicting communities *within* Northern Ireland, but rather the
breach that has emerged *between* North and South, and indeed
the cultural divide between both parts of Ireland and Great Britain. This has the effect of transferring focus away from an inherited sectarianism towards a larger vision of the relations between
all the 'involved' parties. Kitty's taunting of Danny's Belfast
friends – 'I'm the one who's really Irish here' (p. 86) – offers one
example of the skewed and contradictory identifications available
in such a weak political formation. In this respect, then, *Involved*

is a novel about space. The action moves between Cork, Dublin, Belfast and London, thus incorporating into its form the precise geography of the political struggle. In a complex set of resonances and influences, moreover, each of these locations is revealed to be ineluctably connected to the others. Once again, the family functions as the matrix for these resonances and influences, with Kitty's mother Eleanor providing a parallel in the domestic realm to the similarly warped and malignant influence of Eamon. The point is that the 'Troubles' in Northern Ireland may provide the focus for conflict, but the causes and effects of conflict stretch beyond the merely geographical borders in which they are conveniently contained, encompassing wider and deeper levels of significance.

Similarly, although it engages with the discourse of domestic fiction, the novel works to undermine the notion of sexual desire as cure for political desire. Both senses of the word 'involved' connote physical-emotional dimensions, yet as practices they are mutually exclusive, for it is clear that Danny cannot be both politically and sexually 'involved'. The latter (represented by Kitty) offers itself within the text as solution to the former, with the politico-historical discourse (represented by Eamon) depicted as patriarchal, insidious and perverse. However, beginning and ending the narrative with Eamon has the effect of undoing the implicit moral economy of domestic fiction, which would see an unsatisfactory political realm gradually giving way to a domestic realm in which the subject's true identity can emerge. Having lost the battle for Danny's soul (and body) Kitty informs on Eamon and escapes to Canada with Danny's child. But even that minor victory for domestic over political desire will be reversed, as Eamon's chilling last word to his mother – 'Saskatchewan' – reveals.

Involved thus represents a significant advance on the model described by Cleary, in as much as it shifts emphasis from the notion of a fatal sectarianism contained within the Northern Irish state to the issue of inter-state relations, and simultaneously dispels the myth of an apolitical domestic realm where the contradictions of the public sphere can be resolved. At the same time, however, these advances must be weighed against the representation of Eamon, a classic stereotypical portrait of the IRA man – mother-dominated, woman-fixated, emotionally and psychologically disturbed. He has never severed links with his mother, and is thus working out his sexual angst in terms of the sectarian struggle he finds in the immediate environment. His sister Monica tells a family anecdote about Mrs O'Neill chastising Eamon as a child of ten for playing with his penis. 'Touch it again and I'll cut it off' (p. 136). This explains his personality in terms of a sexual psychodrama and suggests that he carries with him a semi-repressed fear of castration. Thus, if the private realm is shown to offer no relief from a debased politics, this latter discourse is revealed to be motivated not by ideology or conviction but by an arrested sexuality displaced into the public sphere, and mitigated not in the least by the fact that it is self-conscious.

6 BORDERLANDS

This chapter engages with one of the most important motifs in modern critical discourse. As characterised in various strands of modern cultural theory, the border is the grey area where established narratives of identity and authenticity come under pressure, where the things which we use to differentiate self from other, past from present, presence from absence, are tested. The border is the place where the very principles of opposition and difference, so important to our received knowledges, are blurred, turned around and sent back to us. In a classic post-structuralist trope, the border is absolutely necessary but at the same time contains within itself its own impossibility – the impossibility of absolute difference which the border was invented to formalise: *here* is where *this* stops and where *this* begins.[1]

Theorised thus, the concept of the border has practical implications for modern Ireland, both in terms of political identity and cultural practice. It is worth quoting at length from a theorist and critic whose work has been very influential in this area, Homi Bhabha:

> The move away from the singularities of 'class' or 'gender' as primary conceptual and organizational categories has resulted in an awareness of the subject positions – of race, gender, generation, institutional location, geopolitical locale, sexual orientation – that inhabit any claim to identity in the modern world. What is theoretically innovative, and politically crucial, is the need to think beyond narratives of originary and initial subjectivities and to focus on those moments or processes that are produced in the articulation of cultural differences. These 'in-between' spaces provide the terrain for elaborating strategies of selfhood – singular or communal – that initiate new signs of identity, and innovative sites of collaboration, and contestation, in the act of defining the idea of society itself.[2]

What this means, again in the words of Bhabha, is that 'the very concepts of homogenous national cultures, the consensual or contiguous transmission of historical traditions, or "organic" ethnic communities – *as the grounds of cultural comparativism* – are in a profound process of redefinition' (p. 5, original emphasis).

In one sense, this book has been an exercise in establishing certain 'grounds of cultural comparativism' with reference to a specific national cultural practice – contemporary Irish fiction. But this discourse is as susceptible to the 'profound process of redefinition' described by Bhabha as any other modern cultural practice emerging from, or looking to engage with, a specific national tradition. Probably more so, in fact, because for the latest generation of writers there already existed an 'established' counter-tradition in Irish culture which refused to be limited by a received national tradition, and which found the most enabling definitions of national identity precisely in those figures and practices which transgress the borders between different styles, genres and traditions.

This counter-tradition had a dual provenance. On the one hand, it arose from the island's colonial history and the will (addressed in Part 1) to resist imposed versions of reality or history. During the nineteenth century, as Terry Eagleton has pointed out, 'Ireland' functioned as a name for the 'blurring of the real and the rhetorical' and this was 'at once an effect of colonialism and a form of resistance to it'.[3] This 'blurring of the real and the rhetorical' has contributed to the emergence of a *fabulist* strand of Irish fiction, observable in texts such as James Stephens's *The Crock of Gold* (1912) and Flann O'Brien's *At Swim-Two-Birds* (1939). On the other hand, there was the zeal with which certain Irish artists embraced modern experimentalism, using art as a weapon to assault the outmoded values of the critical establishment as well as to undermine the borders which structured dominant narratives of identity, national or otherwise. Against a critical discourse which maintained that great art was possessed of 'a kind of value that transcends the particular prejudices and needs of societies at fixed points in time',[4] early twentieth-century Irish modernism asserted a radically performative and transgressive aesthetic. James Joyce, for example, did not try to *describe* new modes of Irishness in his work but to *instantiate* them by experimenting with received and innovative forms of cultural representation. In the words of Samuel Beckett, 'Joyce's writing is not about something; *it is that something itself*.'[5]

These strands combined to form an 'Irish' counter-tradition – encompassing the work of figures such as Oscar Wilde and Bernard Shaw as well as the writers already mentioned, and more recently Aidan Higgins, John Banville and Neil Jordan. This counter-tradition articulates something akin to Bhabha's model of a critical/cultural practice focused 'on those moments or processes that are produced in the articulation of cultural differences'. The work of counter-traditional Irish writers both occupies and engages with the 'in-between' spaces which have been written out of the established national narratives, attempting to imagine the 'new signs of identity' and the 'innovative sites of collaboration, and contestation' demanded by the experience of life on the island during the twentieth century.

I have used the past tense to describe this Irish counter-tradition, not because it has disappeared but rather because its characteristic modes and motifs have been adapted by the new Irish fiction in an effort to engage with the rapid changes overtaking Ireland and Irishness as the century closes. The novelists of the 1980s and 1990s are having to engage with a proliferation of possibilities in which the idea of the border – defined geographically, sexually or culturally, as in the remainder of this chapter – is becoming increasingly important. Moreover, these writers have shown themselves willing to make use of whatever was to hand by way of example – realism, fabulism or experimentalism – in their drive to expand the limits of Irishness. Indeed, the borders between these literary traditions become another of the received structures that has to be transgressed as national identity enters a new and possibly terminal phase.

FAR FROM THE LAND

Exile and emigration have played a fundamental role in the construction of Irish identity at least since the nineteenth century, and arguably long before that. During the 1980s the issue once again came to the top of cultural and political agendas, as a new wave of emigrants from all walks of Irish life began to leave for England, North America and Europe. During this time Mary Robinson initiated the practice of keeping a light burning in the window of the President's official residence for the millions of Irish people abroad as a symbolic confirmation of their spiritual home.

Traditionally, emigration was understood as a colonial

legacy. Constant exportation of the most intelligent, active, courageous and radical young people left the old and the conservative at home, and this had a detrimental effect on the kind of Ireland that emerged after the break with Britain. The revisionist interpretation of the latest wave of emigration stresses a positive dimension, however – the fact that many of the new emigrants are from middle-class rather than working-class or poor rural backgrounds, and that a modern communications network means that emigrants remain more closely connected with the homeland than previous generations. It could be argued, however, that the myth of the 'Ryanair Generation' – a modern cohort of supra-qualified, dynamic young Europeans constituting a mobile, professional work force – hides a much more insidious agenda in which the nation is still merely disposing of its surplus human requirements.[6] As a corollary, the idea of an 'Irish diaspora' has evolved during the 1990s, a vast network of people across the world possessing different kinds and levels of connections with the island. As the critic David Lloyd has pointed out, however, the invocation of an 'Irish diaspora' may be politically retrograde in that it 'has the effect of naturalising the continuing massive outflow of skilled and unskilled labour from Ireland, as if there were some given population level for the island that we have already exceeded'.[7]

To the fact of economic and career migration must be added the condition of voluntary exile chosen by many of the nation's artists, often as an antidote to the prescriptions of cultural nationalism. The key figure here is James Joyce, although Joyce's legacy in this respect is ambivalent (see Chapter 2), in that his example perhaps offers young artists a too readily available alternative to Ireland when continued domicile and intervention may answer the needs of both novelist and nation better. Conversely, Joyce was responsible for consolidating the literary connections between Ireland, Europe and the rest of the world, thereby providing a ready-made tradition for a later generation looking to shake off its isolationist inheritance.[8]

Emigration and exile (although the latter is an increasingly outmoded term) have placed an onus upon the imaginative writer to engage with these different kinds and levels of Irishness. The emigrant challenges the received borders that structure national discourse – the borders between home and abroad, foreigner and native, natural and cultural. The modern emigrant is essentially displaced, mobile and incoherent, and this constitutes a problem for traditional nationalist discourse which works towards more stable and more coherent versions of the national identity. For the emigrant, as Joe O'Connor says, 'when you use the word "home" or "at home" your friends don't really know what you mean. Sometimes you don't know yourself ... Being an emigrant isn't just an address, it's actually a way of thinking about Ireland.'[9] It may be, then, that Irish identity is most fully realised through exclusion from the land, and that the condition sought by those artists wishing to engage with this paradox is of a kind with the one described by Edward Said at the end of his book *Culture and Imperialism*:

> you must have the independence and detachment of someone whose homeland is 'sweet', but whose actual condition makes it impossible to recapture that sweetness, and even less possible to derive satisfaction from substitutes furnished by illusion or dogma, whether deriving from pride in one's heritage or from certainty about who 'we' are.[10]

Home From England (1995) by James Ryan

James Ryan's debut novel explores the contradictions of modern Irish identity as exposed by the experience of emigration. Contradiction is manifested at every level of the narrative – in the relations between men and women, between parents and children, between different styles and levels of narration. Crucially, contradiction and confusion are also revealed to characterise the relations both between and within the discourses which combine in any modern identity. Irish cultural nationalism, we recall, constructed Irish identity in terms of a specific temporal and spatial matrix, investing in notions of homeland, geographical community, observable borders between nations, as well as the idea of the present as part of the narrative linking national past and national future. Emigration, however, upsets this matrix, fatally *displacing* the subject from received concepts of national time and space. In the course of observing his father's pathetic attempts to reconcile an Irish past and an English present, the young unnamed narrator of *Home From England* comes to a sense of the capriciousness of an identity based on these concepts, even as he recognises their importance for those (like his father) to whom national identity constitutes reality itself.

Having spent the first years of his life in a rural Irish community, the narrator and his family are forced through economic
necessity to move to England at the beginning of the 1960s. The
country left behind is one so steeped in its past that it has failed
to grow in the present, sustaining itself with the memory of what
it imagines itself once to have been. The old men sitting on
'Moratorium Row' symbolise a nation postponed:

> They were soldiers once. Most of them fought in the First World War
> and all of them fought in the War of Independence. That is when they
> became heroes, almost fifty years ago, when they won freedom for
> Ireland. At the time everyone thought that when one era ends a new one
> begins. But it didn't turn out like that. It went on being the end of an
> era and the men went on being heroes and everybody waited and waited
> and waiting became an era in itself. (p. 16)

In the early years in England the narrator and his family feel
that 'our real life was taking place elsewhere' (p. 61), thus revealing their preference for the 'then' and 'there' of the Irish past
over the 'here' and 'now' of the English present. The narrator's
father, especially, is locked into a frozen past, for if England is a
place where things happen, then Ireland is the exact opposite: 'all
the people we knew were set into an unchanging story. Every
time he spoke about them they did and said exactly the same
thing' (p. 55). Father comes to rely upon these constant rehears-
als of an unchanging past to sustain him in his 'virtual' life in
England. He demands confirmation from his wife and children
as long as he can, but as their scepticism grows he becomes more
marginalised and more alienated from the present, retreating
further and further into an impotent past over which he remains
master.

The contradictions of emigrant identity are exposed on the
family's first return home for a holiday in 1966 during the celebrations commemorating the fiftieth anniversary of the Easter
Rising. Father receives a 'Freedom Medal' for a conflict in which
he was too young to have fought. The 'freedom' that is being
celebrated, moreover, is the right to live and work in England,
while for those still in thrall to its backward vision 'It was as if
the freedom medal had the power to paralyse anyone around
whose neck it was hung' (p.121). An aura of ambiguity pervades
the entire episode; nothing is decided, nothing fixed, return has
brought only confusion and indirection. Father 'would start out
with a sense of purpose, as if he was going somewhere in particu-

lar, and would arrive back with an air of defeat about him' (p. 91); while the narrator experiences similar impressions of displacement and uncertainty: 'I felt a wave of despair as I felt the fixed points of my landscape tumbling. One by one, our house, Babs, Hegerty, they had all begun to shift' (p. 101).

The holiday is a failure, then, for it exposes the discrepancy between the 'truth' of unchanging memory and the 'truth' of a constantly changing reality. The strain of denying an English present for an Irish past becomes too much. Slowly, the narrator, his sisters and even his mother move away from 'those hollow claims that kept my father looking back' (p. 115). Father becomes a pathetic figure clinging to an image of the past that was never more than the expedient invention of triumphalist nationalism. As he loses his grip on this image, he retreats into silence and half-hearted repetitions of the old lines. When the family discusses an IRA bombing, Father 'said something about freedom but he said it with such little conviction that it almost failed to become a full phrase' (p. 144). He dies unwilling or unable to question 'the beliefs which left him so much at odds with the world in which he lived' (p. 144).

The full extent of Father's self-deception is revealed when his body is returned 'home' for burial. Ireland has continued to change, to the extent that it has embraced a post-nationalism for which the revolutionary generation has become an embarrassment. Dineen, the town's big noise, has bought the 'Big House' which Father was instrumental in destroying during the War of Independence; he even wishes to restore it to its pre-revolutionary glory. Dineen is also responsible for removing the Tricolour from the coffin, because 'in the present situation that flag is an insult' (p. 182). The gap between the discarded Ireland preserved in the memory of the emigrant and the new Ireland is revealed in Father's threadbare epitaph: 'A harmless poor ould divil, home from England, God rest his soul' (p. 183). Although the narrator has escaped his emigrant inheritance, his feelings of sadness and anger at the betrayal of his father encapsulate the fate awaiting all those who remain locked in an impossible vision of the nation.

Cowboys and Indians (1991) by Joseph O'Connor

Whereas *Home from England* is mostly concerned with the disappointments of the returned emigrant, Joseph O'Connor's first novel explores one of the exemplary experiences of modern Irish

life – living and working in London – even if in this case the
emigrant in question is not the rough navvy of popular myth but
a highly educated, fashion-conscious, middle-class Dubliner. The
hero of the novel, Eddie Virago, belongs to the 'Ryanair Generation' – that is, he is a partial emigrant who can (just about) afford
to take advantage of modern transport culture to retain links
with home. Despite this, and despite his post-nationalist obsessions with sex, drugs and rock 'n' roll, Eddie is still an Irishman
in England, and his experiences throughout the novel are
informed by that traditional transnational status. Indeed, one of
the major themes of the novel is the way in which old narratives
are negotiated by new subjects, in this case the old narrative of
Irish life in London as experienced by the class of 1990.

When we first encounter him, Eddie is already embarked on
probably the most famous journey in the Irish popular imagination
– London via Holyhead on the boat-train. Eddie is not primarily an
economic migrant, but a pop music hopeful who like many young
people from throughout the British Isles is simply relocating himself to the European centre of the industry. He has a violent and
passionate affair in Mr Patel's Brightside Hotel with Marion, another Irish emigrant who unbeknownst to Eddie has come to London to have an abortion. When the couple return to Marion's small
home town in the North for her mother's funeral, it is hinted that
the pregnancy was the result of incestuous relations with her father.
Eddie's own family, meanwhile, has also failed to live up to national
propaganda, as his mother has moved to London to live with another man. Her presence in the city, as well as Eddie's reluctance to
visit her, provides one of the novel's major themes.

Eddie's frustration at his failure to break through on the
music scene, Marion's anger and guilt, plus a disastrous visit to
Dublin at Christmas, combine to destroy the relationship. After
Marion leaves, Eddie meets and moves in with a former university acquaintance, the successful and ultra-cool Salome Wilde.
Salome offers an example of an alternative tradition alongside the
more popular image of the sentimental working-class emigrants
whose dreams of home render them incapable of adapting to the
new life. She is in fact a 'NIPPIL', one of the lesser-known
acronyms of the 1980s, standing for 'New Irish Professional Person in London'.[11] By the time Eddie does try to make it up with
Marion she has left London and married Tom Clancy, a spoiled
priest who now runs the Prairie Moon Burger Bar back in her
home town. Mr Patel, who has attended the wedding, compli-
ments Eddie on Ireland's beauty while also remarking upon the

sadness of 'the things that happen over there' and 'the things that you still do to each other' (p. 239). It is clear that he means the 'Troubles' rather than the more mundane ways in which an Irish identity seems to be a passport to all manner of personal and social problems. By the time he turns to his mother, Eddie is as messed up as Marion, and the novel closes with him sitting in drug-induced melancholy in a bar in the centre of London.

Eddie is the last of the Dublin Mohicans, obstinately clinging to his punk haircut fifteen years after it has gone out of fashion. Indeed, the obsession with fashion constitutes probably the most important aspect of the book. Very much a novel of its own time, the text is littered with topical allusions and constant references to current cultural trends. This engagement with fashion means that the text has dated very quickly, although this may in fact be the required effect. The novel gives an in-depth picture of the emigrant experience at one specific moment in the early 1990s, having seemingly few pretensions beyond that. At one point the narrator says of Marion: 'She sounded like a character in some cheap 1970s airport novel' (p. 21), and in some ways this is the status to which *Cowboys and Indians* aspires – a throwaway pulp fiction that exists predominantly in and of its moment.

The engagement with fashion is also a question of narrative technique, as the narrator seems just as concerned as Eddie to consolidate his street credentials. The pace is fast, the tone in-your-face. Much of the narrative is taken up with dialogue, and the narrative remains more or less present-centred and hero-centred throughout. It becomes increasingly difficult, in fact, to separate Eddie's voice zone from that of the narrator; both are simultaneously brash and diffident, confident and self-doubting, always intent on being up-to-the-minute cool. As a consequence there is a somewhat hollow ring to many of the exchanges and scenes, as the worlds of narrative and narration threaten to collapse into each other. When, for example, Eddie goes for a job on a building site, his potential bosses ask him 'if he knew the difference between a joist and a girder. Eddie said yeah, Joyce wrote *Finnegans Wake* and Goethe wrote *Faust*. They didn't see the joke' (p. 183). Now, this is an old joke in Ireland, the point being that the nation's intellectual heritage is lost on a brand of English racist who sees the Irish only as working-class fodder. The joke depends very precisely, moreover, upon the puns made available by the words 'joist' and 'girder', and in that order. However, to the extent that it has a definite discursive status *outside* the fictional narrative – in terms of the *extra*-narrative realm of narrator, author and a specific encoded

Irish reader – the joke detaches itself from the surrounding narrative discourse and compromises the reader's engagement with the story.

Nevertheless, O'Connor's representation of a flawed, fashion-conscious Irishman in London, unwilling to fade into an expatriate ghetto or to turn the other cheek to a residual racism, signals a challenge to the nation's traditional emigrant culture. As the experiences of Eddie and Marion reveal, however, while that culture remains such an integral part of the lives of so many people, England and Englishness will continue to impact upon the possibilities of Ireland and Irishness.

A Farewell to Prague (1995) by Desmond Hogan

A reader looking for one sentence to give the flavour of this enigmatic text could do worse than settle on the following: 'Years later I visited the grey-haired girl in a mental hospital near the border' (p.111). There is nothing particularly striking about these few words taken in isolation, yet in the context of Hogan's 'novel' they operate, to use the text's own dominant image (p. 166), like tiny pieces of a much larger collage, linking up with other pieces and patterns to form an overall impression of motion – paradoxically, an image of movement. Collage is typical of a modernist aesthetics from the early part of the century, as is Hogan's employment of a narrative technique in which, as Seamus Deane wrote of George Moore, the material is organised 'in such a way that his supple prose would achieve cumulative effects by the repetition of phrases and ideas operating like motifs'.[12] Hogan's vision of Ireland and its connections with the rest of the world is very much of the postmodernist 1990s, however, a time and place in which the traditional borders within and between time and place have all but collapsed.

'*Years later* I visited the grey-haired girl in a mental hospital near the border.' There is a discernible story in this book, concerning the breakdown of Des ('I', sometimes 'you') and his relationships with Eleanor, Marek and a host of other pseudo-characters. But the text does not offer any developmental plot in the traditional sense. Instead it is made up of a series of snapshot images and impressions from different periods of the narrator's life, leaping back and forth in a seemingly random manner. The discourse operates through *metaphor* rather than *metonymy* – that is, by a selective and highly intricate pattern of symbolism rather than a quasi-realistic continuity of events.[13] This technique functions at the level of the text as a whole, with certain images and figures (Irish itinerants, Maud Gonne, homosexuality, etc.) recurring in seemingly haphazard fashion, but also at a more local level. For example, in the space of a few hundred words Chartres Cathedral is mentioned as a poster on a student wall (p. 59), as a poster on a Dublin street corner (p. 59), and as the actual French building (p. 60). But the connections between these and other instances are not stated. Rather, one image appears to spark off a series of randomly related moments, the effect being to build up a textual aura rather than offer any discernible meaning. At times, indeed, even the pretence at narrative is abandoned as the text collapses into a series of verbless images (pp. 76, 135).

'Years later I visited the *grey-haired girl* in a mental hospital near the border.' Against the seemingly exhausted modes of narrative and language, the text engages with alternative systems of meaning, most notably colour. The following is typical: 'And the landscape, the clay ochre-red, a vermilion dust in the air from it. I purchased a blue bicycle and cycled the town and got to know people, the old black men beside the signs for Raisin Jacks in Woolworths window, the women with coral pink and squash-coloured hair' (p. 81). In passages such as this, narrative is pared down to its core – a cycle ride – while the surrounding descriptive detail takes on the task of creating layers of meaning through an impressionistic array of colour and light. In fact, Hogan's apparent preference here for a painterly rather than a writerly aesthetic finds many resonances throughout modern Irish fiction, adding to the impression of a continuing mistrust amongst Irish novelists of their own medium, a mistrust which has been exacerbated in recent times by a general postmodernist scepticism regarding narrative's traditional communicative claims.[14]

'Years later I visited the grey-haired girl *in a mental hospital* near the border.' As a text, then, *A Farewell to Prague* is 'mad' in its random, anti-linear, chaotic organisation. But madness also constitutes one of the text's recurring themes – a collective insanity built into Irish and European history, and a personal history of chronic depression and mental instability with which the narrator is trying to cope. Somehow, madness becomes linked in the narrator's mind with the city of Prague:

> I'd known for a long time that I had to get to Prague. I knew that I came from a cruel and hypocritical and unrelenting country. No matter what,

they'd be right. I knew that there was an imminent madness, an
imminent breakdown in me and I knew I had to get there before it
happened ... I looked towards the country of childhood when I'd had a
soul and realized it was possible to get souls back, but only through
long journeys, inner and maybe outer. (p. 229)

Travelling is a means to stave off the madness which is his
national inheritance, but always it is madness which is his constant companion and, in the guise of Prague, his destination.
Hence, 'a farewell to Prague' would be a farewell to madness, a
coming to terms with personal nightmares which are themselves
fatally linked to the barely repressed nightmares of Irish history.

'Years later I visited the grey-haired girl in a mental hospital
near the border.' Hogan's artistic vision refuses to be contained
within the traditional parameters of Irish cultural discourse. Ireland, England and the United States are still significant locations
within the national imagination, but that imagination must expand
to engage with a wider set of geographical possibilities. Crossing
these new geographical borders functions as a metaphor for the
transgression of traditional emotional and sexual borders and the
construction of a broader frame of reference within which the
identity of the Irish subject can be negotiated. As Cherry Smyth,
another Irish writer concerned with the borders between sexualities and states, writes:

I cannot envisage returning for good, nor can I build a future based on a
life in England. I vacillate. I journey back and forth. I take home with
me in a suitcase. I imagine becoming global and that being enough.[15]

QUEER NATION

Homosexuality is one of the central motifs in *A Farewell to
Prague,* and an AIDS-related death appears to be the paradoxical
centre of this centreless text. Hogan's engagement with these
issues leads into the second of our 'Borderlands'. Along with
post-colonialism, 'Queer Studies' has become an area of increasing intellectual interest in recent years. Queer Studies is in fact
one of a number of relatively new disciplines which have
emerged to challenge the constitution of certain conditions, practices and identities as marginal or aberrant. In the modern era,
the west's characteristic mode of subject-identification has operated in terms of a *straightgeist* – that is, a loosely defined public

sphere which works to normalise certain discourses of race, gender, sexuality, age, health and lifestyle, all of which are in fact highly contingent.[16] As its name suggests, Queer Studies is concerned with the positive reappropriation of a historically marginalised homosexuality, but also with the wider project of exploring the systematically suppressed relations between the *straightgeist* and all those discourses positioned as marginal, *other*, charmingly exotic or frighteningly different. Moreover, the predominantly post-structuralist methodologies of the new social movements mean that *otherness* – in this case homosexuality – is invariably discovered at the heart of the *straightgeist*, the central figure of the heterosexual imagination. Thus, 'One in every family' is the cry – part accusation, part celebration – of modern Ireland's queer community.[17]

Spurred on by developments in other parts of the world, Irish homosexual self-awareness grew throughout the 1970s and 1980s. Homosexuality was identified as one of the silenced voices of post-revolutionary Ireland. As Eibhear Walshe writes:

> post-colonial countries, like Ireland, have particular difficulty with the real presence of the homoerotic, because colonialism itself has a gendered power relation and, inevitably, casts the colonizing power as masculine and dominant and the colonized as feminine and passive ... The emergent post-colonial nation perceives the sexually different as destabilizing and enfeebling, and thus the lesbian and gay sensibility is edited out, silenced.[18]

This was not because of any shortage of Irish homoerotic texts – on the contrary, in addition to subjecting the extant canon to re-analysis, research is still in the process of uncovering a great wealth of gay and lesbian Irish writing – but because of the insidious survival of the colonialist *straightgeist* and its dualistic modes of thought in post-colonial Ireland, both North and South.

In June 1993 a coalition government abolished the laws (enacted for the United Kingdom – including Ireland – in 1885 and retained under Free State and Republican law) which criminalised homosexual acts between men. Thus began the process of amendment and rescission which will see the category of (homo)sexuality fully installed in all the laws governing the Republic's citizens. In fact, the new legislation encapsulated perhaps more than anything else official acknowledgement of the need for new modes of political and cultural identity in response to demands arising from the community. However, this process is ongoing and is being resisted, and Ireland's homosexual writers find themselves as a result working within a system that is highly fluid, legally (if precariously) protected yet still subject to a homophobia deeply embedded in the country's social and cultural institutions.

At the same time as they have struggled to find a civic and political voice, Ireland's gay and lesbian writers have also been engaging with a range of literary issues, both textual and institutional. Perhaps the major problem for the homosexual novelist, however, is that, as Declan Kiberd has pointed out, 'the short story is the form which renders the lives of the marginal and the isolated, whereas the traditional novel tends to feature the urbane and complex relationships of a fully "made", calibrated society'.[19] The problem thus confronting the modern Irish homosexual novelist is not dissimilar to the one faced by the Irish novelists of the nineteenth century who tended to employ the novel as part of a specific politico-cultural programme. It should not be surprising, therefore, that in contexts of continuing misrepresentation the temptation to polemicise can sometimes prove too much for the queer novelist. Note, however, that in the passage above Kiberd invokes 'the traditional novel'. The 'problem' may reside not in the admixture of novelistic and polemical discourses, or in some lack of urbanity or complexity which characterises the Irish homosexual experience, but in critical and aesthetic formulations which reflect the perspectives of an established, specifically heterosexual, society.

As Edward Said has pointed out, 'no one today is purely *one* thing'.[20] When 'homosexual' is prefixed by the word 'Irish', and then suffixed by the word 'novelist', the results are bound to be complex. It is these complexities which, as the first legally out generation, Ireland's modern gay and lesbian novelists have begun to address.

Stir-fry (1994) by Emma Donoghue

In recent years Emma Donoghue has become one of Ireland's most public lesbian figures. Scholar, playwright and novelist, Donoghue's work tapped into the wider libertarian movements overtaking the country and in its turn helped to raise the profile of homosexuality throughout Irish life. As well as providing an engaging narrative, her first novel offers an interesting example of the limits of the novel as deliberate social intervention.

The action is set in contemporary Dublin and concerns Maria, a young country woman who has come to the capital to attend university. Desperate to explore the world beyond the narrow familial limits she has hitherto known, Maria takes a room in a flat shared by two older students – Ruth and Jael – unaware, at least at the outset, that they are lesbians. Disappointed by the sexual and emotional roles available in traditional student life, increasingly intrigued by the activities of her flatmates, the novel charts Maria's growing social and sexual awareness amid the complexities of this three-cornered relationship and a wider exploration of the particularities of lesbian subculture.

It seems clear that Donoghue is employing the novel as a tactical weapon in a wider strategy which is concerned with the role and status of lesbians in Irish life. Despite this, she makes strenuous efforts to avoid any 'representative' status for or in her work, or to invoke any special pleading which would detract from the impact of her narratives. In *Stir-fry*, especially, Donoghue seems concerned to *normalise* lesbianism within a society which has come to see same-sex relationships as radically *abnormal*. In this, Donoghue is at odds with more radical lesbian strategies described by Joan McCarthy:

> To be a lesbian, to act and name oneself as a lover of women, presents an unmitigated challenge to the belief system that sustains reality ... If ... we challenge the belief systems that sustain reality, that is, if we take the underlying beliefs to be arbitrary, we begin to understand reality itself as changeable. It is then that we contribute a new structure to reality, rather than argue for the inclusion of our experience in the dominated reality.[21]

It is not clear, however, how such a restructuring of reality could take place, or indeed if simply acting and naming oneself as a lover of women could achieve the impact claimed in this passage. The changes which saw the introduction of such relatively liberal laws on homosexuality resulted, arguably, not from any radical refusal of 'dominated reality' but from a familiarity with, and subsequent exposure of, the underlying contradictions of 'normal' Irish sexual life. Such changes, moreover, may have more to do with the state's desire to shed the inconvenient trappings of its nationalist past in a drive for fuller integration with the European Union than with any sudden discovery of a liberal conscience. The point made in Chapter 1 regarding the cultural

politics of colonial resistance seems relevant here, namely, that a
discourse of resistance which refuses received realities cuts itself
off from effective action, and that the marginalised subject – in
this case, lesbian – must negotiate from within a situation that
she is forced to inhabit. This may lead in time to a questioning
of the arbitrary nature of 'normal' heterosexual discourse, as is
characteristic of contemporary American 'queer theory'; but for a
nascent homosexual formation such as exists in Ireland, getting
the issue of homosexuality onto the relevant agendas would seem
to take precedence over radical assaults on the philosophical
bases of established heterosexual humanism.

The tactics employed by Donoghue as she sets about nor-
malising lesbianism include engagement with traditional narrative modes, concentration on individual psychology and the
avoidance of stereotypes. *Stir-fry* is a variation on the traditional *Bildungsroman* novel, a form which seems particularly
suited to the 'coming-out' narrative so fundamental to modern
homosexual discourse. Maria, as so many novelistic heroes and
heroines before her, leaves the country and the family embrace
to find herself in the city. Through an interwoven process of
social and psychological development she reaches a sense of
that self and with at least one element of her identity finally
named – lesbian. It is unclear if she will manage to come out
to her family, as the novel makes it clear that lesbianism is
still a problem for the traditional religious and familial discourses informing Irish society. But by concentrating on
Maria's self-discovery and the melodrama of the triangular relationship rather than the wider social status of lesbianism, focus
remains on the narrative rather than on the 'issue'. In the
process of rejecting Jael's seduction, Maria realises that she
wants Ruth. The text thus remains true to its *Bildungsroman*
form and reaches a traditional point of closure – the self-
constitution of the central character through recognition of her
significant other.

At the same time as it engages with the familiar elements
of the coming-of-age narrative, *Stir-fry* does not offer uniformly
positive lesbian images and thus try to 'save' the characters for
some extra-narrative political discourse. While the occasionally
grating tone of chirpiness refuses the seriousness of (mainly
heterosexual images of) lesbianism, the text nevertheless
engages with some of the more contentious issues within same-
sex relationships – for example, the status of traditional heterosexual values such as sexual monogamy, and the distress caused

for Irish gays and lesbians who feel compelled to forego the comfort of religion as a result of the Catholic Church's opposition to homosexuality. These issues are broached in *Stir-fry*, and it is at these points in the text that one can see the polemical skeleton beneath the narrative flesh. But neither are the problems of fidelity and religion explained away in terms of some uniform 'alternative' perspective which would turn the text into a handbook for prospective Irish lesbians. Instead, each of the main characters is shown to be working through these issues, negotiating complex manoeuvres between what as lesbians they feel they *should* be doing and saying and thinking, and the practicalities of living as lesbians in modern Ireland. Part of Maria's education involves learning what Jael and Ruth already know despite – or rather precisely because of – their faults, that, in McCarthy's words: 'The revolution will not begin tomorrow, or next week, it is already taking place and we are already on the barricades' (p. 106).

When Love Comes to Town (1993) by Tom Lennon

Tom Lennon's debut novel is an example of the 'coming-out' narrative which despite attempts to avoid flag-waving ends up as something of a documentary about the trials of a homosexual protagonist in a predominantly heterosexual and homophobic society. Neil Byrne is a popular teenager living with his family in a middle-class area of South Dublin. As the narrative opens Neil has already discovered his own sexuality but is worried to the point of depression about how a revelation will affect relations with family and friends. Denied the satisfaction of a real relationship, Neil fantasises, especially about his schoolmate Ian whom he can only otherwise engage on strictly heterosexual terms. Partially out – to his friend Becky and his sister Jackie – Neil takes the plunge and becomes initiated into the rituals and the language of Dublin's queer subculture. He is compensated for getting mugged leaving a gay bar one night by winning the interest of the exotic Shane (from Belfast) with whom a physical relationship is implied but never broached.

Distressed by the reaction of his parents and by the failure of his affair with Shane, Neil gets drunk and makes a half-hearted attempt at suicide before being re-admitted into the family circle, albeit at the price of collusion with his father's version of a non-physical homosexuality. The novel thus ends on an ambiguous note, with Neil receiving acceptance of sorts and learning of Ian's homosexual interest, but at the same time having to accede to a partial lie to retain the family links upon which his peace of mind and security rely. The deliberately 'fictional' happy ending in which Neil gets his man is thus weighed against the non-ending which leaves him stranded between the half-truths of his father's squeamish liberalism. The battle has been won, but at a price, and in the meantime the war continues on other fronts. Irish society is indicted for its inability and/or unwillingness to acknowledge one of its constituent truths: 'We'll love you, providing you hide your love away. We know you've been through hell, but please don't bring us down into that hell. Just pretend' (p. 174).

The argument invoked by his parents against homosexuality is religious – that it flies in the face of God (p. 151). Despite this, Neil frequently draws upon religion, both in the search for the courage to reveal his sexuality and as a subsequent support against the prejudice he encounters. As in Donoghue's novels, *When Love Comes to Town* seems to suggest that it is not the concept of religion that is wrong, only its misuse for discriminatory and basically anti-religious practices. Arguably as significant as religion for gay and lesbian identity, although seldom engaged, is the issue of class. The city depicted in *When Love Comes to Town* (and in Donoghue's novels) is worlds apart from Doyle's Dublin. The social and cultural milieu in which Neil circulates is obviously that of a reasonably well-off middle-class person, and this raises one of the perennial issues of queer theory – the extent to which homosexual existence is dependent upon a class discourse which it inevitably dismisses through appeals to a pre-class sexual essence. It could be argued that modern queer politics (indeed, the politics of all the new radical movements based on gender, race and sexuality) has become the constituency of a social and educational elite which because of its background and training is better positioned to expose the contradictions of the *straightgeist*. By the same token, the privileged middle-class homosexual is as a rule more confident of his/her validity within the community as a whole. But, as one critic has written: 'The preponderance of intellectually-trained people within the new social movements is precisely what has enabled and even required them to construct movement identities in increasingly overt opposition to class-based identity.'[22]

Neil is not yet 'intellectually-trained', although the nature of his university training is another point of contention – he prefers the 'softer' humanities option over the traditionally masculine engineering degree favoured by his father. None the less, Neil is clearly of a different social background from 'Daphne', the outrageous queen of the scene who is dying of an AIDS-related illness. When Neil visits Daphne in his working-class estate on the northside of the city, the narrative invokes the popular images of Dublin working-class life – 'scruffy' street urchins, graffiti, the accent, the earthiness of Daphne's mother and the resemblance of the house to a 'refugee camp' (pp. 141–6). However, the narrative invites the reader to share Neil's surprise at the 'liberalism' of Daphne's family, the effect being to collapse Dublin's class boundaries in the face of an all-encompassing sexual imperative. Having patronised Daphne in his own environment, however, Neil returns to his comfortable suburb to confront an entirely different set of life options based on the interaction between *his* homosexuality and *his* class. Read against itself, Lennon's novel reveals that away from the levelling club scene, class is a fundamental component of a modern Irish homosexual existence. The issue of class, moreover, becomes even more significant in a society such as Ireland where as a category it has been systematically displaced by discourses based on race and geography.

When Love Comes to Town was written in the dark days before the new legislation and seems to have been published with definite social aims in mind. Its target audience is solely Irish – aimed both at young homosexuals requiring assurance of a larger queer community and at the straight majority as a plea for tolerance and understanding. In its invocation of some of the stock characters and scenes of homosexual existence it is also concerned to rehumanise homophobic stereotypes. At times, however, its very worthiness detracts from its formal success. The narrative tense frequently strays into the subjunctive, with Neil constantly wondering what his friends and family *would* think *if* they knew his real feelings. This gives the text a curiously postponed atmosphere as if the real story was taking place elsewhere. In fact, all the characters remain little more than caricatures going through the motions of the familiar coming-out narrative against the background of social ignorance and intolerance. At points its crusading tone descends into a sentimentality and special pleading that seems as likely to alienate as to win over the unconverted section of its intended audience. It would be churlish, however, to indict *When Love Comes to Town* in terms of critical prescriptions which have traditionally occluded the very criterion to which Lennon makes his literary discourse answerable – social efficacy.

Hood (1995) by Emma Donoghue

Having insisted upon normality and visibility with *Stir-fry*, Donoghue's second novel represents a bolder and more formally ambitious exploration of modern Irish lesbian existence. This later text is considerably longer, more intricately structured and, in its graphic depiction of lesbian sex, less concerned to bridge the gap with the *straightgeist* than to engage as fully as possible with the specifics of a lesbian identity. Moreover, in its scrupulous delineation of homosexual widowhood *Hood* also begins the search for a social language that is becoming more and more necessary but which has by and large yet to be described or understood. Despite these differences, however, the novel may be seen as part of a larger critical and imaginative project in which Donoghue is concerned to address the question: 'How is a woman who loves women to live as an Irishwoman?'[23]

The story is simple. Thirty-year-old Pen tells how she met Cara Wall at school and they became lovers, and how despite Cara's occasional affairs they remain together, living in the Walls' house with Cara's father (her mother has left to live in the United States where Kate, Cara's sister and Pen's first crush, also lives). Because of social and familial pressures, they are out only to a small group of lesbian friends. Before the narrative begins, Cara is killed in a car crash as she returns home from a holiday, leaving Pen widowed to all intents and purposes but unable to grieve properly because of the stigma attached to same-sex relationships in Irish society. The narration takes place over the week leading up to Cara's funeral, although much of the narrative is taken up with flashbacks to different points in the relationship. It is not until Pen decides to come out to her unsympathetic mother at the end of the book that she can begin the twin processes of grieving and healing.

The narrative turns on the different meanings attached to the word 'hood'. The earlier connotations are all more or less negative: the hood on the school coats Pen and Cara have to wear to mark their similarity to all the other girls (p. 39); the red riding hood worn by the eponymous fairy-tale character symbolising her archetypally ambiguous female role as sexual aggressor and passive victim; the various kinds of 'hood' available to women in

modern Ireland to categorise themselves – sisterhood, maiden-
hood, widowhood, spinsterhood, wifehood, dykehood (pp.
113–14). However, all these are absorbed and positively re-
activated by the novel's central device (although the concept of
'centrality' with its phallic connotations is precisely what is at
issue):

> The hood of the clitoris was not a hood to take off, only to push
> back. In fact the whole thing was a series of folds and layers, a
> magical Pass the Parcel in which the gift was not inside the wrap-
> pings, but was the wrappings. If you touched the glans directly it
> would be too sharp, like a blow. It was touching it indirectly,
> through and with the hood, that felt so astonishing. (p. 257)

As well as offering practical hints for the lesbian novice, this
passage signals the climax of the sexual discourse which constitutes one of the text's most significant aspects. Starting in a low
key, more or less where *Stir-fry* left off, sex becomes increasingly
important as the narrative progresses. A remarkable early passage
describing a shared bath communicates the intimacy and the
trust between Cara and Pen (pp. 124–6), but with every new
scene the details become more graphic, as if the author is deliberately testing the good faith of the new 'liberal' Ireland. The
climax is reached in Pen's description of oral sex during men-
struation (pp. 253–6), a passage designed to shock complacent
readers into questioning their own values, especially the kind of
reader (such as represented by Neil's father in *When Love Comes
to Town*) who might accept a 'soft' version of homosexuality as an
unavoidable psychological condition but would not wish to be
reminded of its physical aspects. By focusing on the particularities of lesbian sex in this way, Donoghue is insisting that homosexuality cannot be contained by pseudo-liberal jargon about
'different identities' or 'hidden traditions' or 'new Irishness';
rather, it is distinguished precisely by an entirely different
approach to one of the most fundamental aspects of human life –
sex – and it would be as well, the text seems to suggest, for
everyone to acknowledge what this entails.

Alongside this emphasis on the physical realities of lesbian
love, dreams, fantasies and fairy-tales are integral to the organisation and rhythm of the novel. Deprived of a social outlet for her
grief, Pen retreats to her unconscious to make sense of her life
with and without Cara. Dreams function as a sort of grammar
throughout the text, punctuating the 'real' narrative and offering

Pen an alternative realm to that of contemporary Ireland which, to the extent that it is unable to provide a space for her true feelings, is paradoxically unreal. At the same time, Pen's unconscious also appears to be drawing upon a common store of deeply embedded folk images to cope with the loss of Cara. Even more than religion (which plays an understated but significant role throughout), the rituals encapsulated in fairy-tales such as Hansel and Gretel, Rapunzel and Little Red Riding Hood are seen to contain the seeds of a compensatory myth for public lesbian widowhood. These Freudian and Jungian discourses are drawn together in the final dream sequence in which Pen chases an elusive Cara through a maze only to be distracted by another figure:

> I run and run till my lungs are burning up, and finally corner her. She turns, her gauzy hood falling back. Was I expecting decay behind a mask of powder, or the grin of bone? She has my face. It is my own face that looks back at me, almost understandingly. Then she turns and runs on, after Cara. I can hear their laughter in the distance. (p. 302)

In this way Pen learns that she must come to terms not only with Cara's death but also with the loss of the person she used to be when still a part of Cara. This is not really a loss, however, for having resolved in her unconscious what resisted resolution in the real world, Pen has found the strength to re-enter that real world, only this time to take up the challenge of learning to live openly as an Irishwoman who loves women.

BRINGING IT ALL BACK HOME

This book has been concerned by and large with the emergence of a new generation of Irish novelists articulating a range of voices which have been, or which continue to be, marginalised from the mainstream of life throughout the island. It is a frequently remarked irony, however, that in times of rapid change (such as Ireland has been undergoing in the decade or so before the appearance of this book) the traditional and the established can quickly become the marginal; to put it in the theoretical terms of Raymond Williams, as *emergent* voices move into a position of *dominance*, the formerly dominant become *residual* – become, that is, marginal to a new mainstream tradition.[24] This study ends, then, with a brief look at some recent novelistic treatments and examples of certain traditional elements of life in Ireland – land, religion, the construction of the nation in gendered terms and the established novelistic tradition. This is to demonstrate that these staples have not disappeared with the latest generation of writers but have necessarily been adapted to new times and new cultural contexts.

The Bray House (1990) by Eilís Ní Dhuibhne

Land has held a perennial interest for people living on the island of Ireland. On the one hand, it seems reasonable to assume that from the time of the first inhabitants there has been a materialistic interest in the limited amount of available land. Interest became obsession, however, under the colonial dispensation beginning in the twelfth century. In fact, the issue of ownership and organisation of the land may be said to underpin much of the subsequent Irish–British conflict, culminating perhaps in the land agitation of the late nineteenth century but still active at the end of the millennium in the question over the border between the Republic and Northern Ireland.

At the same time, the mythological tales and legends reveal a deep fascination with landscape and with humankind's role in nature. Through the peculiar nomenclature of the Gaelic language, in which places became associated with individuals, events and topographical features, the land became a kind of narrative in itself which required certain skills and protocols from its inhabitants while offering a secure natural base in which to ground identity. But this kind of existence, in which the individual is born into an organic relationship with the local landscape, is increasingly a thing of the past. There are many possible reasons for this – the erosion of the Gaelic language, rural emigration, new agricultural technologies, and so on. It could be argued, however, that these are merely symptoms of larger changes overtaking the whole world towards the end of the twentieth century concerning the radical reorganisation of traditional discourses such as work, family, community and, perhaps most significantly, information.

Taken together, however, these two discourses helped to install 'the Land' as one of the great watchwords of political and cultural nationalism. In the predominantly agrarian society of nineteenth-century Ireland, deprivation of the land was understood both as alienation from a peculiarly Irish form of existence and as an assault on the right to a secure livelihood – a neat argument combining practical and elevated discourses. Moreover, obsession with the land (as observed in Chapter 3), persisted into the post-revolutionary era, producing all manner of (not always salutary) effects in the organisation of Irish life.

It is precisely this Irish obsession with the land which Eilís Ní Dhuibhne explores in *The Bray House* from the perspective of late twentieth-century eco-criticism. Ecology has become an issue of increasing importance as the twentieth century has progressed. The basic point is that the political organisation of new technology has failed to take account of the planet's resources and the larger temporalities into which the natural world is locked. And, despite lip-service to the residual national-ist discourse just described and to the new ecological impera-tive, it appears that Ireland is as guilty as other modern nation-states of the sins of omission and commission which constitute the present threat to the welfare of local environ-ments as well as to the planet as a whole.

The Bray House is set in the early twenty-first century. The British Isles have been destroyed by a chain of explosions follow-ing an accident at a nuclear installation at Ballylumford, just inside the border of Northern Ireland. A Swedish archaeological team of four led by the ambitious and arrogant Robin Lagerlof sails to Ireland to conduct scientific research on the remains of the country. Landing in a town just south of Dublin, the team find and excavate 'The Bray House' and a large part of the novel (Chapters 12–15) is taken up with a pseudo-scientific report on the contents of the house and what it reveals about life in Ireland before the Ballylumford disaster.

However, it becomes clear that this supposedly objective report is in fact highly coloured by Robin's personality which, through her attitudes and actions, is revealed to be deeply scarred by her past. It emerges that the Bray House family was in the process of breaking up just before the incident, and this reflects on the stories which emerge during the narrative concerning Robin's trauma at the loss of her own family and the subsequent failure of her own marriage to the Irishman Michael. Her description of the daughter Fiona (who occupies the same position in the Bray House as Robin did in her own family) as 'an undesirable human being' (p. 165) is particularly revealing. In fact, at the same time as it explodes the myth of scientific rationalism, the archaeological venture shows the breakdown of a community through abuse of power and trust, and thus offers an analogy in miniature to the breakdown of life in pre-Ballylumford Ireland.

At the same time, *The Bray House* is a typical dystopian narrative in that although set in the future it is clearly aimed at the present. Performance at individual and national levels is linked to attitudes towards the environment: 'just as they were falling apart at the seams, torn by internal strife and beset by lack of self-knowledge, so, it would seem, was their country, Ireland' (p. 167). The device of the scientific report creates the illusion of perspective from a future in which certain contemporary trends have led to a range of possible outcomes. Although it is itself suspect, Robin's report demands to be read in terms of the present, and its accusatory tone is aimed at the real reader of the 1990s rather than the implied reader of some thirty years hence. Thus, the reader is asked to measure the country described by Robin against his/her own perceptions, asking if it is really the case that modern Ireland is 'a country of poverty, violence and ignorance ... There seems to have been a lack of will to succeed in making Ireland a safe civilised place to live. Or else some strange lack of ability to do so' (p. 167). And the same self-reflection is demanded by the report's final damning indictment of contemporary complacence: 'If Ireland failed to pay adequate attention to the warnings, who is really to blame, in the final analysis, for her demise?' (p. 168).

The Bray House cannot avoid the problems besetting all thesis novels, although it attempts to compensate by making characters and situations as complex as possible. It demands that modern Ireland re-examine its relations with the land, and that such a re-examination should engage both with older nationalist discourses as well as with Ireland's implication in the contemporary ecological crisis. Crucially, it encourages the individual to recognise and address her/his implication in the trends which feed the deteriorating situation.

Sam's Fall (1995) by Richard Kearney

Although religion has figured significantly in many of the novels discussed so far in this book, nowhere has it been invoked as an intellectual system or examined for its impact on individual identity and the wider cultural consciousness of the community. In his debut novel the philosopher and critic Richard Kearney undertakes just such a task.

Like other aspects of Irish life, religion and the organised churches (it is crucial to distinguish) have been undergoing intense changes in recent years. In the period after the revolution the organised churches came to play a crucial role throughout the island – political and economic as well as cultural and moral.[25] However, they have of late come under pressure from a combination of factors, including falling attendances and an alarming decrease in the number of vocations, which seems to betoken a growing scepticism towards the principle of organised religion. Obviously, the case of Northern Ireland is exceptional, but even there religion tends to function less as a belief system than a form of tribal identification; one seldom encounters a Northern Ireland politician, much less a member of the paramilitary organisations, invoking religious discourse to support a particular point. None the less, religious rancour continues to play a significant role in the social and political life of the province, leading some people to argue that a curtailment of that role would increase the chances for a lasting settlement.

There are a number of possible reasons behind the change in the fortunes of religion in the Republic. It is clear that the Catholic Church is finding it difficult to keep pace with the changes occurring in other areas of Irish life, while grass-roots attempts at reform have tended to be curbed by a conservative hierarchy. At the same time, a number of high-profile scandals involving Catholic clergy has led to a widespread revision of the church's role in the national life. Many Irish people feel betrayed by a church (if not by a religion) which, especially in the crucial areas of celibacy and child-care, has found it difficult to adhere to its own teachings. Perhaps most significantly, however, the Catholic Church is being slowly erased from the national life as part of the nation's movement towards a postmodern secular Europeanism. While religion remains an important factor in Irish life, therefore, its rapidly altering role is a cause of anxiety amongst both clergy and believers, and it is difficult to speculate on its fate over the coming years.

Sam's Fall is a novel about religion that also attempts to work on a number of different levels – mystery, myth, allegory, philosophy, theory. The story concerns twins Jack and Sam Toland growing up in Cork in the 1950s and 1960s before going to the Columbanus Abbey School. At the school the twins come under the influence of the abbot Anselm who tells them of the search for the Priscian Grammar,

a perfect liturgy which might reveal the ways of God to man and
reunite the fragmented word of Christ – a quest that had inspired so
much of Western monasticism from the outset ... The common aim
of their penitential was to disclose God's hidden Word, unifying the
split tongues of Babel and repairing the rents in the garment of the
spirit. (p. 89)

Anselm wishes Jack to undertake research on the Priscian Grammar by analysing a medieval text which has been discovered in
the Abbey's sister monastery in Switzerland and which may hold
the key to the lost language of God. The Swiss monastery was
founded by and named after the seventh-century Irish monk
Gallus who travelled in Europe with his more famous colleague
Columbanus before falling out with him for some unknown reason. When Jack refuses, Anselm recruits Sam who accepts the
task as an opportunity to escape his brilliant brother's shadow
under which he has felt himself to be living.

The narrative is organised around two main discourses – a
journal which tells of Sam's spiritual struggles, his desire for
Jack's girlfriend Raphaëlle and his work on the Priscian Grammar, and Jack's reactions to the journal as he reads it after his
brother's unexplained suicide. Sam's written discourse is thus
punctuated by Jack's thoughts, exposing the 'fictionality' of the
fiction and the extent to which religious concerns with language
and truth are themselves mediated by the contingencies of narrative context. The novel is in fact quite obviously informed by the
author's engagement with the theoretical revolution which has
overtaken European intellectual life since the 1960s. Indeed, in
some respects, *Sam's Fall* may be read as nothing less than a
fictional rendering of the philosophy of Jacques Derrida. It is a
book about books, about language, ultimately a book about itself.
The text is dominated by the principle of opposition initiated by
the Fall – the opposition between Sam and Jack, Anselm and
Raphaëlle, Gallus and Columbanus, eye and ear, speech and
silence, body and soul. Most importantly, the text broaches the
paradoxical opposition between perfection and desire – that is,
between the possibility of a perfect pre-lapsarian moment in
which meaning and language are entirely commensurate (the
religious ideal), and the impossibility of that moment, instanti-
ated in the fatal gap between word and meaning, between language as a signifying system and the reality to which it refers.
This latter point is described, and later exemplified, by the monk
Cilian who has presumably picked up his ideas on the nature of

language during his studies in Paris: 'Learning a language ... was an endless hunt for things that didn't exist, an interminable play of signs, each displacing the other in an infinite game of desire. Language was *desire*, not fulfilment of desire' (p. 93). What Sam eventually learns is that desire is the very condition of human existence, and that although opposites in some respects, *desire* also functions as a fundamental condition for the imagination of *perfection* which has underpinned the entire Christian project. These two discourses are brought together in the quest for the Priscian Grammar, the divine Logos which existed before the descent into Babel.

Thus, however far removed from everyday religious life in modern Ireland, Kearney's novel does offer a relevant point – that precisely because of its contradictions, religious discourse retains a recurring attraction for a species which has desire built into its very existence as a result of the fatal gap between reality and the principal means available to engage with reality – that is, verbal language. More pragmatically, *Sam's Fall* insists that the island's religious practices should be seen within the framework of European history, and that the isolationism which character-ised post-revolutionary Ireland was in fact a degeneration from a much fuller national involvement in the intellectual and social life of the continent.

Amongst Women (1990) by John McGahern

It may seem odd that a study of the new generation of Irish novelists should end with a book by one of Ireland's major estab-lished writers. However, in a text dedicated to the analysis of fictional explorations of marginality, but which has itself by and large ignored (hence, marginalised) established writers, it is appropriate that this tradition should be represented. As it hap-pens, John McGahern's exploration of the interplay between dis-courses of gender, family and nation in *Amongst Women* turns out to be as challenging and as engaged as any of the novels of the latest generation. Moreover, it displays a formal sophistication and a narrative control not always apparent amongst the newer Irish novelists for whom it sometimes appears that publishing opportunities have impeded technical development.

Michael Moran is a complex man living in a complex rural society. Having been a successful revolutionary soldier he finds himself at odds with post-colonial Ireland, refusing to take his national pension and increasingly alienated from life outside the confines of his own family. Moran's bitterness and frustration are due in one respect to the fact that he reached the climax of his life at such an early age, and that life in post-colonial Ireland offers few opportunities for growth or self-exploration. The power and respect he commanded in his youth can only be remembered or lost, eroded but never recovered. His life is thus an echo of what it could be, a constant rehearsal rather than an actual performance; throughout the day of his marriage to Rose, for example, Moran 'felt a violent, dissatisfied feeling that his whole life was taking place in front of his eyes without anything at all taking place' (p. 45).

However, Moran's anger at his self-inflicted exclusion from post-revolutionary Ireland feeds into deeper social and psychological losses. Having failed in the public sphere, Moran attempts to dominate the domestic sphere, thus hoping to compensate for his loss of power by installing himself as a patriarch in his own family. The family offers a theatre of operations which he can marshal, but even there he is frustrated by the rebellion of his sons Luke and Michael who refuse to put up with their father's compulsion to dominate. The family is important to Moran not because it is the cornerstone of the community nor for any genuine regard, but because it is vital to his own identity: 'Families were what mattered, more particularly that larger version of himself – his family' (p. 22).

With the loss of his sons and his few male friends Moran is increasingly 'amongst women' – an ironic reference to the line from the 'Hail Mary' ('Blessed art thou amongst women'), the repeated recitation of which constitutes a major part of the Rosary. The Rosary provides the pulse of the narrative, and the effect of its frequent invocation is that the reader learns to expect it as surely as the dwellers of Great Meadow. Moran employs the Rosary as a signal of the power he retains over and through the family. It is only when his failing health prevents him from orchestrating the prayer that it is rejected, as he tells his wife and daughters to 'shut up' (p. 180). This is the very point, however, at which female power is re-instituted, with Rose taking over the role of leading the prayer and thus taking her 'proper' role as ruler of the domestic sphere.

The narrative reveals that the Rosary was always an ambiguous weapon for an Irishman such as Moran in as much as it constitutes a tacit acknowledgement of the power of women and their centrality to patriarchal discourse. By choosing the domestic sphere as his theatre of operations, Moran confirms rather than mitigates his loss of power. This is because he is engaging with a discourse specifically characterised as female in post-revolutionary Ireland, especially after the Constitution of 1937 which included one article stating that 'the State recognises that by her life within the home, woman gives to the State a support without which the common good cannot be achieved'. *Amongst Women* offers an ambiguous image of life in modern Ireland in which traditional gender roles have been reversed. For the women walking from Moran's grave 'it was as if each of them in their different ways had become Daddy' (p. 183); of the husbands and brothers and sons, on the other hand, Sheila says: 'Will you look at the men. They're more like a crowd of women' (p. 184).

There is in fact a formal and thematic economy at work throughout the narrative which weighs a note of elegy for the loss of Irish manhood against a celebration of the re-empowerment of women and the breakdown of artificial gender borders imposed by the post-colonial state. The narrator gives many clues to Moran's personality, as well as offering the occasional bald summary, for example: 'No matter how favourably the tides turned for him he would always contrive to be in permanent opposition' (p. 163). It is not possible, however, to discern or to adopt a final position regarding Moran from these offerings, and the question of the morality of 'permanent opposition' is left to the individual reader and the particular array of resources brought to bear on the text.

What the novel does achieve, however, is an astute portrayal of a post-colonial life in which disappointment and frustration are the typical informing emotions, at the level of both individual and state. Such a portrayal, moreover, operates not just at the level of plot; rather, through such narrative techniques as intra-textual repetition (for example, the coming of the Wren Boys on pp. 35 and 100) and extra-textual allusion (for example, the Yeatsian echoes on pp. 80 and 84), McGahern creates an organic narrative in which meaning is alive, active and reader-generated rather than passive and author-imposed. *Amongst Women* makes deceptively easy reading, but the balance between what the narrator tells the reader and what the reader is enabled to infer from the characters' actions and words, as well as from the overall structure of the narrative, is brilliantly maintained.

CONCLUSION:
THE POLITICS OF CHANGE

In the years leading up to the millennium, and in all sorts of cultural and political contexts, the words 'modern Ireland' and 'change' seem to have become indissolubly linked. The story goes something like this: from being a backward-looking, under-developed island on the periphery of Europe, Ireland since the mid-1980s has been undergoing a process of rapid and thorough change as it renegotiates relationships with the rest of the world and with its own history. Combining traditional strengths in the area of culture and the arts with an aptitude for new technology and new media, a highly educated population of 'young Europeans' has adapted brilliantly to changes overtaking the organisation of life on the entire globe. At the same time, modern Ireland is also experiencing the downside of these changes as traditional systems are swept unsentimentally aside, with agricultural depression, urban decay and continuing high levels of emigration the obvious results.

To a certain extent, this story is animated by a chiliastic impulse widespread throughout European culture, as if it was the imminence of the millennium itself which was precipitating changes in the present. However, a satisfactory account of the particular form that change is taking in modern Ireland and the impact it is having on life in both North and South would be concerned not so much with the future as with a full and proper appreciation of the island's peculiar history. For although enthusiastically European in one regard, modern Ireland is also operating along a recognisably different historical trajectory from that of the established continental nation-states. This is because for a large part of its history the island experienced a form of systematic colonialism similar to that imposed upon what are now known as 'Third World' countries. This split identity – simultaneously European and not European – has left modern Ireland, in the words of one commentator, as an island of 'anomalous states'.[1] This refers not just to the two political administrations sharing the island but to an amorphous and fluctuating array of physical and psychological states prevalent throughout late twentieth-century Irish society, operating at the level of both individual and community.

It is the delineation of these volatile physical and psychological states which has motivated both the new Irish novelists and this work of criticism. By way of conclusion, three such states are worth mentioning which, in best 'novelistic' fashion emerge from, while reflecting back upon, the critical 'story' that has just been told. First of all, there appears to have been something resembling a pan-Celtic Revival in the years leading up to the millennium, the Irish element of which amounts to little less than another Cultural Renaissance. This revival is apparent throughout Irish cultural life: in music, U2, Clannad, Altan, *Riverdance*; in film, the work of Neil Jordan, Jim Sheridan, the Barrytown trilogy adaptations; in poetry and drama, the success of writers like Seamus Heaney and Brian Friel; and, with the continuing influx of famous tax exiles from Europe and the United States, in the general elevation of Dublin to one of the cultural capitals of Europe.

The resurgence of the Irish novel may also be seen as part of this movement. Ireland has been going through a period of extraordinary attraction in the eyes of publishers since the late 1980s, especially London-based publishers. So whereas in 1987 Roddy Doyle ended up having to give away most of the 3,000 self-published copies of *The Commitments* before being offered £1,200 by Heinemann for the book, in 1996 23-year-old Antonia Logue from Derry was offered around £65,000 by Bloomsbury after she had allowed them to see just six pages of her first novel. As one of these publishers says: 'Irish writing is *the* hot topic. Any country developing culturally as rapidly as Ireland is bound to produce interesting writing.'[2] But interesting to whom, one might be inclined to ask, and for what reasons?

Whether the resurgence of the Irish novel constitutes a grass-roots revival or the work of a coterie of publishers with an eye for the main chance will be the concern of future literary historians. But it may be that 'The New Irish Fiction' is little more than an invention by a loose affiliation of London publishers, creating a critical category (and a market) where before there was only a set of vague impressions. If this is the case, then once again it is possible to see how modern Ireland is still engaging with a metropolitan agenda which is concerned with the kind of culture 'post-colonial' nations *should* be producing. The continuing insecurity and psychological dependence of 'post-colonial' Ireland is apparent also in the fact that despite a relatively healthy domestic publishing industry, Irish writers still appear to defer to London as the measure of critical and popular success. As one critic has said:

> Look at the number of Irish writers who are published abroad; they will say it's about the money. It isn't only about the money, because Irish publishers on the whole pay well; it's also about acclaim, it's about the sense of reaching a vaster audience, it's about the niggardliness and the begrudgery within Ireland, where what we produce is culturally still seen as being somehow a second level production.[3]

Paradoxically, the new Irish novelists have become so successful in London that they are in danger of returning to a cultural insularity similar to that from which they are supposedly leading the escape. So assured has the new generation become of the inherent interest of novelistic representations of Ireland and Irishness that there appears to be little impetus to look beyond the Irish experience at what is happening in other cultures. It might be said, in fact, that modern Ireland is most representatively post-colonial in its unwillingness to place its own history in some kind of comparative context, and that the self-obsession which characterises the new Irish fiction is an indication of the way in which colonialism continues to limit the possibilities of Irish identity decades after the onset of the 'post-colonial' era.

This leads on to another of the 'states' currently animating Irish culture – the question of the role of the artist in society. Through censorship and the narrowness of the socio-cultural base in the post-revolutionary period, many early and mid-twentieth-century writers were forced to adopt positions outside the mainstream of society, criticising the kind of Ireland that had emerged (albeit in the name of the better Ireland it could become). In time, this necessity was converted into a mystique: art could be defined and judged precisely by its distance from merely social concerns. However, the idea of the artist as renegade and outsider, as the sole bastion of freedom in the carceral society is too easily absorbed back into such a society. Against the belief that Irish society has ever in any way been touched by the extreme individualism of the writer, Thomas

Kilroy wrote in 1980:

> Quite the contrary, such individualism, however outrageous, is curiously consoling to the society of liberal aspirations. It is only when the writer assumes a common place in the world about him that that kind of encounter takes place and literature enters into the dynamics of the social process.[4]

It seems clear that the 'Robinsonian' novelist is a much more engaged figure compared with the traditional image of the aloof, alienated Irish artist. With the expansion of Irish society and the willingness to review national performance, the stories that modern Irish novelists tell are geared more towards intervention than reflection, simultaneously allowing silenced voices to speak and questioning the voices which have dominated society since the revolution. Less of an intellectual and more of an artisan, the new Irish novelist is concerned to narrate the nation as it has been and as it is, rather than how it should be or might have been. But if it was a mistake for earlier writers to opt out of society, it may also be a mistake for the current generation to place so much emphasis on intervention. The confessional and anthropological ethos animating many of the texts examined in Part 2 of this book seems undeniable, and one consequence of the development of the novel as social document has been a concomitant loss of focus on technique. It is not yet clear what this might mean for the ways in which novels function and circulate in Irish society. Perhaps we are witnessing a major transmogrification of the form itself, necessitating, in time, fundamental changes to the critical, aesthetic and sociological discourses which have attended the novel.

It would be unwise, moreover, to underestimate the ease with which mainstream society can accommodate critique, howsoever formulated or directed. Writers continue to enjoy special tax concessions in the Republic and while this is certainly welcome (especially when one considers the fate of artists in many other post-colonial countries) official state patronage does rather take the sting out of artistic critique. Indeed, it is alarming how quickly mainstream society jumped onto the bandwagon of 'change' which began to roll through Irish life in the latter part of the 1980s. Change is a threat to the modern state precisely because of its unpredictability, because it is capable of improvising social and cultural discourses which evade the state's ability to control. However, when change becomes narrativised, as in the novel, then this radical potential disappears because the principle of narrativity is precisely what allows the modern state to reproduce itself. It may be, therefore, that every novel delineating the changes overtaking the modern Irish imagination is also part of the process whereby the idea of change is contained.

Perhaps the major effect following on from rapid social and cultural change, however, is the loss of an accepted regime of critical and/or aesthetic value. As the new fiction has taken upon itself the task of thoroughly deconstructing received accounts of political authority, historical authenticity and social accountability, so there has been a similar assault upon traditional literary critical discourses. But while traditional modes and models are becoming less acceptable, nothing has yet been successfully formulated to take its place. In 1991 *The Field Day Anthology of Irish Writing* was published, a massive three-volumed collection which offered itself as a canon of sorts. Here was a body of Irish work in terms of which modern writing might contextualise itself and from which later generations could gain confidence. It was produced, however, at precisely the time when the definitions of 'Irish', 'Writing' and especially 'Irish Writing' were changing most rapidly. Novelists working in a society characterised by instability and incoherence found little purchase in a text which for all its gestures towards difference actually appeared to offer a highly coherent, evolutionary model of Irish writing. While most modern writers would respect the integrity of the project, few, I suggest, could identify with its ethos.

Robinsonian novelists are in fact producing for the most part in a critical vacuum, unsure of every aspect of the writing process – their own role as authors, both the value and the form of the texts they are producing, and the readers at whom their texts are aimed. Critics, whose traditional task it has been to identify particular literary trends and to evaluate texts according to a wide range of socio-aesthetic theories, are just as perplexed as to how to bring text and context together in any kind of meaningful analysis. Such cultural embarrassment reflects the uncertainty obtaining throughout the island at a social and political level as the millennium approaches. But precisely what this might mean for modern Ireland is itself uncertain as novelist and critic, politician and public, find themselves speculating with tools and from within systems that are themselves undergoing rapid change.

It is not clear, however, that uncertainty is necessarily a bad thing. Just as the island was one of the first colonies in the modern sense, so we may be witnessing in modern Ireland the conditions for the emergence of the world's first truly post-colonial state. Asked to define such a state I would say that it would be one in which discourses of change and discourses of continuity have entered into symbiotic relationship, and one which accepts uncertainty as an empowering and creative condition. In modern Ireland, some practices are obviously still evolving from earlier points in the island's history, while others represent entirely new departures. This book has attempted to trace the uncertainty attending the interaction between these two processes as mediated by that most uncertain of cultural forms, the novel.

NOTES

INTRODUCTION

1. Although social and political background is of crucial importance to this book, there is no space for an elaboration of the finer points of modern Irish history. Specific points and trends will emerge throughout, but readers not possessing a basic grasp of the relevant contexts should consult the Bibliography.

2. See for example the chapter entitled 'The Pitfalls of National Consciousness' in Frantz Fanon, *The Wretched of the Earth* (London: Penguin, 1967), pp.119–65; Ashis Nandy, *The Intimate Enemy: Loss and Recovery of Self Under Colonialism* (Delhi: Oxford University Press, 1983); and Edward Said, *Culture and Imperialism* (London: Chatto & Windus, 1993), pp. 316–40.

3. Extracts from 'The Inaugural Speech' in K. Donovan, A.N. Jeffares and B. Kennelly (eds) *Ireland's Women: Writings Past and Present* (London: Kyle Cathie Limited, 1994), pp. 253–4. Further page references will be cited parenthetically.

4. Carol Coulter, *The Hidden Tradition: Feminism, Women and Nationalism in Ireland* (Cork: Cork University Press, 1993), p. 1.

5. Richard Kearney, 'Letters on a New Republic – Three Open Letters to Three Presidents' in D. Bolger (ed.) *Letters from the New Island* (Dublin: Raven Arts Press, 1992), p. 309.

6. Mikhail Bakhtin, *The Dialogic Imagination*, ed. M. Holquist, trs. C. Emerson and M. Holquist (Austin: University of Texas Press, 1981), p. 7.

7. Kevin Barry, 'Lullabies for Insomniacs: The Writer and Contemporary Irish Society', *Irish Review*, No. 2 (1987), p. 8.

8. Joseph O'Connor, *Cowboys and Indians* (London: Flamingo, 1992), p. 137.

CHAPTER 1

1. J.G. Herder *Outlines of a Philosophy of the History of Man,* trs. T. Churchill (London: Johnson, 1800), p. 166.
2. For a good explication of the revisionist position see Edna Longley, 'Introduction: Revising Irish Literature', *The Living Stream: Literature and Revisionism in Ireland* (Newcastle upon Tyne: Bloodaxe Books, 1994), pp. 9–68. On the irony of revisionism's antipathy to postmodernism see Luke Gibbons, 'Challenging the Canon: Revisionism and Cultural Criticism' in S. Deane (Gen. Ed.) *The Field Day Anthology of Irish Writing* (Derry and London: Field Day Publications and Faber, 1991), pp. 561–8.
3. Richard Kearney, 'Postmodernity and Nationalism: A European Perspective', *Modern Fiction Studies*, Vol. 38, No. 3 (Autumn 1992), p. 586.
4. On the wider implications of cultural nationalism's dual orientation see the chapter 'Adulteration and the Nation', in David Lloyd, *Anomalous States: Irish Writing and the Post-Colonial Moment* (Dublin: Lilliput, 1993), pp. 88–124. For the effect on the nineteenth-century Anglo-Irish novel see the chapter 'Form and Ideology in the Anglo-Irish Novel' in Terry Eagleton, *Heathcliff and the Great Hunger: Studies in Irish Culture* (London: Verso, 1995), pp. 145–225.
5. Both quotes from 'Novelists on the Novel – An Interview with Francis Stuart and John Banville by Ronan Sheehan' in M.P. Hederman and R. Kearney (eds) *The Crane Bag Book of Irish Studies* (Dublin: Blackwater, 1981), pp. 408 and 412.
6. On the application to Irish culture of Lionel Trilling's distinction between 'sincerity' and 'authenticity' see Declan Kiberd, *Inventing Ireland* (London: Jonathan Cape, 1995), p. 298.
7. Joseph O'Connor, *The Secret World of the Irish Male* (London: Minerva, 1995), pp. 134 and 136.
8. Fintan O'Toole, 'Introduction: On the Frontier' in D. Bolger, *A Dublin Quartet* (London: Penguin, 1992), p. 1.
9. There is a large body of material on the emergence of the novel, but see especially Nancy Armstrong, *Desire and Domestic Fiction: A Political History of the Novel* (Oxford: Oxford University Press, 1987); Lucien Goldmann, *Towards a Sociology of the Novel*, trs. A. Sheridan (London: Tavistock, 1975); Georg Lukács, *The Theory of the Novel: A His-*

torico-Philosophical Essay on the Forms of the Great Epic Literature, trs. A. Bostock (London: Merlin, 1971); Diana Spearman, *The Novel and Society* (London: Routledge & Kegan Paul, 1966); Dale Spender, *Mothers of the Novel: One Hundred Good Women Writers Before Jane Austen* (London: Pandora, 1986); Ian Watt, *The Rise of the Novel: Studies in Defoe, Richardson and Fielding* (London: Peregrine, 1977).

10. Benedict Anderson, *Imagined Communities: Reflections on the Origins and Spread of Nationalism* (London: Verso, 1983). Further page references will be cited parenthetically.

11. Fredric Jameson *The Political Unconscious: Narrative as a Socially Symbolic Act* (London: Methuen, 1981), p. 141. Further page references will be cited parenthetically.

12. Fredric Jameson, 'Third-World Literature in the Era of Multinational Capitalism', *Social Text*, No. 15 (Fall 1986), p. 69.

13. Jean Franco, 'The Nation as Imagined Community' in H.A. Veeser (ed.) *The New Historicism* (London: Routledge, 1989), p. 205.

14. This is the key thesis of one of the founding texts of modern post-colonial studies, Edward Said's *Orientalism* (London: Peregrine, 1985). See also his *Culture and Imperialism* (London: Chatto & Windus, 1993), a book which, as its title suggests, extends and refines this thesis.

15. On this point see Homi Bhabha, 'Representation and the Colonial Text: A Critical Exploration of Some Forms of Mimeticism' in F. Gloversmith (ed.) *The Theory of Reading* (Sussex: Harvester, 1984).

16. Chinua Achebe, 'The Novelist as Teacher', *Morning Yet On Creation Day* (New York: Anchor Press/Doubleday, 1975), pp. 167–74.

17. On the function of realism in the Irish novelistic tradition see Eagleton, *Heathcliff and the Great Hunger* in which he claims that for such a tradition 'realism, as the fruit of a developed European civilisation, had never been less than profoundly problematic' (p. 225).

18. Helen Tiffin, quoting Wilson Harris, in her essay 'Post-Colonial Literatures and Counter-Discourse' in B. Ashcroft, G. Griffiths and H. Tiffin (eds) *The Post-Colonial Studies Reader* (London: Routledge, 1995), p. 96.

19. On the use of hybridity and related strategies of colonial resistance see the chapters 'Of Mimicry and Men: The Ambivalence of Colonial Discourse' (pp. 85–92), and 'Signs

Taken for Wonders: Questions of Ambivalence and Authority Under a Tree Outside Delhi, May 1817' (pp. 102–22) in
Homi Bhabha, *The Location of Culture* (London: Routledge,
1994). On the history of hybridity as a concept and its function in colonial relations see Robert Young, *Colonial Desire:
Hybridity in Theory, Culture and Race* (London: Routledge,
1995).

20. Such would be the argument of critics such as Arif Dirlik
in 'The Postcolonial Aura: Third World Criticism in the
Age of Global Capitalism', *Critical Inquiry*, No. 20 (Winter
1994), pp. 328–56, and Anne McClintock in 'The Angel of
Progress: Pitfalls of the Term "Post-colonialism"' in P.
Williams and L. Chrisman (eds) *Colonial Discourse and Post-
Colonial Theory: A Reader* (Hemel Hempstead: Harvester/
Wheatsheaf, 1993), pp. 291–304. For the Irish context to
these debates see David Lloyd, *Nationalism and Minor
Literature: James Clarence Mangan and the Emergence of Irish
Cultural Nationalism* (Berkeley: University of California
Press, 1987).

21. This section draws on the essays collected in Mikhail
Bakhtin, *The Dialogic Imagination: Four Essays by M.M.
Bakhtin*, ed. M. Holquist, trs. C. Emerson and M. Holquist
(Austin: University of Texas Press, 1981).

22. On the search for an Irish epic during the nineteenth century see Lloyd, 'Adulteration and the Nation' in *Anomalous
States*.

23. Seamus Heaney, 'The Sense of Place' in *Preoccupations:
Selected Prose 1968–1978* (London: Faber, 1980), p. 132.

24. Bakhtin, *The Dialogic Imagination*, p. 53. Bakhtin's stress on
mimicry and comedy in the essays in this collection also
provides a point of contact with the strategies outlined by
Bhabha in the essays cited above.

25. Lloyd, *Anomalous States*, p. 155.

CHAPTER 2

1. Seamus Deane, *A Short History of Irish Literature* (London:
Hutchinson, 1986), p. 112.

2. Seamus Deane, 'Heroic Styles: The Tradition of an Idea' in
Field Day Theatre Company, *Ireland's Field Day* (London:
Hutchinson, 1985), p. 58.

3. This is the point of departure for *Inventing Ireland* (London:

Jonathan Cape, 1995), Declan Kiberd's massive study of Irish writing in the twentieth century.

CHAPTER 3

1. See the chapter 'Colonial War and Mental Disorders' in Frantz Fanon, *The Wretched of the Earth* (Harmondsworth, Middlesex: Penguin 1969), pp. 200–50.
2. Ashis Nandy, *The Intimate Enemy: Loss and Recovery of Self under Colonialism* (Delhi: Oxford University Press 1983). Further page references will be cited parenthetically.
3. Augustine Martin, *The Genius of Irish Prose* (Cork: Mercier, 1985), p. 112.
4. Vivian Mercier, *The Irish Comic Tradition* (Oxford: Clarendon, 1962).
5. In *Journey Through the Labyrinth: Latin American Fiction in the Twentieth Century* (London: Verso, 1989) Gerald Martin notes the influence of Joyce's later work on magic realism, but not the extent to which Joyce's work drew on ancient Gaelic narrative techniques for his subversive, multi-voiced texts.
6. Richard Haslam, 'Maturin and the Calvinist Sublime' in A. Lloyd Smith and V. Sage (eds) *Gothick Origins and Innovations* (Amsterdam and Atlanta, Ga.: Editions Rodopi, 1994), pp. 44–56.
7. Homi Bhabha, *The Location of Culture* (London: Routledge, 1994), pp. 9–10. Further page references will be cited parenthetically.
8. Siobhán Kilfeather, 'Origins of the Irish Female Gothic', *Bullán: An Irish Studies Journal*, Vol. 1, No. 2 (Autumn 1994), p. 46.
9. Shoshana Felman, *Writing and Madness: Literature, Philosophy, Psychoanalysis*, trs. S. Evans and S. Felman (Ithaca, New York: Cornell University Press, 1985), *passim*. Further page references will be cited parenthetically.
10. On these matters see Julia Kristeva, *Desire in Language: A Semiotic Approach to Literature and Art*, ed. L.S. Roudiez, trs. T. Gora, A. Jardine and L.S. Roudiez (Oxford: Basil Blackwell, 1981).
11. John Banville, *Birchwood* [1973] (London: Minerva, 1992), p. 174.
12. C.L. Innes, *Woman and Nation in Irish Literature and Society, 1880–1935* (Athens, Ga.: University of Georgia Press, 1993), p. 10.

13. Ernest Renan, from *The Poetry of the Celtic Races* [1859], quoted in M. Storey (ed.) *Poetry and Ireland Since 1800: A Source Book* (London: Routledge, 1988), p. 58.

14. Matthew Arnold, *On The Study of Celtic Literature* (London: Smith, Elder & Co., 1900), p. 90.

15. *Bunreacht na hÉireann* (*Constitution of Ireland*) (Dublin: Stationery Office, 1937), p. 138.

16. On the diversity of Irishwomen's relations with nationalism see Margaret Ward (ed.) *In Their Own Voice: Women and Irish Nationalism* (Dublin: Attic, 1996). For a modern theoretical analysis of these issues see R. Radhakrishnan, 'Nationalism, Gender and the Narrative of Identity' in A. Parker et al. (eds), *Nationalism and Sexualities* (London: Routledge, 1992), pp. 77–95.

17. Leo Flynn, 'The Missing Body of Mary McGhee: The Constitution of Woman in Irish Constitutional Adjudication', *Journal of Gender Studies*, Vol. 2, No. 2 (November 1993), pp. 238–52.

18. Declan Kiberd, *Inventing Ireland* (London: Jonathan Cape, 1995), p. 570. Further page references will be cited parenthetically.

19. David Lloyd, 'Adulteration and the Nation', *Anomalous States: Irish Writing and the Post-Colonial Moment* (Dublin: Lilliput, 1993), p. 105.

20. Raymond Williams, *The Country and the City* (St Albans, Herts: Paladin, 1975).

21. Fintan O'Toole, 'Going West: The City Versus the Country in Irish Writing', *The Crane Bag*, Vol. 9, No. 2 (1985), p. 113. Further page references will be cited parenthetically.

22. For two classic novelistic representations of the banality of Irish rural life see *The Valley of the Squinting Windows* [1918] (Dublin: Anvil Books, 1991) by Brinsley MacNamara, and *Tarry Flynn* (London: Pilot Press, 1948) by Patrick Kavanagh.

23. Luke Gibbons, *Transformations in Irish Culture* (Cork: Cork University Press, 1996), p. 169.

24. On the role of the city in the development of modern literature see the chapter 'Petersburg: The Modernism of Underdevelopment' in Marshall Berman, *All That Is Solid Melts Into Air: The Experience of Modernity* (London: Verso, 1983), pp. 173–286.

25. Shaun Richards, 'Northside Realism and the Twilight's Last

Gleaming' *Irish Studies Review*, No. 2 (Winter 1992), pp. 18–20.

CHAPTER 4

1. Shaun Richards, 'Northside Realism and the Twilight's Last Gleaming', *Irish Studies Review*, No. 2 (Winter 1992), p. 20.
2. Joseph O'Connor, 'Barrytown International: The World of Roddy Doyle', *The Secret World of the Irish Male* (London: Minerva, 1995), p. 139.
3. Roddy Doyle, *The Barrytown Trilogy* (London: Minerva, 1992), pp. 122–3. Further page references to this and to novels referenced throughout the remainder of this book will be cited parenthetically.
4. Ferdia MacAnna, 'The Dublin Renaissance: An Essay on Modern Dublin and Dublin Writers', *Irish Review*, No. 10 (Spring 1991), p. 28.
5. 'Introduction' in Dermot Bolger (ed.) *Letters from the New Island* (Dublin: Raven Arts Press, 1991), p. 12.
6. Declan Kiberd, *Inventing Ireland* (London: Jonathan Cape, 1995), p. 609.
7. Katie Donovan, 'Irish Women Writers: Marginalised by Whom?' in D. Bolger (ed.) *Letters from the New Island*, pp. 105–6.

CHAPTER 5

1. Joe Cleary, '"Fork-Tongued on the Border Bit": Partition and the Politics of Form in Contemporary Narratives of the Northern Irish Conflict', *South Atlantic Quarterly*, Vol. 95, No.1 (Winter 1996), p. 236. Further page references will be cited parenthetically.
2. Niall McGrath, 'Interview with Glenn Patterson', *Edinburgh Review*, No. 93 (Spring 1995), p. 50.
3. See for example Gerald Seymour, *Harry's Game* (London: Fontana, 1977) and Tom Clancy, *Patriot Games* (London: HarperCollins, 1987); Neil Jordan's movie *The Crying Game* (1992) samples these 'boys' games' for ironic effect. On the modern 'Troubles Thriller' see Bill Rolston, 'Mothers, Whores and Villains: Images of Women in Novels of the

Northern Ireland Conflict', *Race and Class*, Vol. 31, No. 1 (1989), pp. 41–57.

4. Eve Patten, 'Fiction in Conflict: Northern Ireland's Prodigal Novelists' in I.A. Bell (ed.) *Peripheral Visions: Images of Nationhood in Contemporary British Fiction* (Cardiff: University of Wales Press, 1995) p. 30. Further page references will be cited parenthetically.

5. See, however, Edna Longley, 'The Writer and Belfast', in Maurice Harmon (ed.) *The Irish Writer and the City* (Gerrards Cross, Bucks: Colin Smythe, 1984) on novelistic engagements with the city of Belfast and its history: 'the fact that Birmingham, McLaverty, Bell and Moore have all written historically suggests a search for what went wrong in the evolution of the city, or for the missed moment – 1798, 1921, 1941' (p. 79).

6. Edna Longley, *The Living Stream: Literature and Revisionism in Ireland* (Newcastle upon Tyne: Bloodaxe Books, 1994), p. 188.

CHAPTER 6

1. The major source for modern cultural theory's infatuation with the border is the work of the French philosopher Jacques Derrida, especially his book *Of Grammatology*, trs. G.C. Spivak (Baltimore: Johns Hopkins University Press, 1976).

2. Homi Bhabha, *The Location of Culture* (London: Routledge, 1994) pp. 1–2. Further page references will be cited parenthetically.

3. Terry Eagleton, *Heathcliff and the Great Hunger: Studies in Irish Culture* (London: Verso, 1995), p. 170.

4. Harold Bloom, *The Western Canon: The Books and School of the Ages* (New York: Harcourt Brace, 1994), p. 62.

5. Samuel Beckett et al., *Our Exagmination Round His Factification For Incamination Of Work In Progress* (London: Faber, 1961), p. 14, original emphasis.

6. See Jim MacLaughlin, 'Outwardly Mobile: The Sanitising of Emigration', *Irish Reporter: Ireland – The Global Nation?*, No. 13 (1994), pp. 9–11.

7. David Lloyd, 'Making Sense of the Dispersal', *Irish Reporter: Ireland – The Global Nation?*, No. 13 (1994), p. 4.

8. Vivian Mercier, 'European-Irish Literary Connections in the

Twentieth Century', *Modern Irish Literature: Sources and Founders* (Oxford: Clarendon, 1994), pp. 327–44.

9. Joseph O'Connor, 'Introduction' in D. Bolger (ed.) *Ireland in Exile: Irish Writers Abroad* (Dublin: Raven Arts Press, 1993), pp. 13–14.

10. Edward Said, *Culture and Imperialism* (London: Chatto & Windus, 1993), p. 407.

11. Eamonn Hughes, '"Lancelot's Position": The Fiction of Irish-Britain', in A. Robert Lee (ed.) *Other Britain, Other British: Contemporary Multicultural Fiction* (London: Pluto Press, 1995), p. 146.

12. Seamus Deane, *A Short History of Irish Literature* (London: Hutchinson, 1986), p. 174.

13. See David Lodge, *The Modes of Modern Writing: Metaphor, Metonymy and the Typology of Modern Literature* (London: Edward Arnold, 1977).

14. For some examples of the use of painterly motifs and themes in modern Irish fiction see Jennifer Johnston, *The Railway Station Man* (Harmondsworth, Middlesex: Penguin, 1984); Deirdre Madden, *Nothing is Black* (London: Faber, 1994), John Banville, *Athena* (London: Secker & Warburg, 1995); Colm Tóibín, *The South* (London: Picador, 1990). On the use of colour as an alternative signifying system see the essay 'A New Type of Intellectual: The Dissident' in T. Moi (ed.) *The Kristeva Reader* (Oxford: Basil Blackwell, 1986).

15. Cherry Smyth, 'Keeping it Close: Experiencing Emigration in Britain' in Í. O'Carroll and E. Collins (eds) *Lesbian and Gay Visions of Ireland: Towards the Twenty-First Century* (London: Cassell, 1995), p. 232.

16. The term *straightgeist* was employed by Alan Sinfield in his lecture, 'Subculture and Dissidence: Stating the Queer/ Queering the State' delivered at the 'Citizenship and Cultural Frontiers Conference', Staffordshire University, 14–17 September 1994.

17. Hence the title of a book looking to raise the profile of homosexuality in Ireland – Carole Wardlaw, *One in Every Family: Dispelling the Myths about Lesbian and Gay Men* (Dublin: Basement, 1996).

18. Eibhear Walshe, 'Oscar's Mirror' in O'Carroll and Collins (eds) *Lesbian and Gay Visions of Ireland*, p. 149.

19. Declan Kiberd, *Inventing Ireland* (London: Jonathan Cape, 1995), p. 494.

20. Said, *Culture and Imperialism*, p. 407.

21. Joan McCarthy, 'Identity, Existence and Passionate Politics' in O'Carroll and Collins (eds), *Lesbian and Gay Visions of Ireland*, p. 105.
22. Andrew Milner, *Literature, Culture and Society* (London: University College London Press, 1996), p. 186.
23. Emma Donoghue, 'Noises from Woodsheds: Tales of Irish Lesbians, 1886–1989' in O'Carroll and Collins (eds), *Lesbian and Gay Visions of Ireland*, p. 160.
24. Raymond Williams, *Marxism and Literature* (Oxford: Oxford University Press, 1977), pp. 121–7.
25. See Dermot Keogh, *Ireland and the Vatican: The Politics and Diplomacy of Church–State Relations, 1922–1960* (Cork: Cork University Press, 1995).

CONCLUSION

1. David Lloyd, *Anomalous States: Irish Writing and the Post-Colonial Moment* (Dublin: Lilliput, 1993).
2. The quote is from Alison Walsh, an Irish publisher working for the London firm Phoenix (itself a division of the multi-national Orion publishing group) and is reproduced in Katie Donovan, 'Novel Sums: Big Advances for Young Sensations', *Irish Times: Weekend* (16 November 1996), p. 1.
3. Ailbhe Smyth, quoted in Mary O'Connor, 'The Thieves of Language in Gaol?', *Krino*, No. 15 (Spring 1994), p. 38.
4. Thomas Kilroy, 'The Irish Writer: Self and Society, 1950–80' in p. Connolly (ed.) *Literature and the Changing Ireland* (Gerrards Cross, Bucks: Colin Smythe, 1982), p. 186.

BIBLIOGRAPHY

Place of publication is London unless otherwise stated. Original publication date is given in square brackets if different from copy cited.

Selected bibliography of modern Irish novels plus: (i) significant earlier titles; (ii) titles mentioned in this book; (iii) full career citations as far as possible for novelists discussed in Part 2.

Patricia Aakhus McDowell *The Voyage of Mael Duin* (Dublin: Wolfhound, 1991)
Laura Anderson *Cuckoo* (Bodley Head, 1986)

John Banville *Birchwood* [1973] (Minerva, 1992), *Ghosts* [1993] (Minerva, 1994), *Athena* [1995] (Minerva, 1996), *The Untouchable* (Picador, 1997)
Vincent Banville *Death the Pale Rider* (Dublin: Poolbeg, 1995)
Leland Bardwell *There We Have Been* (Dublin: Attic, 1989)
Sheila Barrett *A View to Die For* (Dublin: Poolbeg, 1997)
Colin Bateman *Divorcing Jack* (HarperCollins, 1995), *Cycle of Violence* (HarperCollins, 1995), *Of Wee Sweetie Mice and Men* (HarperCollins, 1996)
Mary Beckett *A Belfast Woman* (Swords, Dublin: Poolbeg, 1980), *Give Them Stones* (Bloomsbury, 1987),
Brendan Behan *Borstal Boy* (Hutchinson,1958)
Ronan Bennett *The Second Prison* (Hamish Hamilton, 1991)
George Birmingham *The Red Hand of Ulster* (Smith, Elder & Co., 1912)
Dan Binchy *Fireballs* (Century, 1993)
Maeve Binchy *Evening Class* (Orion, 1996)
Sean Martin Blain *The Chameleon* (Signet, 1996)
Dermot Bolger *Night Shift* [1985] (Penguin, 1993), *The Woman's Daughter* [1987] (Penguin, 1992), *The Journey Home* [1990] (Penguin, 1991), *Emily's Shoes* [1992] (Penguin, 1993), *A Second Life* [1994] (Penguin, 1995), *Father's Music* (Flamingo, 1997)

Elizabeth Bowen *The Last September* [1929] (Harmondsworth, Middlesex: Penguin, 1983)

Clare Boylan *Home Rule* (Penguin, 1992)

Una Brady *Love in Grafton Street* (Dublin: Brookside, 1995)

Catherine Brophy *Dark Paradise* (Dublin: Wolfhound, 1991)

Christy Brown *Down All The Days* [1970] (Pan, 1972)

Declan Burke-Kennedy *Leonie* (Dublin: Poolbeg, 1995)

Mary Rose Callaghan *The Awkward Girl* (Dublin: Attic, 1990)

William Carleton *Traits and Stories of the Irish Peasantry* [1831] (George Routledge and Sons Ltd, no date)

Paul Carson *Scalpel* (Dublin: Poolbeg, 1996)

Philip Casey *The Fabulists* (Serif, 1994)

Tom Clancy *Patriot Games* (HarperCollins, 1987)

A.P. Clarke *The Way of the Bees* (Dublin: Basement, 1996)

Tom Coffey *Don't Get Mad, Get Even* (Dublin: Marino, 1996)

Evelyn Conlon *Stars in the Daytime* (Dublin: Attic, 1989)

Shane Connaughton *The Run of the Country* [1991] (Penguin, 1992)

Emma Cooke *Wedlocked* (Dublin: Poolbeg, 1994)

Mary Costello *Titanic Town* (Mandarin, 1992)

Linda Cullen *The Kiss* (Dublin: Basement, 1990)

Peter Cunningham *Tapes of the River Delta* (Arrow, 1996)

Michael Curtin *The Plastic Tomato Cutter* (Fourth Estate, 1991)

Ita Daly *All Fall Down* (Bloomsbury, 1992)

Caroline D'Arcy *Passion Flowers* (Dublin: Marino, 1996)

John F. Deane *Flightlines* (Dublin: Poolbeg, 1995)

Seamus Deane *Reading in the Dark* (Jonathan Cape, 1996)

Frank Delaney *A Stranger in their Midst* (HarperCollins, 1996)

Martin Dillon *The Serpent's Tail* [1995] (Fourth Estate, 1996)

Emma Donoghue *Stir-fry* [1994] (Penguin, 1995), *Hood* [1995] (Penguin, 1996)

Mary Dorcey *The River that Carries Me* (Galway: Salmon Publishing, 1995)

Roddy Doyle *The Commitments* [1987], *The Snapper* [1990], *The Van* [1991], published as *The Barrytown Trilogy* (Secker & Warburg, 1992), *Paddy Clarke Ha Ha Ha* (Secker & Warburg, 1993), *The Woman Who Walked Into Doors* (Jonathan Cape, 1996)

Catherine Dunne *In the Beginning* (Jonathan Cape, 1997)

John Dunne *Purtock* (Dublin: Anna Livia, 1992)

Seamus Dunne *The Gardener* (Dublin: Wolfhound, 1993)

Christine Dwyer Hickey *The Gambler* (Dublin: Marino, 1996)

Maria Edgeworth *Castle Rackrent* [1800] and *The Absentee* [1812]
    (Ware, Herts: Wordsworth Classics, 1994)
Anne Enright *The Wig My Father Wore* [1995] (Minerva, 1996)
Martina Evans *The Glass Mountain* (Sinclair-Stevenson, 1997)

Kathleen Ferguson *The Maid's Tale* [1994] (Dublin: Poolbeg, 1995)
Katie Flynn *From Clare to Here* (Heinemann, 1997)

Carlo Gébler *Life of a Drum* (Hamish Hamilton, 1991)
Máire Geoghegan-Quinn *The Green Diamond* (Dublin: Marino,
    1996)

Hugo Hamilton *Headbanger* (Secker & Warburg, 1997)
Lara Harte *First Time* (Phoenix, 1995)
Anne Haverty *One Day as a Tiger* (Chatto & Windus, 1997)
Katy Hayes *Curtains* (Phoenix, 1997)
Dermot Healy *A Goat's Song* [1994] (Flamingo, 1995)
Aidan Higgins *Bornholm Night-ferry* (Allison & Busby, 1983)
Niki Hill *Death Grows On You* (Michael Joseph, 1990)
Desmond Hogan *A Farewell to Prague* (Faber, 1995)

Heather Ingman *Sara* (Dublin: Poolbeg, 1994)

Jennifer Johnston *The Railway Station Man* (Penguin, 1984)
Neil Jordan *Sunrise with Sea Monster* (Vintage, 1995)
James Joyce *A Portrait of the Artist as a Young Man* [1916] (St
    Albans, Herts: Triad/Panther, 1977), *Ulysses* [1922] (Oxford:
    Oxford University Press, 1993)

Patrick Kavanagh *The Green Fool* (Michael Joseph, 1938), *Tarry
    Flynn* (Pilot Press, 1948)
John B. Keane *The Bodhrán Makers* (Dingle: Brandon, 1986)
Molly Keane *Good Behaviour* (André Deutsch, 1981)
Colbert Kearney *The Consequence* (Belfast: Blackstaff, 1993)
Richard Kearney *Sam's Fall* [1995] (Sceptre, 1996)
Maeve Kelly *Florrie's Girls* (Michael Joseph, 1989)
Marian Keyes *Lucy Sullivan is Getting Married* (Dublin: Poolbeg,
    1996)
Benedict Kiely *Proxopera* (Gollancz, 1977)
Kevin Kiely *Mere Mortals* (Swords, Dublin: Poolbeg Press and
    Odell and Adair, 1989)

Mary Lavin *Mary O'Grady* (Michael Joseph, 1950)

Emily Lawless *Hurrish: A Study* [1886] (Belfast: Appletree, 1992)

Joseph Sheridan Le Fanu *Uncle Silas* [1864] (Oxford: Oxford University Press, 1981)

Maurice Leitch *Gilchrist* (Secker & Warburg, 1994)

Mary Leland *The Killeen* (New York: Atheneum, 1986)

Tom Lennon *When Love Comes to Town* (Dublin: O'Brien, 1993)

Fergus Linehan *Under the Durian Tree* (Macmillan, 1995)

Mike Lunnon-Wood *Dark Rose* (HarperCollins, 1996)

Liam Lynch *The Pale Moon of Morning* (Dublin: Wolfhound, 1991)

Ferdia MacAnna *The Ship Inspector* [1994] (Penguin, 1995)

Brinsley MacNamara *The Valley of the Squinting Windows* [1918] (Dublin: Anvil Books, 1991)

Sam McAughtry *Touch and Go* (Belfast: Blackstaff, 1993)

Eugene McCabe *Death and Nightingales* [1992] (Minerva, 1993)

Patrick McCabe *Carn* [1989] (Picador, 1993), *The Butcher Boy* [1992] (Picador, 1993), *The Dead School* (Picador, 1995)

Anne McCaffrey *Damia's Children* (Corgi, 1994)

Colum McCann *Songdogs* (Phoenix, 1995)

Mike McCormack *Crowe's Requiem* (Jonathan Cape, 1997)

Moy McCrory *The Fading Shrine* (Jonathan Cape, 1990)

John McGahern *The Barracks* (Faber, 1963), *The Dark* (Faber, 1965), *The Leavetaking* [1974] (Faber, revised edition, 1984), *The Pornographer* (Faber, 1979), *Amongst Women* (Faber, 1990)

Patrick McGinley *The Lost Soldier's Song* (Sinclair-Stevenson, 1994)

Eamonn McGrath *The Fish in the Stone* (Belfast: Blackstaff, 1994)

John McKenna *Clare* (Belfast: Blackstaff, 1993)

Bernard MacLaverty *Cal* (Jonathan Cape, 1983)

Bryan MacMahon *The Master* (Dublin: Poolbeg, 1992)

Liz McManus *Acts of Subversion* (Dublin: Poolbeg, 1991)

Eoin McNamee *The Last of Deeds and Love in History* (Penguin, 1992), *Resurrection Man* (Picador, 1994)

Deirdre Madden *Hidden Symptoms* [1986] (Faber, 1988), *The Birds of the Innocent Wood* (Faber, 1988), *Remembering Light and Stone* (Faber, 1992), *Nothing is Black* (Faber, 1994), *One by One in the Darkness* (Faber, 1996)

Maureen Martella *Bugger Bucharest* (Dublin: Basement, 1995)

Emer Martin *Breakfast in Babylon* (Dublin: Wolfhound, 1996)

Aidan Mathews *Muesli at Midnight* (Secker & Warburg, 1990)

Charles Maturin *Melmoth the Wanderer* [1820] (Oxford University Press, 1968)

Lia Mills *Another Alice* (Dublin: Poolbeg, 1996)
Frances Molloy *No Mate for the Magpie* (Virago, 1985)
Brian Moore *The Mangan Inheritance* (Jonathan Cape, 1979)
George Moore *The Lake* [1905] (Gerrard's Cross, Bucks: Colin
    Smythe, 1980)
Danny Morrissey *On The Back of the Swallow* (Cork: Mercier, 1994)
Mary Morrissey *Mother of Pearl* (Jonathan Cape, 1996)
Val Mulkerns *Very Like a Whale* (John Murray Publishers, 1986)
Iris Murdoch *The Red and the Green* (Chatto & Windus 1965)
Tom Murphy *The Seduction of Morality* [1994] (Abacus, 1995)

Eilís Ní Dhuibhne *The Bray House* (Dublin: Attic, 1990)
Christopher Nolan *Under the Eye of the Clock* (Weidenfield &
    Nicolson, 1987)

Edna O'Brien *House of Splendid Isolation* (Weidenfield &
    Nicolson, 1994)
Flann O'Brien *At Swim-Two-Birds* [1939] (Penguin, 1967), *The
    Third Policeman* [1967] (Flamingo, 1993)
Kate O'Brien *Mary Lavelle* [1936] (Virago, 1984), *That Lady*
    (Heinemann, 1946)
Brendan O'Carroll *The Granny* (Dublin: O'Brien, 1996)
Clairr O'Connor *Love in Another Room* (Dublin: Marino, 1995)
Joseph O'Connor *Cowboys and Indians* [1991] (Flamingo, 1992),
    Desperadoes (Flamingo, 1994)
Mary O'Donnell *Virgin and the Boy* (Dublin: Poolbeg, 1996)
Julia O'Faolain *Women in the Wall* [1975] (Virago, 1985), *The
    Irish Signorina* (Harmondsworth, Middlesex: Penguin, 1984)
Sean O'Faolain *Bird Alone* (Jonathan Cape, 1936)
Kathleen O'Farrell *The Fiddler of Kilbroney* (Dingle: Brandon,
    1994)
Liam O'Flaherty, *The Informer* [1925] (New English Library, 1971)
Sheila O'Flanagan *Dreaming of a Stranger* (Dublin: Poolbeg, 1997)
J.M. O'Neill *Commissar Connell* (Hamish Hamilton, 1992)
Joan O'Neill *Daisy Chain War* (Dublin: Attic, 1990)
Kate O'Riordan *Involved* (Flamingo, 1995)
T.S. O'Rourke *Ganglands* (Dublin: Breffni Books, 1996)
Mark O'Sullivan *Melody for Nora* (Dublin: Wolfhound, 1995)
Sydney Owenson (Lady Morgan), *The Wild Irish Girl* [1806]
    (Pandora, 1986)

David Park *Stone Kingdoms* (Phoenix, 1996)
Glenn Patterson *Burning Your Own* (Chatto & Windus, 1988), *Fat

Lad [1992] (Minerva, 1993), *Black Night on Big Thunder
Mountain* (Chatto & Windus, 1995)
Chris Petit *The Psalm Killer* (Macmillan, 1996)
Tom Phelan *In the Season of the Daisies* (Dublin: Lilliput, 1993)
James Plunkett *Strumpet City* (Hutchinson, 1969)
Una Power *The Spellbinder* (Century, 1993)
Terry Prone *Racing the Moon* (Dublin: Marino, 1996)

Patrick Quigley *Borderland* (Dingle: Brandon, 1994)
John Quinn *Generations of the Moon* (Dublin: Poolbeg, 1996)
Niall Quinn *The Café Cong* (Dublin: Wolfhound, 1991)

Moya Roddy *The Long Way Home* (Dublin: Attic, 1992)
Frank Ronan *Dixie Chicken* (Hodder & Stoughton, 1994)
Seán Rooney *Early Many a Morning* (Dingle: Brandon, 1994)
George Ryan *Time for a Smile* (Athlone: Temple, 1996)
James Ryan *Home from England* (Phoenix, 1995)

Patricia Scanlan *Promises, Promises* (Dublin: Poolbeg, 1996)
Gerald Seymour *Harry's Game* (Fontana, 1975), *Field of Blood*
(Collins, 1985)
Bernard Share *The Finner Faction* (Swords, Dublin: Poolbeg,
1989)
Gaye Shortland *Turtles All the Way Down* (Dublin: Poolbeg,
1997)
Edith Somerville and Martin Ross, *The Real Charlotte* [1894]
(Rutgers University Press, 1987)
Pádraig Standún *Celibates* (Swords, Dublin: Poolbeg, 1993)
James Stephens *The Crock of Gold* [1912] (Macmillan, 1926), *The
Charwoman's Daughter* [1912] (Dublin: Gill and Macmillan,
1972)
John Stephenson *The Virgin* (Dublin: Marino, 1996)
Laurence Sterne *Tristram Shandy* [1759–67] (Norton, 1980)
Bram Stoker *Dracula* [1897] (Ware, Herts: Wordsworth Classics,
1993)
Eithne Strong *The Love Riddle* (Dublin: Attic, 1993)
Francis Stuart *Black List, Section H* (Carbondale: Southern
Illinois University, 1971)
Jonathan Swift *Gulliver's Travels* [1726] (Oxford: Oxford
University Press, 1994)

Colm Tóibín *The South* [1990] (Picador, 1990), *The Heather
Blazing* (Pan, 1992), *The Story of the Night* (Picador, 1996)

Edward Toman *Dancing in Limbo* (Flamingo, 1995)
William Trevor *Felicia's Journey* (Penguin, 1994)

Dolores Walsh *Fragile We Are* (Dublin: Wolfhound, 1996)
Robert Welch *The Kilcolman Notebook* (Dingle: Brandon, 1994)
Oscar Wilde *The Picture of Dorian Gray* [1891] (Ware, Herts: Wordsworth Classics, 1992)
Robert MacLiam Wilson *Ripley Bogle* [1989] (Picador, 1990), *Manfred's Pain* (Picador, 1992), *Eureka Street* (Secker & Warburg, 1996)

Criticism and Theory – Irish Context

Acheson, J. (ed.) *The British and Irish Novel Since 1960* (St Martin's, 1991)
Arnold, M. *On The Study of Celtic Literature* [1867] (Smith, Elder & Co., 1900)

Barry, K. 'Lullabies for Insomniacs: The Writer and Contemporary Irish Society', *Irish Review*, No. 2 (1987), pp. 7–13
Beckett S. et al. *Our Exagmination Round His Factification For Incamination Of Work In Progress* [1929] (Faber, 1961)
Bolger, D. (ed.) *Invisible Cities: The New Dubliners: A Journal Through Unofficial Dublin* (Dublin: Raven Arts Press, 1990)
—— (ed.) *Letters from the New Island* (Dublin: Raven Arts Press, 1992)
—— *A Dublin Quartet* (Penguin, 1992)
—— (ed.) *The Picador Book of Contemporary Irish Fiction* (Pan, 1993)
—— (ed.) *Ireland in Exile: Irish Writers Abroad* (Dublin: Raven Arts Press, 1993)
Bornstein, G. 'Afro-Celtic Connections: From Frederick Douglass to *The Commitments*', in Tracey Mishkin (ed.) *Literary Influence and African-American Writers* (New York: Garland Publishing, 1996), pp. 171–88.
Brady, C. (ed.) *Interpreting Irish History: The Debate on Historical Revisionism* (Dublin: Irish Academic Press, 1993)
Brown, T. *Ireland: A Social and Cultural History 1922–1985* (Fontana, 1987)
Bunreacht na hÉireann (*Constitution of Ireland*) (Dublin: Stationery Office, 1937)

Cahalan, J. *Great Hatred, Little Room: The Irish Historical Novel* (Dublin: Gill and Macmillan, 1983)
—— *The Irish Novel: A Critical History* (Dublin: Gill and Macmillan, 1988)
Cairns, D. and Richards, S. *Writing Ireland: Colonialism, Nationalism and Culture* (Manchester: Manchester University Press, 1988)
Candy, C. *Priestly Fictions: Popular Irish Novelists of the Early 20th Century* (Dublin: Wolfhound, 1996)
Carlson, J. (ed.) *Banned in Ireland: Censorship and the Irish Writer* (Athens, Ga.: University of Georgia Press, 1990)
Clarke, D.M. *Church and State* (Cork: Cork University Press, 1984)
Cleary J. '"Fork-Tongued on the Border Bit": Partition and the Politics of Form in Contemporary Narratives of the Northern Irish Conflict', *South Atlantic Quarterly*, Vol. 95, No. 1 (Winter 1996), pp. 227–76
Connolly, P. (ed.) *Literature and the Changing Ireland* (Gerrards Cross, Bucks: Colin Smythe, 1982)
Coulter, C. *The Hidden Tradition: Feminism, Women and Nationalism in Ireland* (Cork: Cork University Press, 1993)
Cronin, J. *The Anglo-Irish Novel: The Nineteenth Century* (Belfast: Appletree, 1980)

Dawe, G. and Williams, J. (eds) *Krino 1986–1996: An Anthology of Modern Irish Writing* (Dublin: Gill & Macmillan, 1996)
Deane, S. *Celtic Revivals* (Faber, 1985)
—— *A Short History of Irish Literature* (Hutchinson, 1986)
—— (Gen. Ed.) *The Field Day Anthology of Irish Writing* (Derry and London: Field Day Publications and Faber, 1991)
Donovan, K. 'Novel Sums: Big Advances for Young Sensations', *Irish Times: Weekend* (16 November 1996), p.1
Donovan, K., Jeffares, A.N. and Kennelly, B. (eds) *Ireland's Women: Writings Past and Present* (London: Kyle Cathie Ltd, 1994)

Flanagan, T. *The Irish Novelists, 1800–1850* (New York: Columbia University Press, 1959)
Flynn, L. 'The Missing Body of Mary McGhee: The Constitution of Woman in Irish Constitutional Adjudication', *Journal of Gender Studies*, Vol. 2, No. 2 (November, 1993), pp. 238–52
Foster, J.W. *Forces and Themes in Ulster Fiction* (Dublin: Gill and Macmillan, 1974)
Foster, R. *Modern Ireland, 1600–1972* (Penguin, 1988)
—— *Paddy and Mr Punch: Connections in Irish and English History* (Allen Lane, 1993)

Gibbons, L. *Transformations in Irish Culture* (Cork: Cork University Press, 1996)

Harmon, M. (ed.) *The Irish Writer and the City* (Gerrards Cross, Bucks: Colin Smythe, 1984)

Haslam, R. 'Maturin and the Calvinist Sublime' in A. Lloyd Smith and V. Sage (eds) *Gothick Origins and Innovations* (Amsterdam and Atlanta, Ga.: Editions Rodopi, 1994), pp. 44–56

Heaney, S. *Preoccupations: Selected Prose 1968–1978* (Faber, 1980)

Hederman, M.P. and Kearney, R. (eds) *The Crane Bag Book of Irish Studies* (Dublin: Blackwater, 1981)

Hughes, E. '"Lancelot's Position": The Fiction of Irish-Britain', in A. Robert Lee (ed.) *Other Britain, Other British: Contemporary Multicultural Fiction* (Pluto Press, 1995), pp. 142–60.

Imhof, R. (ed.) *Contemporary Irish Novelists* (Gunter Narr Verlag Tübingen, 1990)

Innes, C.L. *Woman and Nation in Irish Literature and Society, 1880-1935* (Athens, Ga.: University of Georgia Press, 1993)

Kearney, R. (ed.) *The Irish Mind: Exploring Intellectual Traditions* (Dublin: Wolfhound, 1985)
—— *Transitions: Narratives in Modern Irish Culture* (Manchester: Manchester University Press, 1988)
—— (ed.) *Migrations: The Irish at Home and Abroad* (Dublin: Wolfhound, 1990)
—— 'Postmodernity and Nationalism: A European Perspective', *Modern Fiction Studies*, Vol. 38, No. 3 (Autumn 1992), pp. 581–93

Kenneally, M. (ed.) *Cultural Contexts and Literary Idioms in Contemporary Irish Literature* (Gerrards Cross, Bucks: Colin Smythe, 1988)

Keogh, D. *Ireland and the Vatican: The Politics and Diplomacy of Church-State Relations, 1922–1960* (Cork: Cork University Press 1995)

Kiberd, D. *Inventing Ireland* (Jonathan Cape, 1995)

Kilfeather, S. 'Origins of the Irish Female Gothic', *Bullán: An Irish Studies Journal*, Vol. 1, No. 2 (Autumn 1994), pp. 35–46

Lee, J.J. *Ireland 1912–1985: Politics and Society* (Cambridge: Cambridge University Press, 1989)

Lloyd, D. *Nationalism and Minor Literature: James Clarence Mangan and the Emergence of Irish Cultural Nationalism* (Berkeley: University of California Press, 1987)
—— *Anomalous States: Irish Writing and the Post-Colonial Moment* (Dublin: Lilliput, 1993)
—— 'Making Sense of the Dispersal', *Irish Reporter: Ireland – The Global Nation?*, No. 13, (1994), pp. 3–4
Longley, E. *The Living Stream: Literature and Revisionism in Ireland* (Newcastle upon Tyne: Bloodaxe Books, 1994)

McGrath, N. 'Interview with Glenn Patterson', *Edinburgh Review*, No. 93, (Spring 1995), pp. 41–50
MacLaughlin, J. 'Outwardly Mobile: The Sanitising of Emigration', *Irish Reporter: Ireland – The Global Nation?*, No. 13 (1994), pp. 9–11
—— *Ireland: The Emigrant Nursery and the World Economy* (Cork: Cork University Press, 1995)
Martin, A. *The Genius of Irish Prose* (Cork: Mercier, 1985)
Mercier, V. *The Irish Comic Tradition* (Oxford: Clarendon, 1962)
—— *Modern Irish Literature: Sources and Founders* (Oxford: Clarendon, 1994)

Nolan, E. *James Joyce and Nationalism* (Routledge, 1994)

O'Carroll, Í. and Collins, E. (eds) *Lesbian and Gay Visions of Ireland: Towards the Twenty-First Century* (Cassell, 1995)
O'Casey, S. *Three Plays* (Macmillan, 1963)
O'Connor, J. *The Secret World of the Irish Male* [1994] (Minerva, 1995)
O'Connor, M. 'The Thieves of Language in Gaol?', *Krino*, No. 15 (Spring 1994), pp. 30–42
O'Dowd M. and Valiulis, M. *Engendering Irish History* (Dublin: Wolfhound, 1996)
O'Toole F. 'Going West: The Country Versus the City in Irish Writing', *The Crane Bag*, Vol. 9, No. 2 (1985), pp. 111–16

Patten, E. 'Fiction in Conflict: Northern Ireland's Prodigal Novelists' in I.A. Bell (ed.) *Peripheral Visions: Images of Nationhood in Contemporary British Fiction* (Cardiff: University of Wales Press, 1995), pp. 28–48
Paulin, T. *Ireland and the English Crisis* (Newcastle upon Tyne: Bloodaxe Books, 1984)

Rafroidi, P. and Harmon, M. (eds) *The Irish Novel in Our Time* (Lille: Publications De L'Universite De Lille, 1975–76)

Richards, S. 'Northside Realism and the Twilight's Last Gleaming' *Irish Studies Review*, No. 2 (Winter 1992), pp. 18–20

Rolston, B. 'Mothers, Whores and Villains: Images of Women in Novels of the Northern Ireland Conflict', *Race and Class*, Vol. 31, No. 1 (1989), pp. 41–57

Ronsley, J. (ed.) *Myth and Reality in Irish Literature* (Waterloo, Ontario: Wilfred Laurier University Press, 1977)

Rose, K. *Diverse Communities: The Evolution of Gay and Lesbian Politics in Ireland* (Cork: Cork University Press 1994)

Sloan, B. *The Pioneers of Anglo-Irish Fiction 1800–1850* (Gerrards Cross, Bucks: Colin Smythe, 1986)

Storey, M. (ed.) *Poetry and Ireland Since 1800: A Source Book* (Routledge, 1988)

Vance, N. *Irish Literature: A Social History* (Oxford: Basil Blackwell, 1990)

Walshe, E. (ed.) *Sex, Nation and Dissent: Essays* (Cork: Cork University Press, 1995)

Ward, M. (ed.) *In Their Own Voice: Women and Irish Nationalism* (Dublin: Attic, 1996)

Wardlaw, C. *One in Every Family: Dispelling the Myths about Lesbian and Gay Men* (Dublin: Basement, 1996)

Welsh, R. *Changing States: Transformations in Modern Irish Writing* (Routledge, 1993)

Criticism and Theory – General

Achebe, C. *Morning Yet On Creation Day* (New York: Anchor Press/Doubleday, 1975)

Ahmad, A. 'Jameson's Rhetoric of Otherness and the "National Allegory"', *Social Text*, No. 17 (Fall 1987), pp. 3–25

Anderson, B. *Imagined Communities: Reflections on the Origin and Spread of Nationalism* [1983] (Revised Edition, Verso, 1991)

Armstrong, N. *Desire and Domestic Fiction: A Political History of the Novel* (Oxford: Oxford University Press, 1987)

Ashcroft, B., Griffiths, G. and Tiffin, H. (eds) *The Post-Colonial Studies Reader* (Routledge, 1995)

Bakhtin, M. *The Dialogic Imagination*, ed. M. Holquist, trs. C.

Emerson and M. Holquist (Austin: University of Texas Press, 1981)

Berman, M. *All That Is Solid Melts Into Air: The Experience of Modernity* [1982] (Verso, 1983)

Bhabha, H.K. 'Representation and the Colonial Text: A Critical Exploration of Some Forms of Mimeticism', in F. Glover-smith (ed.) *The Theory of Reading* (Sussex: Harvester, 1984), pp. 93–122

—— (ed.) *Nation and Narration* (Routledge, 1990)

—— *The Location of Culture* (Routledge, 1994)

Bloom, H. *The Western Canon: The Books and School of the Ages* (New York: Harcourt Brace, 1994)

Derrida, J. *Of Grammatology* [1967], trs. G.C. Spivak (Baltimore: Johns Hopkins University Press, 1976)

Dirlik, A. 'The Postcolonial Aura: Third World Criticism in the Age of Global Capitalism', *Critical Inquiry*, No. 20 (Winter 1994), pp. 328–56

Fanon, F. *The Wretched of the Earth* [1961], trs. C. Farrington (Harmondsworth, Middlesex: Penguin, 1969)

Felman, S. *Writing and Madness: Literature, Philosophy, Psychoanalysis* [1978], trs. S. Evans and S. Felman (Ithaca, New York: Cornell University Press, 1985)

Gellner, E. *Nations and Nationalism* (Oxford: Basil Blackwell, 1983)

Gilman, S. *Difference and Pathology: Stereotypes of Sexuality, Race and Madness* (Ithaca, New York: Cornell University Press, 1985)

Gilroy, P. 'It Ain't Where You're From, It's Where You're At ... The Dialectics of Diasporic Identification', *Third Text*, No. 13 (1990/91), pp. 3–16

Goldmann, L. *Towards a Sociology of the Novel*, trs. A. Sheridan (Tavistock, 1975)

Herder, J.G. *Outlines of a Philosophy of the History of Man* [1784–91], trs. T. Churchill (Johnson, 1800)

Jameson, F. *The Political Unconscious: Narrative as a Socially Symbolic Act* (Methuen 1981)

—— 'Third-World Literature in the Era of Multinational Capitalism', *Social Text*, No. 15 (Fall 1986), pp. 65–88.

Kristeva, J. *Desire in Language: A Semiotic Approach to Literature and Art*, ed. L.S. Roudiez, trs. T. Gora, A. Jardine and L.S. Roudiez (Oxford: Basil Blackwell, 1981)

Lodge, D. *The Modes of Modern Writing: Metaphor, Metonymy and the Typology of Modern Literature* (Edward Arnold, 1977)
Lukács, G. *The Theory of the Novel: A Historico-Philosophical Essay on the Forms of the Great Epic Literature*, trs. A. Bostock (Merlin, 1971)

Martin, G. *Journey Through the Labyrinth: Latin American Fiction in the Twentieth Century* (Verso, 1989)
Milner, A. *Literature, Culture and Society* (University College London Press, 1996)
Moi, T. (ed.) *The Kristeva Reader* (Oxford: Basil Blackwell, 1986)

Nandy, A. *The Intimate Enemy: Loss and Recovery of Self Under Colonialism* (Delhi: Oxford University Press, 1983)

Parker, A. et al. (eds) *Nationalism and Sexualities* (Routledge, 1992)

Said, E. *Orientalism* [1978] (Peregrine, 1985)
—— *Culture and Imperialism* (Chatto & Windus, 1993)
Spearman, D. *The Novel and Society* (Routledge & Kegan Paul, 1966)
Spender, D. *Mothers of the Novel: One Hundred Good Women Writers Before Jane Austen* (Pandora, 1986)

Veeser, H.A. (ed.) *The New Historicism* (Routledge, 1989)

Watt, I. *The Rise of the Novel: Studies in Defoe, Richardson and Fielding* [1957] (Harmondsworth, Middlesex: Penguin, 1977)
Williams, P. and Chrisman, L. (eds) *Colonial Discourse and Post-colonial Theory: A Reader* (Harvester/Wheatsheaf, 1993)
Williams, R. *The Country and the City* [1973] (St Albans, Herts: Paladin, 1975)
—— *Marxism and Literature* (Oxford: Oxford University Press, 1977)

Young, R.J.C. *Colonial Desire: Hybridity in Theory, Culture and Race* (Routledge, 1995)

INDEX

(See Contents page to find entries for specific texts and/or novelists.)